BLACK & DECKER ®

THE COMPLETE GUIDE TO
WINDOWS & DOORS

Step-by-Step Projects for
Adding, Replacing & Repairing
All Types of Windows & Doors

CREATIVE
PUBLISHING
international

CHANHASSEN, MINNESOTA

www.creativepub.com

Contents

Copyright © 2002
Creative Publishing international, Inc.
18705 Lake Drive East
Chanhassen, Minnesota 55317
1-800-328-3895
www.creativepub.com
All rights reserved

Printed on American Paper by:
R. R. Donnelley
10 9 8 7 6 5 4 3 2 1

President/CEO: Michael Eleftheriou
Vice President/Publisher: Linda Ball
Vice President/Retail Sales & Marketing: Kevin Haas

Executive Editor: Bryan Trandem
Creative Director: Tim Himsel
Managing Editor: Michelle Skudlarek
Editorial Director: Jerri Farris

Lead Editor: Barbara Harold
Senior Editor: Phil Schmidt
Editors: Thomas G. Lemmer, Dane Smith
Copy Editor: Janice Cauley
Art Director: Kari Johnston
Mac Designer: Jon Simpson
Technical Illustrator: Earl Slack
Technical Photo Editor: Paul Gorton
Project Manager: Julie Caruso
Studio Services Manager: Jeanette Moss McCurdy
Photo Team Leader: Tate Carlson
Photographers: Andrea Rugg, Chuck Nields
Scene Shop Carpenter: Randy Austin
Director of Production Services: Kim Gerber
Production Manager: Stasia Dorn

THE COMPLETE GUIDE TO WINDOWS & DOORS
Created by: The Editors of Creative Publishing international, Inc.,
in cooperation with Black & Decker. Black & Decker is a trademark
of The Black & Decker Corporation and is used under license.

Library of Congress
Cataloging-in-Publication Data

The complete guide to windows &
doors : step by step projects for adding,
replacing & repairing all types of windows
& doors.
    p. cm. -- (Complete guides)
Includes index.
  ISBN 1-58923-045-0 (soft cover)
1. Windows. 2. Doors. I. Creative
Publishing International. II. Complete
guides (Chanhassen, Minn.)
  TH2270 .C65 2002
  690'.1823--dc21

            2002073809

Portions of *The Complete Guide to Windows
& Doors* are taken from the Black & Decker®
books *Carpentry: Remodeling, Carpentry:
Tools • Shelves • Walls • Doors, Exterior Home
Repairs & Improvements, Customizing Your
Home.* Other titles from Creative Publishing
international include:

*The New Everyday Home Repairs; Basic
Wiring & Electrical Repairs; Building Decks;
Home Masonry Projects & Repairs; Work-
shop Tips & Techniques; Home Plumbing
Projects & Repairs; Advanced Home Wiring;
Advanced Deck Building; Bathroom Remod-
eling; Built-In Projects for the Home; Land-
scape Design & Construction; Refinishing &
Finishing Wood; Building Porches & Patios;*

*Flooring Projects & Techniques; Advanced
Home Plumbing; Remodeling Kitchens;
Finishing Basements & Attics; Stonework
& Masonry Projects; Sheds, Gazebos &
Outbuildings; Building & Finishing Walls &
Ceilings; The Complete Guide to Home
Plumbing; The Complete Guide to Home
Wiring; The Complete Guide to Building
Decks; The Complete Guide to Painting &
Decorating; The Complete Guide to Creative
Landscapes; The Complete Guide to Home
Masonry; The Complete Guide to Home
Carpentry; The Complete Guide to Home
Storage; The Complete Guide to Home
Repair; The Complete Photo Guide to
Home Improvement; The Complete Photo
Guide to Outdoor Home Improvement.*

Windows & Doors

Introduction

Few elements of your home are more important than the windows and doors. They serve crucial, and somewhat contradictory, roles. Windows and doors are both the link to—and the shield against—the outside world. When called upon, they must allow free passage to desired elements—friends and family members, sunlight and fresh air—but they also must protect against elements you don't want—human intruders, animal pests, inclement weather.

And no remodeling work has a greater impact on the livability and value of your home than replacing, adding, or renovating windows and doors. Window and door work is a major part of many remodeling projects, but homeowners in ever greater numbers are looking to window and door replacement as a valuable remodeling project in its own right. And for good reason. The paybacks are many: improved home value, better security, lower energy costs, better light and ventilation—an all-around better quality of life.

The Complete Guide to Windows & Doors is the first truly comprehensive guide to all aspects of window and door work—from initial planning to decorative finish work. You'll learn how to choose the technologies and styles best suited to your house, how to plan and install all types of windows and doors, and how to keep your windows and doors in perfect operating condition. The book is arranged in seven convenient sections to make it easy to use.

"A Portfolio of Window & Door Ideas," the first section, has dozens of inspiring photos that show how windows and doors can reinforce the architectural style and create an intended mood or setting within your home.

"Planning" will help you focus and organize the ideas you've gathered from books and magazines. You'll learn how to evaluate your window and door needs, how to choose from the variety of styles available, and how to measure and draw plans for your project. A special section shows how to use the principles of barrier-free living and universal design for your specific project needs.

"Site Preparation" reviews general procedures that can be a part of many projects. Included are step-by-step instructions for removing wallboard, plaster, and exterior surfaces. You'll also learn how to remove windows and doors, how to create temporary supports when enlarging or

creating window and door openings, and how to finish and patch interior and exterior wall surfaces.

"Replacing Windows & Doors" takes you right into some popular projects. In full step-by-step detail, you'll learn how to frame openings and how to install all types of window and door styles—including bay windows, glass block, skylights, garden windows, French doors, sliding patio doors, and space-saving pocket doors.

"Finishing" presents full instructions on trimming, painting, and finishing windows and doors. You'll also learn how to install a garage door opener. The section concludes with several security projects that will make you feel more comfortable and safe in your home.

"Repairing Windows & Doors" is a complete maintenance section including all the information you'll need to keep your existing and new windows and doors in good operating condition for many years. Among the included projects, you'll learn how to trouble-shoot and repair wood and metal storm windows, replace thresholds for barrier-free living, and repair garage doors.

"Decorative Window Treatments" is a delightful extra section that gives nearly a dozen beautiful and ingenious crowning touches. You'll learn how to install ready-made shutters, make a cornice, and build plant shelves, for example. Looking for alternative windows treatments? Then try etching window glass yourself, or making an antique stained-glass window frame.

Thank you for choosing *The Complete Guide to Windows & Doors*. If you have questions or problems that aren't answered by this book, please feel free to e-mail us at DIY@creativepub.com. We'll be glad to help, if we can.

NOTICE TO READERS

For safety, use caution, care, and good judgment when following the procedures described in this book. Neither the Publisher nor Black & Decker® can assume responsibility for any damage to property or injury to persons as a result of misuse of the information provided.

Consult your local Building Department for information on building permits, codes, and other laws as they apply to your project.

Photo next page courtesy of Andersen Windows, Inc.
Photo previous page ©Bill Tijerina

A Portfolio of Window & Door Ideas

Photo courtesy of Morgan Door, part of the JELD-WEN family

The perfect door is more than a hard-working, well-used part of your home. An entry door often makes a style statement, in addition to its main function as an opening to your home. An interior passage door serves to provide security and privacy while echoing elements of the home's architectural style.

The perfect window does more than just let light in. It adds personality and charm to a room's decor as it controls exposure to air and sunlight. Your needs for privacy, energy efficiency, and traffic patterns will influence the type, style, and placement of the windows in your home.

The dazzling photographs in this section feature many types and styles of windows and doors in creative and dramatic displays. They are sure to spark your imagination and help you make choices that will meet your remodeling needs perfectly.

This entry door, with leaded-glass panels and sidelights, is an elegant welcome to visitors, as well as residents. The soft but ample lighting extends a silent invitation into the home.

The cheerful decor of this child's room (above) is the perfect setting for a lovely bay window. The window seat doubles as a shelf and a play area. Snap-on muntins have been added to the casement windows, complementing the traditional style of the wainscoting.

The size and type of windows combine with the distinctive architecture, manicured lawn, and plantings to enhance this home's appeal (right). The white-painted accents at the roof peak and porch pillars continue the theme of the double-hung window trim.

There's no doubt that the egress windows in this basement area (above) make a world of difference in how people think about and use the room. With minimal window treatments, the large expanses of glass let in lots of natural light. And the slider windows can let in fresh outside air for increased ventilation.

When the owners of this home need a quiet place, they can simply close the interior French doors (right) to the study. The glass panels create quiet without a feeling of isolation. A simple window treatment can offer added privacy.

The size and shape of a window grouping (left) transforms an ordinary room into an extraordinary space. This fixed "picture" window is flanked by double-hung windows, plus a double-hung on each adjacent wall. The fixed windows near the ceiling add an elegant touch.

Various shapes and styles of windows and doors (below) combine to provide an exquisite beach view. Window treatments may be used to increase privacy and shield the interior of the home from the hot sun.

11

Curved doors and transom windows (above) create an interesting counterpoint to the overall square lines of a traditional style. French doors can be used for passage between rooms as well as for entry into the house from the outdoors.

Any nook that would benefit from more natural light is the perfect location for a window (right). This oval fixed window with decorative leading and ornate trim is an unexpected surprise at the foot of the staircase.

This multiple-window grouping perfectly enhances the off-square, angular look of the kitchen layout. The upper two triangle-shaped windows are fixed, and let in huge amounts of light for the pots of orchids on the shelves above the countertop work area. The lower three awning-style windows can be opened for extra circulation of fresh air.

(above) ©Andrea Rugg, (below) Photo courtesy of Milgard Windows

Natural light and ventilation are sometimes difficult to achieve in a bathroom (left) that also needs privacy. This homeowner has solved this dilemma with a lovely combination of two styles of window. The fixed round window gracefully accents the architecture of the ceiling while brightening the whole room with sunlight. And the double-hung with lightly frosted panes can be opened a little or a lot to let in fresh air while preserving privacy.

Living in a cold climate (below) brings special challenges, such as weatherization. Replacing windows and doors to gain energy efficiency is a great idea. And there are many other easy, do-it-yourself projects to help keep your home cozy and comfortable. Some of them are barely noticeable in the home, until you pay the (lower!) energy bill.

Double doors (right) make it a breeze to move furniture or other large objects in and out of a room. Here, the casual style of the wood panels fits right in with the rustic look of the bunk-bed set in this child's bedroom.

In this dining area (below), the window trim coordinates with the table. If you look closely, you'll see that this homeowner cleverly added a window seat, with several storage cubbies near the floor. Casement windows come in a variety of shapes. These are nearly square, each providing a large glass area for enjoying the view and catching a breeze.

Stately trees provide plenty of privacy for the lucky owners of this home. The many fixed windows bring the outdoors inside. And even if the breezes are slight, awning windows catch whatever is available. Open windows near the floor and near the ceiling work well together to keep the home cool in summer.

If the sun warms this breakfast nook (left) too much, the blinds on the double-hung windows can be easily closed to shade the area. For more privacy, the blinds can be lowered fully. The pattern of the true muntins on the lower windows is echoed in the muntins of the half-circle fixed window overhead.

There are few better places to enjoy the evening than relaxing in front of floor-to-ceiling windows that seem to surround you with nature. The tall casement windows (below) can be opened to let in fresh air, as well as the gentle sounds of the outdoors. The fabric and color of the window cornices coordinate with the room's decor. And the upper pairs of fixed windows draw the night sky into the vista.

The cathedral style of this family room's window grouping (above) elegantly echoes and balances the architecture of the massive floor-to-ceiling fireplace. The two casement windows flanking a fixed pane provide plenty of ventilation for the room. And the two upper rows of fixed windows let in plenty of natural light.

Many modern-style kitchens have minimal window areas. With a little out-of-the-box thinking, you can make the most of the opening by extending it all the way to the ceiling (left). The small triangular shelf is perfect for fresh blooms in small vases, and the muntins add a certain stylish feel to the room.

The curve of the door tops (right) mirrors the shape of the side window and the gable window above. Decorative brick accents reinforce the design motif. The color of the pillars, window shutters, and gable trim all work effectively as a cozy welcome to guests.

The single-hung windows (only the bottom half moves up; the top half is fixed) are perfect for this traditional-style home (below). The ornate trim above the windows and the red accent paint fit the architectural period perfectly. The large cupola and bay window bump-out help make the home unique.

ELEVATION
1/2"=1'-0"

3-SEASON
PORCH

Planning for New Windows & Doors

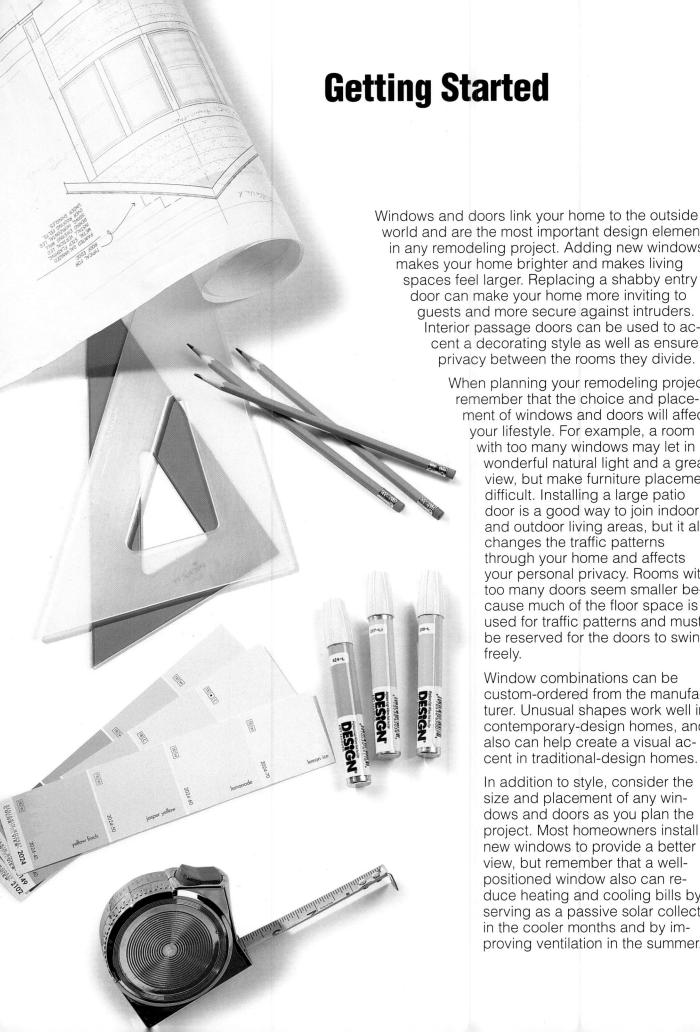

Getting Started

Windows and doors link your home to the outside world and are the most important design elements in any remodeling project. Adding new windows makes your home brighter and makes living spaces feel larger. Replacing a shabby entry door can make your home more inviting to guests and more secure against intruders. Interior passage doors can be used to accent a decorating style as well as ensure privacy between the rooms they divide.

When planning your remodeling project, remember that the choice and placement of windows and doors will affect your lifestyle. For example, a room with too many windows may let in wonderful natural light and a great view, but make furniture placement difficult. Installing a large patio door is a good way to join indoor and outdoor living areas, but it also changes the traffic patterns through your home and affects your personal privacy. Rooms with too many doors seem smaller because much of the floor space is used for traffic patterns and must be reserved for the doors to swing freely.

Window combinations can be custom-ordered from the manufacturer. Unusual shapes work well in contemporary-design homes, and also can help create a visual accent in traditional-design homes.

In addition to style, consider the size and placement of any windows and doors as you plan the project. Most homeowners install new windows to provide a better view, but remember that a well-positioned window also can reduce heating and cooling bills by serving as a passive solar collector in the cooler months and by improving ventilation in the summer.

Choose new windows and doors that match the style and shape of your home. For traditional home styles, strive for balance when planning for windows and doors. In the colonial-style home shown on the left, carefully chosen window units match the scale and proportions of the structure, creating a pleasing symmetry. In the home on the right, mismatched windows conflict with the traditional look of the home.

Casement windows and doors are available in both right-hand and left-hand models, indicating the swing direction, which must be specified when ordering. Double window units often have one of each. If you are installing a single window, choose the one that will catch prevailing breezes when it is opened.

Divided window panes in windows and doors lend a traditional appearance to a home and create interesting lighting patterns in a room. An alternative to true divided-pane windows are snap-in grilles (shown). They are available for most windows and doors, and are an inexpensive way to achieve this effect.

Evaluating Your Needs

There are many good reasons a homeowner may choose to replace windows and doors. All or some of the ones discussed in this section might apply to your project, or you may have other reasons. Those reasons may change as your living situation changes, producing new opportunities to use different projects.

Especially in older homes, the need to reduce energy loss is high on the list. This section discusses many of the telltale signs that indicate a home is not as efficient as it could be. Installing the newer styles of window with the advanced technology of low-E glass and increased insulation factors is certainly one way to lower energy costs year-round. Entry doors can be a source of energy loss also, and today's variety of well-insulated units can satisfy almost any need.

Weatherizing your existing windows and doors is an instant way of making your home more

energy-efficient. This section gives you some easy weatherizing tips.

Increasing light and ventilation are other ways new windows can enhance the comfort and usability of your home. Well-placed windows can take advantage of natural exposure and prevailing breezes. They also can work to limit those factors, as you wish. Doors with glass panels offer stylish new ways to connect rooms within the home. They can make rooms seem more accessible while still providing separation.

Perhaps a room needs an additional exit. A new door can certainly provide another avenue to the rest of the home. A window can increase the use of a basement area, for instance, by meeting the code requirements to use it as a sleeping room.

For many people, security is a concern. New windows and doors with state-of-the-art construction and locks can help put your mind at ease. There are also a multitude of ways to make your home more secure without replacing windows and doors. This section discusses several tips and illustrates how to install various safety devices.

Improving the usability of a space warrants adding or replacing windows and doors. Sometimes the sheer aesthetics of having a new unit is all the reason you need.

Windows play an integral part in the interior design of your home. They can enhance your lifestyle by influencing the way you use a room, making the outdoors seem to come inside, and becoming a focal point of the room. A new entry door can certainly make a home more inviting to guests, as well as to the residents.

As with any remodeling project, be sure to check with your local building inspector to find out whether you need permits before beginning the work.

Detecting Energy Loss

Some of the indications that your home is not energy-efficient will be obvious, such as draftiness, fogged or frosted windows, ice dams, gaps around windows in the foundation wall, and high energy bills. However, it can be more difficult to detect problems such as inadequate wall insulation or the loss of warm air around attic vents. The following are some ways to identify where your home may be losing energy:

• Measure the temperature in different parts of a room. A difference of more than one or two degrees indicates that the room is poorly sealed. The solution is to update the weatherstripping around the windows and doors (pages 217 and 227).

• Check for drafts around windows and doors by holding a tissue next to the jambs on a windy day. If the tissue flutters, the weatherstripping is inadequate. Another sign is outside light coming in around the jambs.

• Conduct an energy audit. Most power companies will provide you with an audit kit or conduct an audit for you.

• Monitor your energy usage from year to year. If there's a significant increase that can't be explained by variations in the weather, consider hiring a professional to conduct an energy audit.

The average home has many small leaks, which collectively may add up to the equivalent of a 2-ft. hole in the wall. The air that leaks through these cracks can account for as much as one-third of your total energy loss.

Condensation or frost buildup on windows is a sign of poor weatherstripping and an inadequate storm window.

Weatherstripping and insulation may begin to deteriorate. Telltale signs include crumbling foam or rubber.

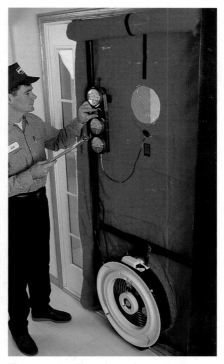

Energy audits done by power companies may use a blower door to measure airflow and detect leaks.

Before buying a basement window well cover, measure the widest point of the window well and note its shape.

Weatherizing

No matter whether you live in a hot or a cold climate, weatherizing your home's windows and doors can pay off handsomely. Heating and cooling costs may account for over half of the total household energy bill.

Since most weatherizing projects are relatively inexpensive, you can recover your investment quickly. In fact, in some climates, you can pay back the cost of a weatherproofing project in one season.

If you live in a cold climate, you probably already understand the importance of weatherizing. The value of keeping warm air inside the house during a cold winter is obvious. From the standpoint of energy efficiency, it's equally important to prevent warm air from entering the house during summer.

Weatherizing your home is an ideal do-it-yourself project, because it can be done a little at a time, according to your schedule. In cold climates, the best time of the year to weatherize is the fall, before it turns too cold to work outdoors.

Whether you're concerned about the environment, or want to spend less on your utility bills, some simple adjustments around your home can help you accomplish your goal.

Most weatherizing projects deal with windows (pages 215 to 217) and doors (pages 225 to 227), because these are the primary areas of heat loss in most homes. Here are a few simple suggestions you might consider for the exterior of your home:

Minimize heat loss from basement window wells by covering them with plastic window well covers (left, top). Most window well covers have an upper flange designed to slip under the siding. Slip this in place, then fasten the cover to the foundation with masonry anchors, and weigh down the bottom flange with stones. For extra weatherizing, seal the edges with caulk.

Adding caulk is a simple way to fill narrow gaps in interior or exterior surfaces. It's also available

Use a caulk that matches your home exterior to seal the window and door frames.

A felt door sweep can seal out drafts, even if you have an uneven floor or a low threshold.

in a peelable form, which can be easily removed at the end of the season.

When buying caulk, estimate half a cartridge per window or door, four for an average-size foundation sill, and at least one more to close gaps around vents, pipes, and other openings.

Caulk around the outside of the window and door frames to seal any gaps (page 26, center). For best results, use a caulk that matches or blends with the color of your siding.

There are many different types of caulk and weatherstripping materials. All are inexpensive and easy to use, but it's important to get the right materials for the job, as most are designed for specific applications.

Generally, metal and metal-reinforced weatherstripping is more durable than products made of plastic, rubber, or foam. However, even plastic, rubber, and foam weatherstripping products have a wide range of quality. The best rubber products are those made from neoprene rubber—use this whenever it's available.

A door sweep (page 26, bottom) attaches to the inside bottom of the door to seal out drafts. A felt or bristle sweep is best if you have an uneven floor or a low threshold. Vinyl and rubber models are also available.

A door bottom fits around the base of the door. Most have a sweep on the interior side and a drip edge on the exterior side, to direct water away from the threshold.

A threshold insert seals the gap between the door and the threshold. These are made from vinyl or rubber, and can be easily replaced.

Self-adhesive foam strips (below, left) attach to sashes and frames to seal the air gaps at windows and doors.

Reinforced felt strips (below, right) have a metal spine that adds rigidity in high-impact areas, such as doorstops.

Self-adhesive foam strips are an easy way to seal air gaps around window sashes and door frames.

A reinforced felt strip can add rigidity in high-impact areas, such as doorstops, that tend to develop air gaps.

Natural Light & Ventilation

Here are a few guidelines to keep in mind if you are considering new windows to increase the light and ventilation in a room:

- Windows must open and operate from inside, and they must exit to a street, alley, yard, court, or porch.

- Windows must equal at least 8% of the floor area in habitable rooms. The minimum openable area of a window must equal at least 4% of the room's floor area.

- In bathrooms, windows must be at least 3 sq. ft., and at least half of the window must open.

- Glass block, frosted, leaded, and stained glass are specialty glasses that also can be used to bring in natural sunlight, while preserving privacy.

- Casement windows are best for ventilation; they circulate the most air because the entire window opens.

Exits & Openings

Remember that sleeping rooms and habitable basements must have at least one egress window or exterior door for emergency escape. Occupants must be able to open the exit from inside the home, without a key or tool. Here are a few other guidelines:

- An egress window must provide a clear opening of at least 5.7 sq. ft., with a minimum height of 24" and a minimum width of 20".

- Windowsills on egress windows cannot be more than 44" above the floor.

- Egress windows below ground level must have window wells. If the wells are deeper than 44", they must have permanent ladders or steps. The steps can project up to 6" into the well but must be usable when the window is fully opened. Steps must be at least 12" wide and project at least 3" from the wall. Ladder rungs must be less than 18" apart.

- Exit doors must be at least 3 ft. wide and 6 ft., 8" high. They must provide direct outside access and operate without special knowledge or tools.

Home Security

When thinking about the security of your home, the most obvious component is the exterior entry door. It should have secure hinges and a good lockset attached; a deadbolt is best. You should also have at least one way to see who is outside the door. If the door does not have a window that provides a clear view of visitors, then add a sidelight or a peephole.

Specialty doors such as sliding patio doors and French doors have some unique security challenges because of their large size and the fact that they are mostly glass. Think of them as big windows, and add extra locks and install screws to prevent the panels from being pried from their tracks.

Most local hardware or home stores carry a large variety of inexpensive locks and security devices available for any type of window or door you may have in your home.

Photo courtesy of Simpson Door Company

Building Codes & Permits

Building permits are required for any remodeling project that involves a change or addition to your home's structure or mechanical systems.

Most simple window and door replacements do not require building permits. Check with your local building department if you're unsure about how the regulations might apply to your project.

Building permits are issued to ensure your remodeling project meets local building codes, which establish material standards, structural requirements, and installation guidelines for your project. In short, they ensure that your work is done properly.

Building permits are required by law, and getting caught without them can result in fines from the city and possibly trouble with your insurance company. Also, work done without permits can cause problems if you try to sell your home.

Most local building codes follow the national codes, such as the National Electrical Code, but are adapted to meet the demands of local conditions and legislation. Keep in mind that local codes always supersede national codes.

Before issuing permits, your local building department will require plans and cost estimates for your project. After your plans have been

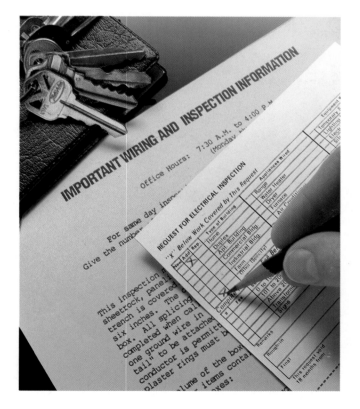

approved, you must pay permit fees, which are based on the cost of the project. You'll also learn what inspections are required and when you should call for them.

Once issued, a building permit typically is good for 180 days.

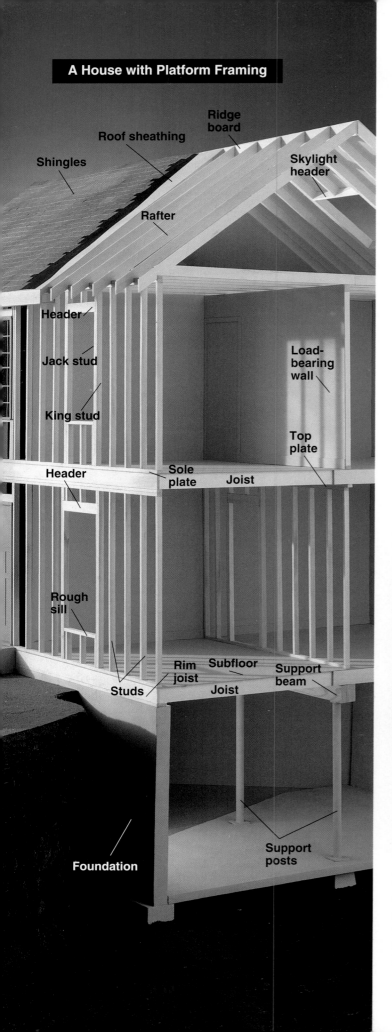

A House with Platform Framing

Shingles

Roof sheathing

Ridge board

Rafter

Skylight header

Header

Jack stud

King stud

Load-bearing wall

Top plate

Header

Sole plate

Joist

Rough sill

Rim joist

Subfloor

Support beam

Studs

Joist

Foundation

Support posts

Anatomy of a House

Enlarging openings or creating new openings for windows, skylights, or doors requires that you familiarize yourself with a few basic elements of home construction and remodeling. Take some time, before you begin, to get comfortable with the terminology of the models shown on the next few pages. The understanding you will gain in this section will make it easier to plan your project, buy the right materials, and clear up any confusion you might have about the internal design of your home.

If your project includes modifying exterior walls or interior load-bearing walls, you must determine if your house was built using platform- or balloon-style framing. The framing style of your home determines what kind of temporary supports you will need to install while the work is in

Platform Framing

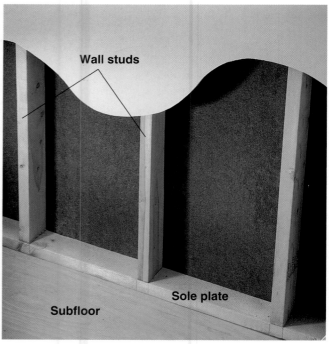

Wall studs

Sole plate

Subfloor

Platform framing (left and above) is identified by the floor-level sole plates and ceiling-level top plates to which the wall studs are attached. Most houses built after 1930 use platform framing. If you do not have access to unfinished areas, you can remove the wall surface at the bottom of a wall to determine what kind of framing was used in your home.

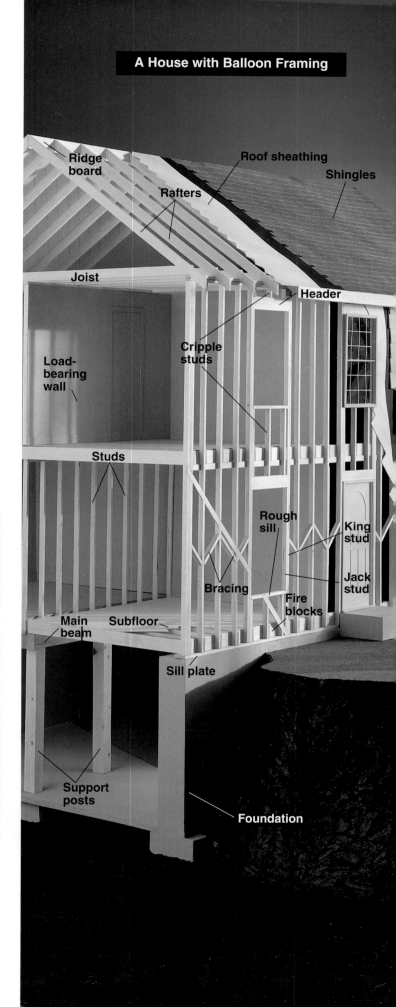

progress. If you have trouble determining what type of framing was used in your home, refer to the original blueprints, if you have them, or consult a building contractor or licensed home inspector.

Framing-in a new door or window on an exterior wall normally requires installing a header. Make sure that the header you install meets the requirements of your local building code, and always install cripple studs where necessary.

There are two types of walls: load-bearing and partition (non-load-bearing). Load-bearing walls require temporary supports during wall removal or framing of a door or window. Partition walls carry no structural load and do not require temporary supports.

Balloon Framing

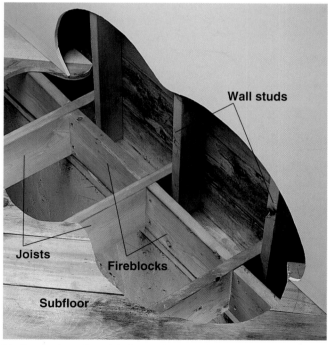

Balloon framing (right and above) is identified by wall studs that run uninterrupted from the roof to a sill plate on the foundation, without the sole plates and top plates found in platform-framed walls (page opposite). Balloon framing was used in houses built before 1930.

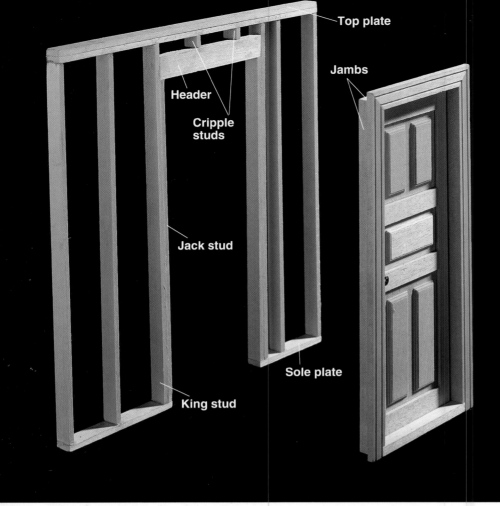

Top plate

Jambs

Header

Cripple studs

Jack stud

King stud

Sole plate

Door opening: The structural load above the door is carried by cripple studs that rest on a header. The ends of the header are supported by jack studs (also known as *trimmer studs*) and king studs that transfer the load to the sole plate and the foundation of the house. The rough opening for a door should be 1" wider and ½" taller than the dimensions of the door unit, including the jambs. This extra space lets you adjust the door unit during installation.

Anatomy Details

Many remodeling projects, like adding new doors or windows, require that you remove one or more studs in a load-bearing wall to create an opening. When planning your project, remember that new openings require a permanent support beam called a *header* above the removed studs, to carry the structural load.

The required size for the header is set by local building codes and varies according to the width of the rough opening. For a window or door opening, a header can be built from two pieces of 2" dimensional lumber sandwiched around ½" plywood (chart, right). When a large portion of a load-bearing wall (or an entire wall) is removed, a laminated beam product can be used to make the new header.

If you will be removing more than one wall stud, make temporary supports to carry the structural load until the header is installed.

Recommended Header Sizes

Rough Opening Width	Recommended Header Construction
Up to 3 ft.	½" plywood between two 2 × 4s
3 ft. to 5 ft.	½" plywood between two 2 × 6s
5 ft. to 7 ft.	½" plywood between two 2 × 8s
7 ft. to 8 ft.	½" plywood between two 2 × 10s

Recommended header sizes shown above are suitable for projects where a full story and roof are located above the rough opening. This chart is intended for rough estimates only. For actual requirements, contact an architect or your local building inspector.

Window opening: The structural load above the window is carried by cripple studs resting on a header. The ends of the header are supported by jack studs and king studs, which transfer the load to the sole plate and the foundation of the house. The rough sill, which helps anchor the window unit but carries no structural weight, is supported by cripple studs. To provide room for adjustments during installation, the rough opening for a window should be 1" wider and ½" taller than the window unit, including the jambs.

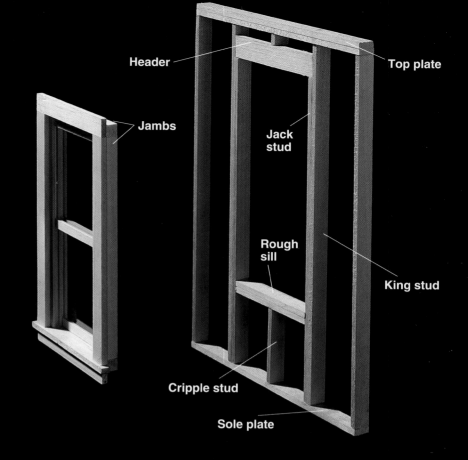

Header

Jambs

Jack stud

Rough sill

Top plate

King stud

Cripple stud

Sole plate

Framing Options for Window & Door Openings (new lumber shown in yellow)

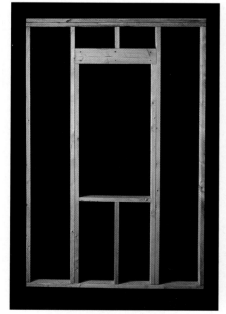

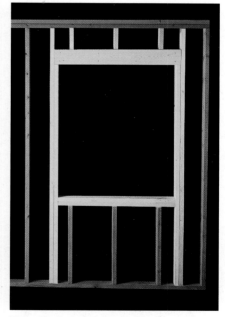

Using an existing opening avoids the need for new framing. This is a good option in homes with masonry exteriors, which are difficult to alter. Order a replacement unit that is 1" narrower and ½" shorter than the rough opening.

Enlarging an existing opening simplifies the framing. In many cases, you can use an existing king stud and jack stud to form one side of the new opening.

Framing a new opening is the only solution when you're installing a window or door where none existed or when you're replacing a unit with one that is much larger.

33

Barrier-free Living & Universal Design

Barrier-free living and universal design are intended for all people. While standard home and product design are based on the "average" person—that is, the average adult male—not everyone fits into that category. Some people are short, some tall; some have difficulty walking, while others walk ably but find bending difficult. And physical abilities change constantly, as do family situations. By incorporating the concepts of barrier-free living and universal design into your remodeling plans, you can create spaces that work better for everyone who lives in or visits your home, regardless of their size, age, or ability.

These "people-friendly" or "high-access" concepts are simply good design that improves everyday situations. For example, wide doorways make passage easier for a person carrying a load of laundry as well as for someone in a wheelchair or using a walker; windows that are easy to open enable people to better ventilate a room, even the entire home. More a way of thinking than a set of rules, barrier-free living and universal design can be applied to any area of your home—from room layouts to door hardware. In all cases, these design concepts encourage independent living by creating a safe, comfortable environment.

Photo courtesy of Dave Regel Construction/Access One, Inc.

Replacing windows and doors can be one of your first steps toward accommodating changes in the household—before those changes become problems. Adapting ideas that promote barrier-free living and universal design will make your everyday life easier. And, it will also make your home more appealing to a wide range of potential buyers, if you choose to sell.

Much of the information provided here comes from universal design specialists, specialty builders, and product manufacturers.

For more help with planning for barrier-free living and universal design adaptations, contact a qualified professional. See page 280 for a list of additional resources.

As always, be sure that all aspects of your project meet local building code requirements.

Checking the Room Layout

Careful planning can make your new windows and doors more accessible and easier to operate. Make sure they all have clear approach spaces and that windows are positioned at heights that accommodate small people and people in wheelchairs. See pages 36 to 37 for tips on selecting new doors, windows, and their hardware when you're remodeling to incorporate for universal design.

• Plan a clear approach space to each window, 30" deep × 48" wide.

• Position view windows at a maximum sill height of 30" to 36", so that children and seated people can see out. Lower sills may pose a safety risk to children; be sure to choose your window heights accordingly.

• Choose tempered glass for windows less than 18" from the floor or within 24" of a door, when required by local building codes.

• Position windows so that hardware is at a maximum height of 48" if the window is operable.

• Provide a clear, 48 × 48" approach space in front of each door. This includes an 18"- to 24"- wide space between the latch side of the door and an adjacent wall—to allow users room to maneuver.

• Frame doorless openings at a minimum of 32" wide (36" preferred).

• Consider the swing direction when choosing doors that will open into the room.

Before You Begin

Be sure to check for hidden mechanicals in the work area before you begin the actual work on any project. You may need to shut off and reroute electrical wiring, plumbing pipes, and other utility lines. If you are not comfortable performing these tasks, hire a professional.

Then, to be absolutely sure of your drawings, you will want to physically plot out the locations for new windows and doors with masking tape. Always mark the full swinging arc of hinged doors. Use newspaper or cardboard to make full-sized cutouts of furniture, and use them to experiment with different room layouts. For barrier-free living and universal design, your floor plan should allow ample room around furniture: 22" around a bed; 36" around couches, chairs, and tables; 40" in front of dressers, chests, and closets.

Walk through the room along different paths to judge how the room elements will interact. Remember to allow a 40"-wide path for foot traffic across a room. Once you have found a pleasing layout, make final floor plan and elevation drawings (pages 46 to 47).

Selecting Windows & Doors

Because windows and doors serve very basic purposes, consider your options carefully before making any purchases (some designs are far from universal). Lever door handles and remote or slide-bolt locks are good examples of universal design: they make opening a door easier for a person carrying packages as well as for someone lacking manual dexterity.

Doorways and doorless openings should be a minimum of 32" wide, but 36" is preferred.

Hardware alone can make the difference between a door that serves as a passageway and one that acts only as a barrier. The type of windows or doors you select may dictate the general style of hardware you install.

As with doors, your design considerations will affect which window styles you select; consider your family's situation before purchasing. Keep in mind the size and strength of those who will operate the windows, and remember that the hardware must be reachable by those users.

• Casement windows offer many attractive design features. Well-built models are easy to operate, and some come equipped with tandem latches or single-lever locking systems. Unfortunately, most casement windows do not accept window air conditioners.

• Many horizontal sliding sash windows have improved in recent years. Some manufacturers now produce models with quality sliding mechanisms and offset hardware. These windows can accept air conditioners and screens.

• Double-hung windows (or vertical sliding sash windows) are good options due to their availability and affordability, and they accept air conditioners and screens. High-quality models are easy to operate and many come with convenient features, such as tilt-in design for easy cleaning.

• Window hardware is often determined by the type of window you select.

Tandem latches, which operate multiple locks on a window with one motion, may be optional on some models; they simplify use considerably. Where possible, opt for larger handles or automatic openers. For other types of hardware, investigate adapters that make windows easier to operate.

• Because glass doors can appear to be open when they are closed, glass doors—sliding or hinged—are dangerous to some people.

Sliding doors can be difficult to operate from a seated position, and as these doors age and dirt accumulates in the tracks, they become even more difficult to open. Also, thresholds on sliding doors typically are high, which creates barriers for walkers and wheelchairs.

Photo courtesy of Milgard Windows

Casement windows are easy to open and close, using their single-lever latches. Automatic openers can also be fitted to most models.

Photo courtesy of Marvin Windows & Doors

Sliding windows are a snap to open and close, requiring minimal strength and little dexterity.

French doors are a good option for interiors, as long as each door is at least 32" wide. There are many styles of this type of glass door (see pages 138 to 141).

• A hinged door requires swing space equal to the width of the door plus 18" to 24" of clear space on the latch side for maneuvering (see page 35). Consider the swing direction, available swing space, and whether the swing of the door will interrupt the flow of traffic in a hallway. Many experts recommend that hinged bathroom doors swing outward, so a person who has fallen inside the bathroom cannot block the door.

Choose entry doors with low thresholds or no thresholds (see pages 230 to 233). The front edge of the threshold should be no more than ¼" high if it's square, ½" high if it's beveled.

A hinged sidelight makes a front entry door easier to navigate, especially when moving large objects.

• Lever handles require less exacting hand placement and are easier to use than knobs or pulls. Locks vary widely. For exterior locks, a key-less entry system is an ideal way to eliminate fumbling with keys in cold weather. For interior locks, slide bolts typically are preferred over standard deadbolts, because they are easier to operate.

You can gain space in all hinged-door openings by installing swing-clear hinges. These have L-shaped leaves that allow the door to swing away from the jamb, increasing the clear opening by the thickness of the door.

• A swinging door with no latch requires swing space on both sides. Because they require no hardware to open and close, swinging doors may be a good option in situations where latches or locks are unnecessary. As with a standard hinged door, consider the door's swing space and whether the swing will interrupt traffic flow.

• Perhaps the best alternative to a hinged or sliding door is a pocket door. It saves space, requires no threshold, and can be equipped with hardware that is easy to use. Pocket doors require special framing considerations; because the door slides into the wall, the rough opening is about twice the width of a standard door opening.

Standard recessed hardware for pocket doors is difficult to use, so install D-pulls instead (page 145). They also provide more room for fingers when the door is closed.

Pocket door units can be custom-built or purchased as prehung units (see pages 142 to 145).

Photo courtesy of Marvin Windows & Doors

Double-hung windows can be used with most home styles and come in many sizes and shapes.

Photo courtesy of Morgan Door, part of the JELD-WEN family

Lever door handles on hinged passage doors facilitate access to other rooms of the home. The handles come in a variety of sizes and design.

Window & Door Placement

One of the important considerations when deciding exactly where to install your new windows and doors is the environment. In some parts of the country, weather conditions change dramatically from season to season, as well as throughout the day and night.

Minimizing the number of windows and doors on the north side of a home may be important if you live with harsh winters. If you must deal with extreme heat or long hours of bright sunshine, you may consider fewer windows on the south and west sides of the home. No matter how energy-efficient your new windows and doors are, you will benefit from placing them to your best advantage.

Of course, prudent landscaping with trees, the use of eaves and overhangs, and controlling ventilation are other components to making your home comfortable year-round.

Changing the position of a door, or adding a second one, will definitely change the traffic pattern within a room. Be sure to consider whether that change will be positive or negative. Changing or adding windows may not change traffic movement through the room but it may well dramatically alter the focal point of the room. More or larger windows can highlight a great view, but they can also reveal a poor view. Be sure to look outside the proposed window location to see what you might be bringing inside.

A unique type of interior design called "Feng Shui" has grown in popularity in recent years. It is an ancient Chinese method of constructing and optimizing residences to bring about happiness, abundance, and harmony. The goal of Feng Shui is to increase the amount of ch'i—or universal life force—in the home. It is believed that correctly placing windows and doors within a home encourages ch'i to circulate through the home, which has a positive influence on the residents.

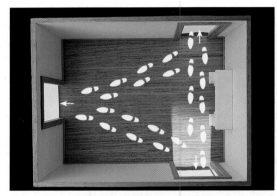

Traffic patterns through the home are determined by the placement of doors. Rooms with many doors seem smaller because traffic patterns consume much of the available space (top). When planning room layout, reserve plenty of space for doors to swing freely.

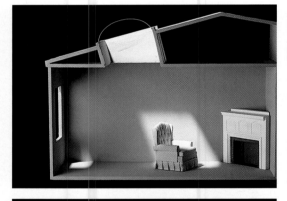

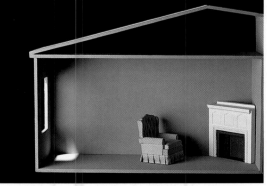

Consider the effect of sunlight when planning window positions. For example, when installing one skylight, choose a location and build the shaft to direct the light where you want it. A bank of several skylights can also dramatically change the ambience of the room.

Window & Door Styles

The following pages contain examples of some of the types of windows and doors you may consider for your home. Your imagination may lead you to other options, and combinations of options.

Casement windows pivot on hinges mounted on the side. They have a contemporary look, and offer good ventilation. Whether your window has exposed or concealed sash locks, casements have a reputation for weather-tight construction.

Double-hung windows slide up and down, and have a traditional appearance. The newer-style, spring-mounted operating mechanism is virtually trouble-free. The dividers (muntins) may divide individual panes of glass, or snap on for decoration.

Bay windows consist of three parts: a central window, usually fixed, parallel to the existing wall, and two side windows (often casements or double-hungs), each set at a 30-, 45-, or 60-degree angle. The deep sill area makes a handy shelf space.

Bow windows have four or more units set at incremental angles to one another. The effect is a subtle, curved look. When large units are used, the bow window may become an extension of the room, even taking the place of a wall.

Garden windows bring the outside in by creating shelf space and letting in sunshine as well as fresh air. Many types are easy-to-install kits that fit into an existing window space. They can be added to any room in the home.

Sliding windows are inexpensive and require little maintenance, but provide restricted ventilation, since only half the window can be open at one time. But that may be an acceptable trade-off for a large, unobstructed view.

Window & Door Styles (continued)

Photos © Andrea Rugg

Awning windows pivot on hinges mounted at the top. Awning windows work well in combination with other windows, and because they provide ventilation without letting moisture in, they are a good choice in damp climates.

© Brad Daniels

Fixed windows do not open, and can be any size and shape, used in any room. They may be flanked by other fixed windows or opening styles, such as awning, casement, or double-hung.

© Brad Daniels

Window groupings in an endless number of shapes and sizes may be used to dramatic effect in a home. They can become the focal point of a room, serving to highlight a spectacular view and let in lots of sunshine.

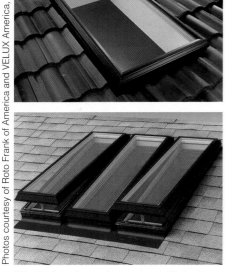

Photos courtesy of Roto Frank of America and VELUX America, Inc. (top)

Skylights introduce extra light into rooms that have limited wall space. Skylights serve as solar collectors on sunny days, and those that also can be opened improve ventilation in the home.

© Brad Daniels

Sliding patio doors offer good visibility and lighting. Because they slide on tracks and require no floor space for operation, they are a good choice for cramped spaces where swinging doors do not fit.

Photo courtesy of Simpson Door Company

French doors open on hinges, so your room design must allow space for them to swing. Weather-tight models join indoor and outdoor living areas, while indoor models link two rooms.

Photo courtesy of Woodport Interior Doors® by Heritage Products, USA

Interior panel doors are also known as raised-panel, stile-and-rail doors. They have a traditional look, and are available in many panel designs and configurations.

Interior flush-design doors may have a hollow or solid core. Both types may be prehung and have a contemporary look. The surface is smooth hardboard or wood veneer facing, which can receive a clear finish or be painted.

Bifold doors are very convenient where there is little room for the swing space of a hinged interior door. The sections' surfaces can be flush, paneled, even partially or completely louvered to assist with airflow.

Photo courtesy of Morgan Door, part of the JELD-WEN family

Entry doors may be made of steel, wood, fiberglass, or a range of new composite materials. Each appeals to the buyer in different ways—from energy efficiency to practicality to cost to durability.

Entry doors with sidelights brighten a dark entry hall and give an inviting look to your home. The sidelights often contain tempered, double-pane glass for better security and energy efficiency.

Storm doors can improve the energy efficiency and appearance of your entry. A storm door prolongs the life of an expensive entry door by protecting it from the elements.

Tips for Choosing Windows & Doors

Before buying new windows, you need to decide on a window style, choose framing and glazing (glass) materials, and compare energy efficiency ratings. You'll also find that several manufacturers offer a variety of decorative treatments, including beveled and stained-glass panels.

Installing a skylight may be another option. Skylights can be operable (capable of being opened) or fixed (non-opening).

If you don't like the window style you're replacing, or you want to add some windows, look for new ideas by studying other homes similar to yours, or by asking a window dealer or contractor for advice.

When buying new doors—whether for the interior or exterior of the home—most people choose prehung units with the door already attached to the jambs. Installing a prehung door is usually easier than installing a door and jambs separately, but both projects can be frustrating if you don't take time to be sure the door is plumb, square, and level throughout the project.

Interior passage doors are not only a focal element of interior design, but also a hard-working and often-used feature of the home.

Replacing inexpensive hollow-core interior doors with new solid-core ones makes a noticeable difference. A solid-core door feels more substantial, closes with less rattle, insulates against sound more effectively, and withstands hard use more readily. However, a solid-core door almost always costs considerably more than a hollow-core model. Your budget may help you make the decision.

Exterior entry doors are usually the most expensive door in the home. Whatever material your entry door is made of, the added protection of a storm door will extend its life and keep it looking new.

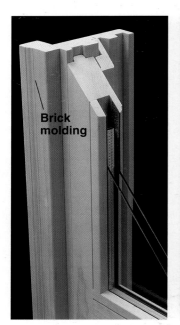 

Brick molding

Aluminum or vinyl shell

Wood frames (left) are a good choice for windows and patio doors used in remodeling projects. Their preattached exterior brick moldings blend well with the look of existing windows. **Clad-frame** windows and doors (right) feature an aluminum or vinyl shell on the exterior side of the window. Most are attached with nailing flanges that fit underneath the siding.

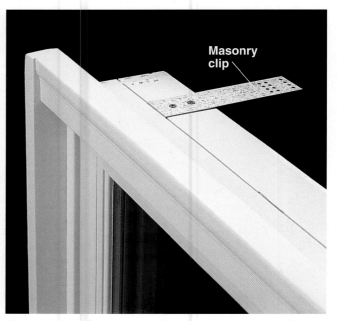

Masonry clip

Polymer coatings are optional on some wood-frame windows and doors. Polymer-coated windows and doors are available in a variety of colors, and do not need painting. To avoid using casing nails, which would pierce the weatherproof coating, anchor polymer-coated units with masonry clips that are screwed to the jambs and to the interior framing members (page 91).

Several types of glass are available from window and door manufacturers. Single-pane glass (A) is suitable only in very mild climates. Double-panes (B) have a sealed air space between the layers of glass to reduce heat loss. They are available in several variations with improved insulating ability, including "low-E" glass with an invisible coating of metal on one surface, and gas-filled windows containing an inert gas, such as argon. In southern climates, double-glazed tinted glass (C) reduces heat transfer. Tempered (or "safety") glass (D) has extra strength for use in patio doors, storm doors, and large picture windows.

Whatever the type of framing or glass in your window, the pane can be one piece, or divided into smaller panes by muntins. True muntins actually hold individual pieces of glass, while snap-on muntins can be easily removed, for cleaning the glass or to change the look of the window.

Window & Door Inspection Tips

Here are a few things to look for when you inspect your new window or door, before you begin the installation:

- Hardware is sturdy and all pieces are present.

- Sash lock or opening mechanism is operable.

- There are no glass cracks or cloudy areas.

- The window weatherstripping is uniform and "tight."

- All door hinges operate easily.

- The doorknob hole is correctly positioned.

- There are no unsightly woodgrain blemishes.

- Each has a seal of quality from one or more of these industry testing organizations: National Woodwork Manufacturers Association, Architectural Aluminum Manufacturers Association, American National Standards Institute, American Wood Window Institute. The National Fenestration Rating Council tests windows and doors for heat loss (U-value), R-value, and solar heat gain.

R-values of windows and doors, listed in manufacturers' catalogs, indicate the energy efficiency of the unit. Higher R-values indicate better insulating properties. Top-quality windows can have an R-value as high as 4.0. Exterior doors with R-values above 10 are considered energy-efficient.

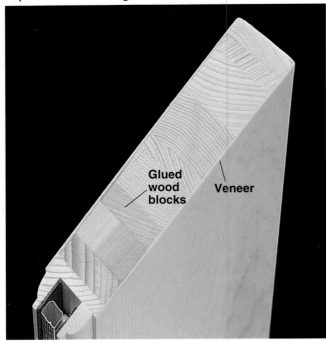

4 %₁₆" jamb for 2 × 4 wall construction

6 %₁₆" jamb for 2 × 6 wall construction

Glued wood blocks **Veneer**

Look for "core-block" construction when choosing exterior wooden doors. Core-block doors are made from layers of glued or laminated wood blocks covered with a veneer. Because the direction of the wood grain alternates, core-block doors are not likely to warp.

Before ordering, find your wall thickness by measuring the jamb width on an existing window or door. Manufacturers will customize the frame jambs to match whatever wall construction you have. Many companies also build custom doors up to 14 ft. tall and 5 ft. wide.

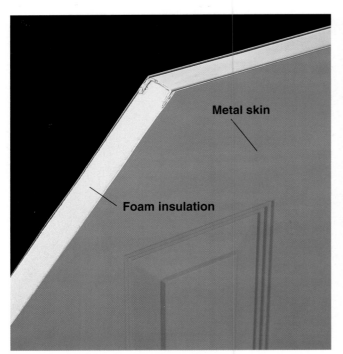

Metal skin

Foam insulation

Steel entry doors are well insulated. Steel doors are less expensive than wooden doors and require little maintenance. Although steel is susceptible to dents and rust, it is used for about 70% of all exterior doors sold to homeowners.

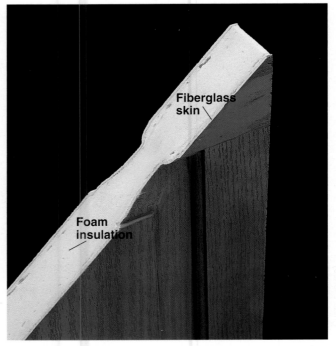

Fiberglass skin

Foam insulation

Fiberglass doors are expensive, but they are sturdy, have excellent insulating values, and require little maintenance. The fiberglass surface is designed to have the texture of wood and can be stained or painted different colors.

Adding a storm door will increase your home's energy efficiency, even if you purchased the best-insulated exterior door available. Manufacturers offer a variety of attractive designs.

Entry doors with an operable sidelight are a recent innovation. In addition to the width of the open main door, one hinged sidelight panel can also open as wide as 14". Moving furniture and other large items has never been so convenient.

A flush-design interior door may have a core of medium-density particleboard and a solid wood frame, or it may be made of a cardboard honeycomb grid separating and stiffening a thin wood veneer or hardboard skin.

True stile-and-rail interior door construction is very popular. But if the door will be painted, you can install a molded-panel door instead. The difference in appearance will be negligible and you can save a few dollars.

Pocket doors can be of flush or raised-panel design. One advantage is that they save floor space in tight quarters. They also allow you to hide the door when it's not in use.

Measuring Windows & Doors & Working with Plans

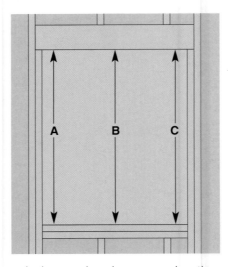

Floor plan annotations:

24'-6"

DECK
8 x 12'

6'-0" SLIDING
GLASS DOOR

ELECTRICAL
OUTLETS

FOYER
8'6 x 14'

LIVING RM
14 x 18'

4'-0" BAY
WINDOW

REMOVE THIS
WALL

50'-6"

BED RM
10 x 12'

DINNING RM
14 x 17'6'

BATH

BED RM
10 x 12'

KITCHEN
9'6 x 12'

MAIN FLOOR - PLAN

A

B

C

A   B   C

Determine the exact size of your new window or door by measuring the opening carefully. For the width (left), measure between the jack studs in three places: near the top, at the middle, and near the bottom of the opening. Use the same procedure for the height (right), measuring from the header to the sill near the left edge, at the middle, and near the right edge of the opening. Use the smallest measurement of each dimension for ordering the unit.

An important early step in your remodeling project is to carefully measure the windows and doors that you wish to replace. You will use these measurements to purchase the new unit, and you must be sure it will fit in the opening.

To finalize your project ideas and make sure they will really work, the next step is to put all the information down on paper. There are two basic types of construction drawings: floor plans and elevation drawings. These drawings may be required if your project needs a building permit.

Floor plans show a room as seen from above. These are useful for showing overall room dimensions, layouts, and the relationship between neighboring rooms. Elevation drawings show a side view of a room, usually with one wall per drawing. Elevations are made for both the interior and exterior of a house and generally show more architectural detail than floor plans.

Both floor plans and elevation drawings provide you with a method for planning and recording structural and mechanical systems for your project. They also help the local building department to ensure your project meets code requirements.

If you will be doing several projects in a short time, you may want to draw a plan of each complete floor of the home. If you're doing one isolated project, you may want to draw the plan of just that room.

To create floor plans, draw one story at a time. First, measure each room from wall to wall. Transfer the room's dimensions on ¼" grid paper, using a scale of ¼" = 1 ft. Label each room for its use and note its overall dimensions. Include wall thicknesses, which you can determine by measuring the widths of window and door jambs—do not include the trim.

Next, add these elements to your drawings:

• Windows and doors; note which way the doors swing.

• Stairs and their direction as it relates to each story.

• Permanent features, such as plumbing fixtures, major appliances, countertops, built-in furniture, and fireplaces.

• Overhead features, such as exposed beams, or wall cabinets—use dashed lines.

• Plumbing, electrical, and HVAC elements. You may want a separate set of drawings for these mechanical elements and service lines.

• Overall dimensions measured from outside the home. Use these to check the accuracy of interior dimensions.

To create elevation drawings, use the same ¼" = 1 ft. scale, and draw everything you see on one wall (each room has four elevations). Include:

• Ceiling heights and the heights of significant features such as soffits and exposed beams.

• Windows, including the height of the sills and tops of the openings, and widths.

• Doors, including the heights (from the floor to the top of the opening) and widths.

• Trim and other decorative elements.

When your initial floor plans and elevations are done, use them to sketch your remodeling layout options. Use tissue overlays to show hidden elements or proposed changes to a plan. Photographs of your home's interior and exterior may also be helpful. Think creatively, and draw many different sketches; the more design options you consider, the better your final plans will be.

When you have completed your remodeling plans, draft your final drawings and create a materials list for the project.

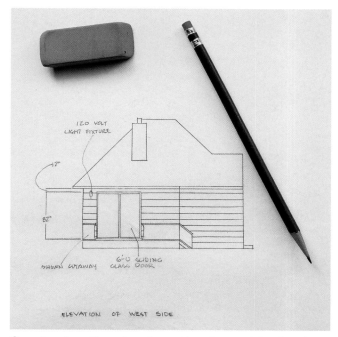 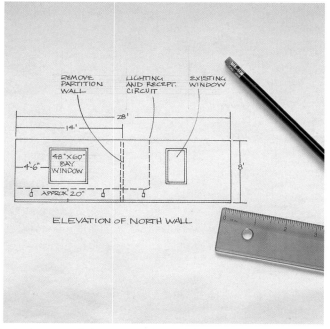

Create elevation drawings showing a side view layout of windows and doors, as viewed from both inside and outside the home. Indicate the size of windows and doors, ceiling heights, and the location of wiring and plumbing fixtures.

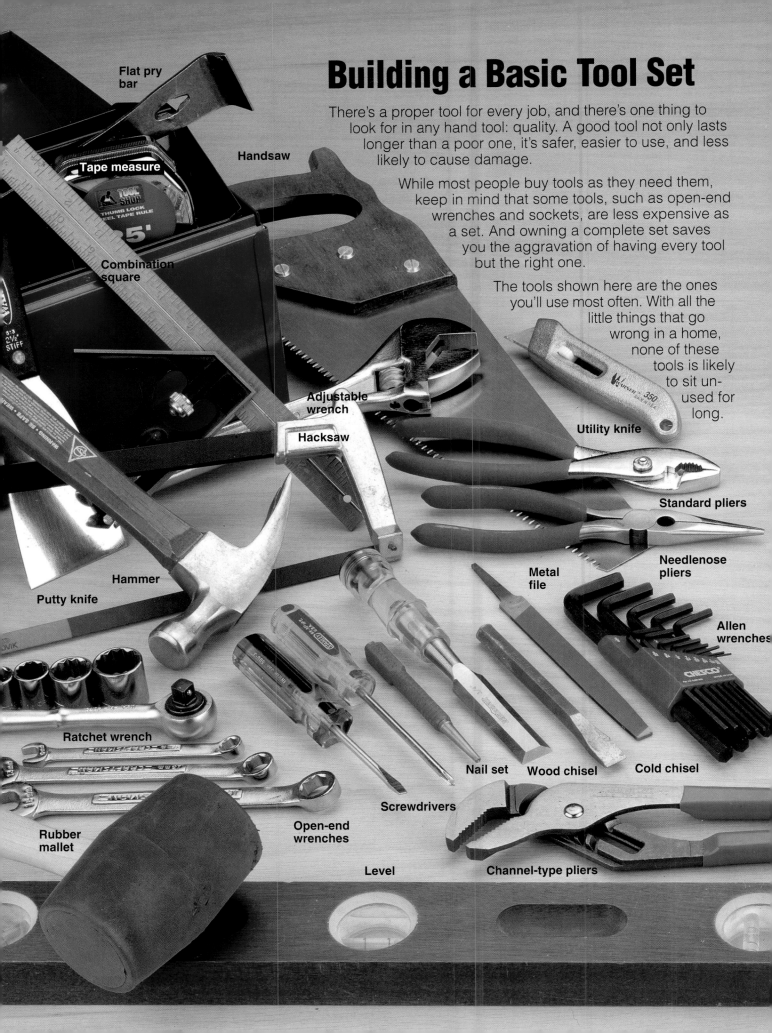

Building a Basic Tool Set

There's a proper tool for every job, and there's one thing to look for in any hand tool: quality. A good tool not only lasts longer than a poor one, it's safer, easier to use, and less likely to cause damage.

While most people buy tools as they need them, keep in mind that some tools, such as open-end wrenches and sockets, are less expensive as a set. And owning a complete set saves you the aggravation of having every tool but the right one.

The tools shown here are the ones you'll use most often. With all the little things that go wrong in a home, none of these tools is likely to sit unused for long.

Flat pry bar

Tape measure

Handsaw

Combination square

Adjustable wrench

Hacksaw

Utility knife

Standard pliers

Needlenose pliers

Metal file

Hammer

Putty knife

Allen wrenches

Nail set

Wood chisel

Cold chisel

Ratchet wrench

Screwdrivers

Rubber mallet

Open-end wrenches

Channel-type pliers

Level

Despite the higher price as compared with hand tools, power tools are a great value. You'll know this as soon as you put one to use. The time it takes to complete repetitive tasks, like drilling, sawing, and sanding, is reduced dramatically by a good power tool. And for many jobs, power tools are more accurate and easier to use than their manual counterparts—try using a handsaw to make a straight cut through plywood, for example.

For basic home repairs you won't need a fully equipped workshop, but a few of the standard tools will come in handy. A circular saw is ideal for any straight wood cuts, square or beveled; jig saws cut curves, holes, and slots in most materials; a palm sander makes short work of laborious sanding tasks; cordless screwdrivers are quick on screws and easy on your wrists; and a cordless drill, with a keyless chuck and adjustable speed, is one of the handiest power tools available.

Circular saw

Palm sander

Jig saw

Cordless screwdriver

Cordless drill

Site Preparation

Preparing the Work Area

When planning a door or window installation—or any carpentry project—you will need to consider and choose from dozens of design and construction options.

Consider hiring professionals for some parts of your project if you are unsure of your own skills.

Organize your project into stages, such as layout and planning, permit application (if required), shopping, site preparation, construction, and inspection. Smaller stages help you work efficiently and let you break large projects into a series of smaller, daily tasks.

If your project requires permits from the local building inspector, do not begin work until the inspector has approved your plans and issued the permits. Shopping is easier once you've obtained permits required for the job. Make a detailed materials list and make all of your purchases at the outset.

During the preparation phase, try to salvage or recycle materials when possible. Window and door units that are in good shape can be used elsewhere or sold to salvage yards. Most raw metals, such as the frames on old aluminum storm windows, are accepted at recycling centers.

Most carpentry projects share the same basic preparation techniques and follow a similar sequence. Start by checking for hidden mechanicals in the work area and shutting off and rerouting electrical wiring, plumbing pipes, and other utility lines. If you are not comfortable performing these tasks, hire a professional.

Test all electrical outlets before beginning any demolition of walls, ceilings, or floors. Shovel all demolition debris away from the work area. Clear away the debris whenever materials begin to pile up during the construction of a project. For larger jobs, consider renting a dumpster.

Everything You Need

Tools: screwdrivers, broom, flat pry bar, trash containers, neon circuit tester, electronic stud finder, channel-type pliers.

Materials: finish nails, masking tape, building paper, plywood, drop cloths.

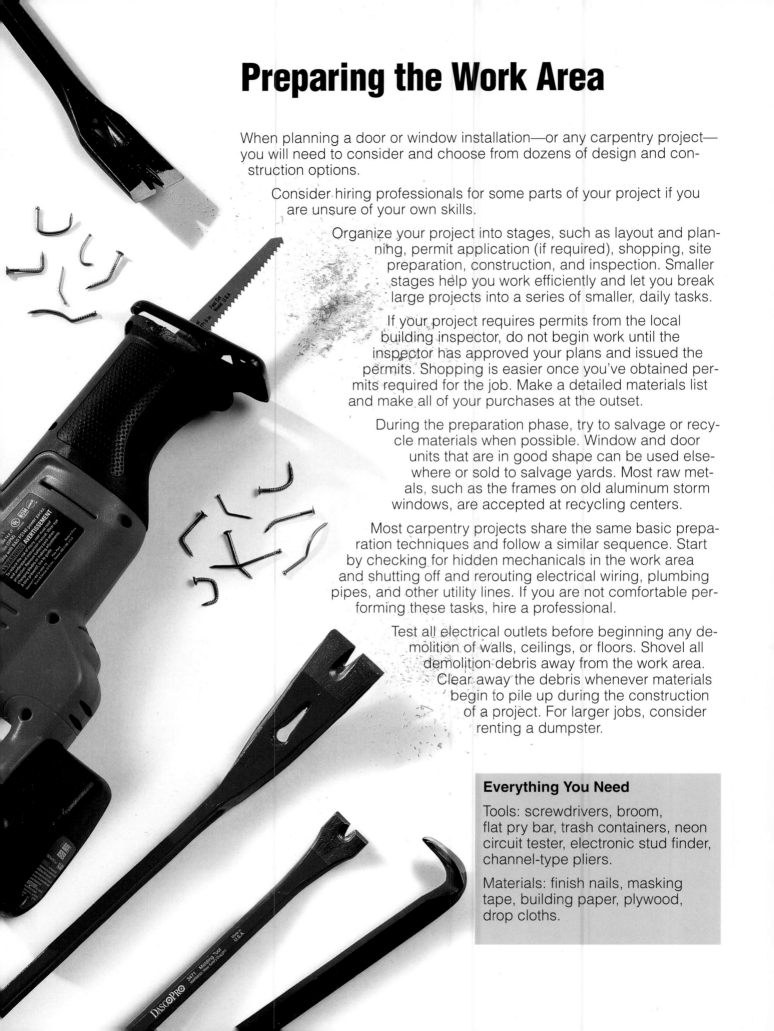

How to Prepare the Work Area

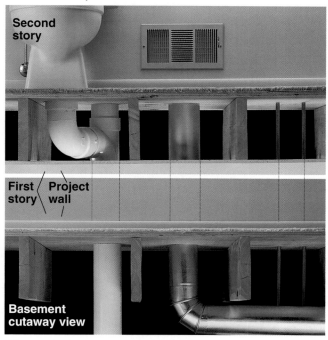

Check for hidden plumbing lines, ductwork, and gas pipes before you cut into a wall to create or enlarge a door or window opening. To determine the location of the pipes and ducts, examine the areas directly below and above the project wall. In most cases, pipes, utility lines, and ductwork run through the wall vertically between floors.

Disconnect electrical wiring before you cut into walls. Trace the wiring back to a fixture outside the cutout area, then shut off the power and disconnect the wires leading into the cutout area. Turn the power back on and test for current with a circuit tester before cutting into walls.

Locate framing members using a stud finder or by knocking on the wall and feeling for solid points. Verify the findings by driving finish nails through the wall surface. After finding the center of one stud, measure over 16" to locate neighboring studs.

Shovel debris through a convenient window into a wheelbarrow to speed up demolition work. Use sheets of plywood to cover shrubs and flower gardens next to open windows and doors. Cover adjoining lawn areas with sheets of plastic or canvas to simplify cleanup.

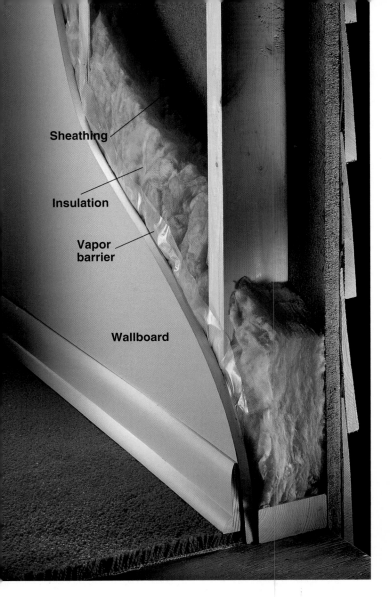

Sheathing

Insulation

Vapor
barrier

Wallboard

Removing Wallboard

You must remove interior wall surfaces before starting the framing work for many window and door projects. Most often, the material you'll be removing is wallboard. Demolishing a section of wallboard is a messy job, but it is not difficult. Before you begin, shut off the power and inspect the wall for wiring and plumbing.

Remove enough surface material so that there is plenty of room to install the new framing members. When framing for a window or door, remove the wall surface from floor to ceiling and all the way to the first wall studs on either side of the planned rough opening.

NOTE: If your walls are covered in wood paneling, remove it in full sheets if you intend to reuse it. It may be difficult to find new paneling to match the old style.

Everything You Need

Tools: screwdrivers, tape measure, pencil, stud finder, chalk line, utility knife, pry bar, circular saw with demolition blade, hammer, protective eyewear.

How to Remove Wallboard

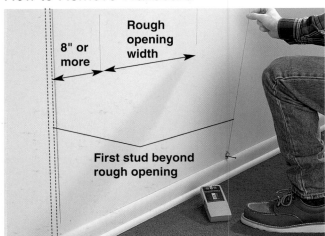

Rough opening width

8" or more

First stud beyond rough opening

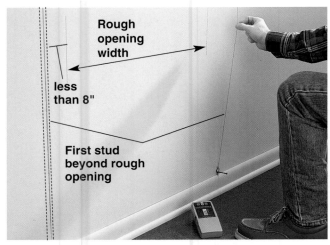

Rough opening width

less than 8"

First stud beyond rough opening

1 Mark the width of the rough opening on the wall and locate the first stud on either side of the planned rough opening. If the rough opening is more than 8" from the next stud, use a chalk line to mark a cutting line on the inside edge of the stud. During framing, an extra stud will be attached to provide a surface for anchoring the new wallboard.

Tip: If the rough opening is less than 8" from the next stud, you will not have room to attach an extra stud. Use a chalk line to mark the cutting line down the center of the wall stud. The exposed portion of the stud will provide a surface for attaching new wallboard when finishing the room.

2 Remove baseboards and other trim, and prepare the work area (pages 52 to 53). Make a ½"-deep cut from floor to ceiling along both cutting lines, using a circular saw. Use a utility knife to finish the cuts at the top and bottom and to cut through the taped horizontal seam where the wall meets the ceiling surface.

3 Insert the end of a pry bar into the cut near one corner of the opening. Pull the pry bar until the wallboard breaks, then tear away the broken pieces. Take care to avoid damaging the wallboard outside the project area.

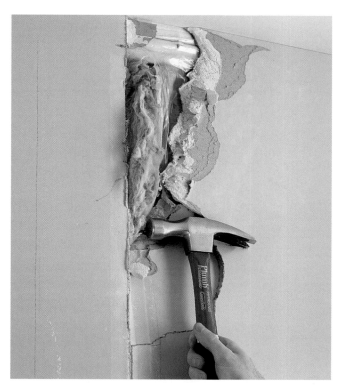

4 Continue removing the wallboard by striking the surface with the side of a hammer, and pulling the wallboard away from the wall with the pry bar or your hands.

5 Remove nails, screws, and any remaining wallboard from the framing members, using a pry bar. Remove any vapor barrier and insulation.

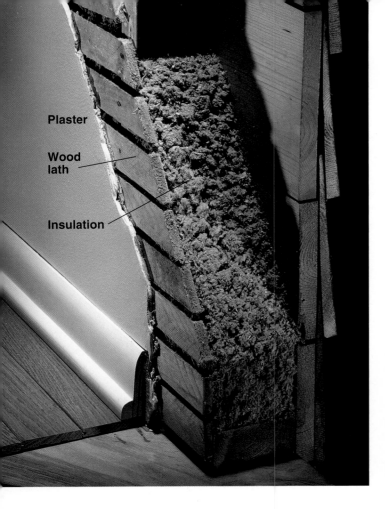

Plaster

Wood lath

Insulation

Removing Plaster

Plaster removal is a dusty job, so always wear eye protection and a particle mask during demolition, and use sheets of plastic to protect furniture and to block open doorways. Plaster walls are very brittle, so work carefully to avoid cracking the plaster in areas that will not be removed.

If the material being removed encompasses most of the wall surface, consider removing the whole interior surface of the wall. Replacing the entire wall with wallboard is easier and produces better results than trying to patch around the project area.

Everything You Need

Tools: straightedge, pencil, chalk line, pry bar, utility knife, particle mask, hammer, aviation snips, work gloves, reciprocating saw or jig saw, protective eyewear.

Materials: masking tape, scrap 2 × 4.

How to Remove Plaster

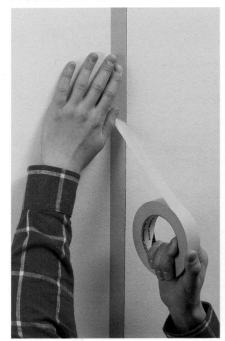

1 Shut off the power and inspect the wall for wiring and plumbing. Mark the wall area to be removed by following the directions on page 54. Apply a double layer of masking tape along the outside edge of each cutting line.

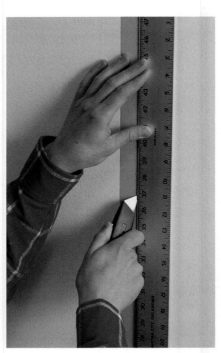

2 Score each line several times with a utility knife, using a straightedge as a guide. Scored lines should be at least ⅛" deep.

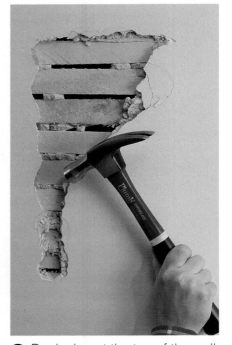

3 Beginning at the top of the wall in the center of the planned opening, break up the plaster by striking the wall lightly with the side of a hammer. Clear away all plaster from floor to ceiling to within 3" of the marked lines.

4 Break the plaster along the edges by holding a scrap piece of 2 × 4 on edge just inside the scored line, and rapping it with a hammer. Use a pry bar to remove the remaining plaster.

5 Cut through the lath along the edges of the plaster, using a reciprocating saw or jig saw.

Metal lath

Variation: If the wall has metal lath laid over the wood lath, use aviation snips to clip the edges of the metal lath. Press the jagged edges of the lath flat against the stud. The cut edges of metal lath are very sharp; be sure to wear work gloves.

6 Remove the lath from the studs, using a pry bar. Pry away any remaining nails, and remove any vapor barrier and insulation.

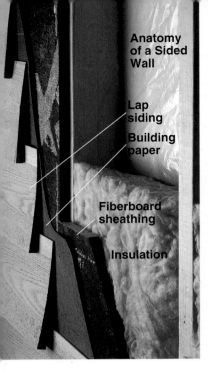

Anatomy of a Sided Wall

Lap siding

Building paper

Fiberboard sheathing

Insulation

Anatomy of a Stuccoed Wall

Stucco

Metal lath

Building paper

Sheathing

Everything You Need

Tools: stapler, flat pry bar, zip tool, drill, chalk line, circular saw, reciprocating saw, masonry chisel and hammer, masonry-cutting blade, masonry bit, aviation snips.

Materials: building paper, nails, 1 × 4.

Brick molding comes pre-attached to most wood-frame window and door units. To remove molding, pry along the outside of the frame to avoid marring exposed parts of the jambs and molding.

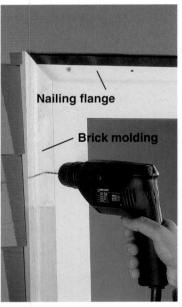

Nailing flange

Brick molding

Nailing flanges provide a means of attachment for most vinyl windows. After installation, the nailing flanges are covered with brick molding, 1 × exterior trim, or channel trim for vinyl or metal siding.

Removing Exterior Surfaces

Exterior surfaces must be removed when you create or enlarge an opening for a window or door in an exterior wall. Determine the best method for your project based on the exterior surface you have and the type of window or door unit you plan to install.

Wood siding can be cut in place or removed in full pieces to expose the area for the window or door opening. For windows and doors with brick molding, you can temporarily set the unit in place, trace around the brick molding onto the wood siding, then cut the siding to fit exactly around the molding. This method is shown on pages 160 to 161.

An alternative method is to remove the brick molding from the window and door unit, then cut the siding flush with the framed rough opening. After the unit is installed, temporarily set the molding in place and trace around it onto the siding. Cut the siding, then permanently attach the molding to the unit frame. Use this method to install a window with nailing flanges, but be sure to remove enough siding during the initial cut to provide room for the flanges (pages 92 to 93).

With vinyl or metal siding, it's best to remove whole pieces of siding to expose the opening, then cut them to fit after the unit and molding are installed. Be aware that vinyl and metal siding typically require special trim around openings. Check with the siding manufacturer before cutting anything, to make sure all of the necessary pieces are available.

Stucco surfaces can be cut away so that brick molding is recessed into the wall surface and makes contact with the sheathing. Or, you can use masonry clips (see page 91) and install the unit with the molding on top of the stucco.

If you're installing a window and door in a new framed opening, don't remove the exterior surface until the framing is complete.

Tips for Removing Siding

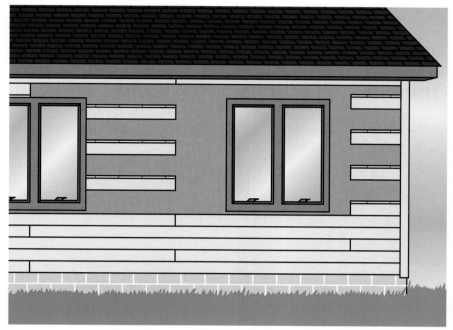

Remove whole pieces of siding to expose the area around a window or door opening. Siding is installed in a staggered pattern so that joints between successive rows do not line up. Number the siding pieces as you remove them to simplify reinstallation.

Patch-in building paper after removing siding. Loosen building paper above patch area, slip the top of the patch underneath, and attach it with staples. Use roofing cement to patch small holes or tears.

To remove a piece of wood siding, start by prying up the piece above, using a flat pry bar near nail locations. Knock the top piece back down with a hammer to expose the raised nails, then pull the nails. Insert spacers between the siding and sheathing to make it easier to access work areas. Use a hacksaw blade or a cold chisel to shear any difficult nails.

Vinyl and metal siding pieces have a locking J-channel that fits over the bottom of the nailing strip on the piece below. Use a zip tool (inset) to separate siding panels. Insert zip tool at overlapping seam nearest removal area. Slide zip tool over J-channel, pulling outward slightly, to unlock joint from the siding below. Remove nails from panel, then push panel down to unlock it. CAUTION: Metal siding will buckle if bent too far.

How to Make an Opening in Wood Siding

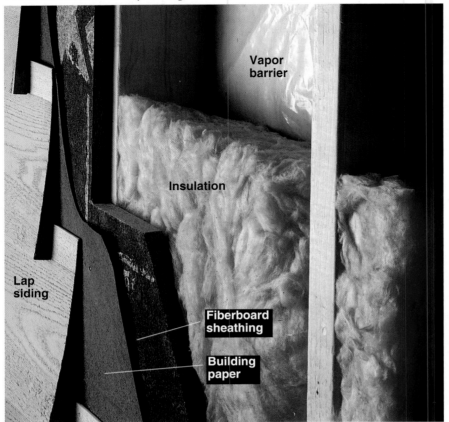

Vapor barrier

Insulation

Lap siding

Fiberboard sheathing

Building paper

Tip: Always shut off the power and reroute utility lines, remove any interior surfaces, and frame-in the new opening before removing an exterior surface. To protect the wall cavities against moisture, enclose the new opening as soon as you remove the old siding.

Everything You Need

Tools: drill with an 8"-long ³/₁₆" twist bit, hammer, tape measure, chalk line, circular saw with remodeling blade, reciprocating saw, eye protection.

Materials: 8d casing nails, straight 1 × 4.

1 From inside the home, drill through wall at corners of the framed opening. Push casing nails through the holes to mark their location. For round-top windows, drill holes around the curved outline (see variation, page 61).

2 Measure the distance between the nails on outside of home to make sure the dimensions are accurate. Mark cutting lines with a chalk line stretched between nails. Push nails back through the wall.

3 Nail a straight 1 × 4 flush with the inside edge of the right cutting line. Sink nail heads with a nail set to prevent scratches to the foot of the saw. Set depth of circular saw so it cuts through the siding and sheathing.

4 Rest the saw on the 1 × 4, and cut along the marked line, using the edge of the board as a guide. Stop the cuts about 1" short of the corners to keep from damaging the framing members.

5 Reposition the 1 × 4, and make the remaining straight cuts. Drive nails within 1½" of the inside edge of the board, because the siding under this area will be removed to make room for window or door brick moldings.

Variation: For round-top windows, make curved cuts using a reciprocating saw or jig saw. Move the saw slowly to ensure smooth, straight cuts. To draw an outline for round-top windows, use a cardboard template (page 87).

6 Complete the cuts at the corners with a reciprocating saw or jig saw. Be careful not to cut beyond the corner marks.

7 Remove the cut wall section. If you wish, remove the siding pieces from the sheathing and save them for future use.

How to Make an Opening in Stucco

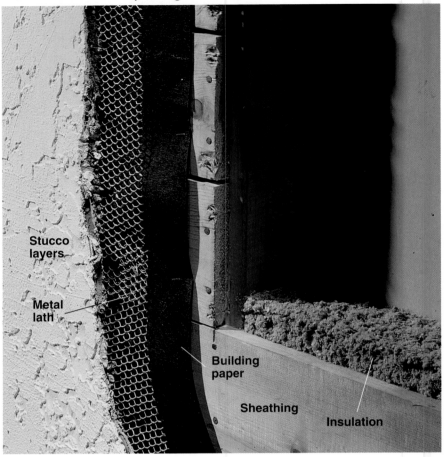

Stucco layers

Metal latH

Building paper

Sheathing

Insulation

Tip: Stucco is a multiple-layer cement product applied to metal lath. Building paper is sandwiched between the metal lath and the sheathing to create a waterproof barrier. Stucco is extremely durable due to its cement base. But if you don't do the removal carefully, it's easy to crack the stucco past the outline for the new window or door.

Everything You Need

Tools: drill with an 8"-long 3/16" twist and masonry bits, tape measure, chalk line, compass, masonry hammer, eye and ear protection, circular saw and blades (masonry-cutting and re-modeling), masonry chisels, pry bar, aviation snips.

Materials: 8d casing nails.

1 From inside the home, drill through the wall at the corners of the framed opening. Use a twist bit to drill through the sheathing, then use a masonry bit to finish the holes. Push casing nails through the holes to mark their locations.

2 On the outside wall, measure the distance between the nails to make sure the rough opening dimensions are accurate. Mark cutting lines between the nails, using a chalk line.

Side jamb

Brick molding

3 Match the distance between the side jambs and the edge of the brick molding on a window or door with the legs of a compass.

4 Drill corners and mark cutting lines with a chalk line. Measure out from the chalk line the same distance as the width of the molding on the window or door unit. Make a second set of lines at the outer marks (the added margin will allow the brick molding to fit tight against the wall sheathing). Score the stucco surface around the outer lines, using a masonry chisel and hammer. The scored grooves should be at least ⅛" deep.

5 Make straight cuts using a circular saw and masonry-cutting blade. Make several passes with the saw, gradually deepening the cuts until the blade just cuts through the metal lath, causing sparks to fly. Stop the cuts just ahead of the corners to avoid damaging the stucco past the cutting line; complete the cuts with a masonry chisel.

Variation: For round-top windows, mark the outline on the stucco, using a cardboard template (page 87), and drill a series of holes around the outline, using a masonry bit. Complete the cut with a masonry chisel.

6 Break up the stucco with a masonry hammer or sledgehammer, exposing the underlying metal lath. Use aviation snips to cut through the lath around the opening. Use a pry bar to pull away lath and attached stucco.

7 Outline the rough opening on the sheathing, using a straightedge as a guide. Cut the rough opening along the inside edge of framing members, using a circular saw or reciprocating saw. Remove the cut section of sheathing.

Masking tape used to keep windows from shattering

Removing Windows & Doors

If your remodeling project requires removing old windows and doors, do not start this work until all preparation work is finished and the interior wall surfaces and trim have been removed. You will need to close up the wall openings as soon as possible, so make sure you have all the necessary tools, framing lumber, and new window or door units before starting the final stages of demolition. Be prepared to finish the work as quickly as possible.

Windows and doors are removed using the same basic procedures. In many cases, old units can be salvaged for resale or later use, so use care when removing them.

Everything You Need

Tools: utility knife, flat pry bar, screwdriver, hammer, reciprocating saw.

Materials: plywood, masking tape, screws.

If wall openings cannot be filled immediately, protect your home by covering the openings with scrap pieces of plywood screwed to the framing members. Plastic sheeting stapled to the outside of the openings will prevent moisture damage.

How to Remove Doors

1 Using a pry bar and hammer, gently remove the interior door trim. Save the trim to use after the new door is installed.

2 Cut away the old caulk between the exterior siding and the brick molding on the door frame, using a utility knife.

3 Use a flat pry bar or a cat's paw to remove the casing nails securing the door jambs to the framing. Cut stubborn nails with a reciprocating saw (see step 2, below). Remove the door from the opening.

How to Remove Windows

1 Carefully pry off the interior trim around the window frame. For double-hung windows with sash weights, remove the weights by cutting the cords and pulling the weights from the weight pockets near the bottom of the side jambs.

2 Cut through the nails holding the window jambs to the framing members, using a reciprocating saw. Place tape over the window panes to prevent shattering, then remove the window unit from the opening.

Nailing flange

Variation: For windows and doors attached with nailing flanges, cut or pry loose the siding material, then remove the nails holding the unit to the sheathing. See pages 32 to 35 for more information on removing siding.

65

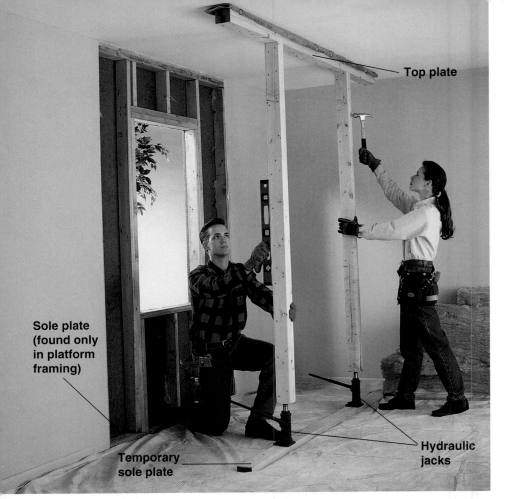

Top plate

Sole plate
(found only
in platform
framing)

Temporary
sole plate

Hydraulic
jacks

Temporary supports for a platform-framed house must support the ceiling joists, since the ceiling platform carries the load of the upper floors. Platform framing can be identified by the sole plate to which the wall studs are nailed.

Whaler

Braces

Planned
rough
opening

Temporary supports for a balloon-framed house support the wall studs, which carry the upstairs load. The temporary support header, called a whaler, is anchored to the wall studs above the planned rough opening, and is supported by wall studs and bracing adjacent to the rough opening. Balloon framing can be identified by long wall studs that pass uncut through the floor to a sill plate resting on the foundation.

Making Temporary Supports

If your project requires you to remove more than one stud in a load-bearing wall, temporary supports will be needed while you do the framing. The technique for making temporary supports varies, depending on your house's construction. See pages 30 to 31 to easily identify wall types and other framing anatomy.

Removal of load-bearing interior walls requires temporary support on both sides of the wall.

To make temporary supports for platform framing, use hydraulic jacks or a temporary stud wall (page 68). The stud wall method is a better choice if the supports must remain in place for more than one day.

To make temporary supports for balloon framing, see page 69.

The project shown involves working on an exterior wall on the first floor of a balloon-framed house. Consult a professional if you want to alter an interior load-bearing wall or an exterior wall on an upper floor of a balloon-framed house.

Hire a professional to remove any wall over 12 ft. long.

Everything You Need

Tools: tape measure, level, circular saw, hammer, ratchet, drill and spade bit, hydraulic jacks.

Materials: 2 × 4 lumber, shims, 3" and 4" lag screws, 2" wallboard screws, 10d nails, cloth.

How to Support Platform Framing with Hydraulic Jacks (Joists Perpendicular to Wall)

1 Measure the width of the planned rough opening and add 4 ft. so the temporary support will reach well past the rough opening. Cut three 2 × 4s to length. Nail two of the 2 × 4s together with 10d nails to make a top plate for the temporary support; the remaining 2 × 4 will be the sole plate. Place the temporary sole plate on the floor, 3 ft. from the wall, centering it on the planned rough opening.

2 Set the hydraulic jacks on the temporary sole plate, 2 ft. in from the ends. (Use three jacks if the opening will be more than 8 ft. wide.) For each jack, build a post by nailing together a pair of 2 × 4s. The posts should be about 4" shorter than the distance between the ceiling and the top of the jacks. Attach the posts to the top plate, 2 ft. from the ends, using countersunk lag screws.

Direction of joists

3 Cover the top of the plate with a thick layer of cloth to protect the ceiling from marks and cracks, then lift the support structure onto the hydraulic jacks.

4 Adjust the support structure so the posts are exactly plumb, and raise the hydraulic jacks until the top plate just begins to lift the ceiling. Do not lift too far, or you may damage the floor or ceiling.

How to Support Platform Framing with a Temporary Stud Wall (Joists Perpendicular to Wall)

1 Build a 2 × 4 stud wall that is 4 ft. wider than the planned wall opening and 1¾" shorter than the distance from floor to ceiling.

2 Raise the stud wall and position it 3 ft. from the wall, centered on the planned rough opening.

3 Slide a 2 × 4 top plate between the temporary wall and the ceiling. Check to make sure the wall is plumb, and drive shims under the top plate at 12" intervals until the wall is wedged tightly in place.

How to Support Platform Framing with Hydraulic Jacks (Joists Parallel to Wall)

1 Follow directions on page 67, except: Build two 4-ft.-long cross braces, using pairs of 2 × 4s nailed together. Attach the cross braces to the double top plate, 1 ft. from the ends, using counter-sunk lag screws.

2 Place a 2 × 4 sole plate directly over a floor joist, then set hydraulic jacks on the sole plate. For each jack, build a post 8" shorter than jack-to-ceiling distance. Nail posts to the top plate, 2 ft. from ends. Cover braces with cloth, and set support structure on jacks.

3 Adjust the support structure so the posts are exactly plumb, and pump the hydraulic jacks until the cross braces just begin to lift the ceiling. Do not lift too far, or you may damage the ceiling or floor.

How to Support Balloon Framing

1 Remove the wall surfaces around the rough opening from floor to ceiling (pages 54 to 57). Make a temporary support header (called a whaler) by cutting a 2 × 8 long enough to extend at least 20" past each side of the planned rough opening. Center the whaler against the wall studs, flush with the ceiling. Tack the whaler in place with 2" screws.

2 Cut two lengths of 2 × 4 to fit snugly between the bottom of the whaler and the floor. Slide the 2 × 4s into place at the ends of the whaler, and attach them with nailing plates and 10d nails.

3 Drill two ³⁄₁₆" holes through the whaler and into each stud it spans. Secure the whaler with ⅜ × 4" lag screws.

4 Drive shims between the bottom of each 2 × 4 and the floor to help secure the support structure.

69

Installing & Finishing Wallboard

Use wallboard panels both to finish new walls and to patch existing wall areas exposed during the installation of a window or door.

Openings in smooth plaster walls usually can be patched with wallboard, but if you need to match a textured plaster surface, it is best to hire a plasterer to do the work.

Wallboard panels are available in 4 × 8-ft. or 4 × 10-ft. sheets, and in ⅜", ½", and ⅝" thicknesses. For new walls, ½" thick is standard.

Use all-purpose wallboard compound and paper joint tape. Lay out wallboard panels so that seams fall over the center of openings, not at sides, or use solid pieces at openings. Insulate all framing cavities around each opening.

Everything You Need

Tools: tape measure, utility knife, wallboard T-square, 6" and 12" wallboard knives, 150-grit sanding sponge.

Materials: wallboard, wallboard tape, 1¼" coarse-thread wallboard screws, wallboard compound, metal inside corner bead.

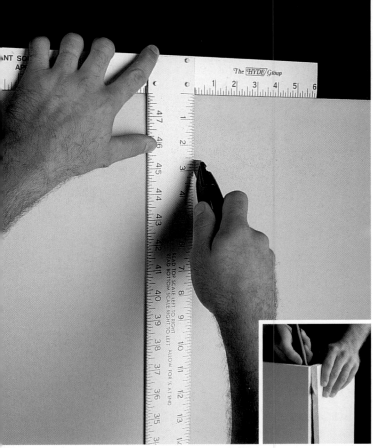

Score wallboard face paper with a utility knife, using a wallboard T-square as a guide. Bend the panel away from the scored line until the core breaks, then cut through the back paper (inset) with a utility knife, and separate the pieces.

How to Install & Finish Wallboard

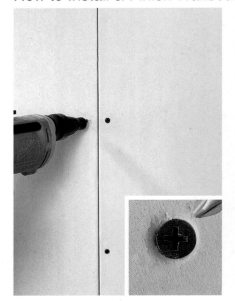

1 Install panels with their tapered edges butted together. Fasten with 1¼" screws, driven every 8" along the edges, and every 12" in the field. Drive screws deep enough to dimple surface without ripping face paper (inset).

2 Finish the seams by applying an even bed layer of compound over the seam, about ⅛" thick, using a 6" taping knife.

3 Center the tape over the seam and lightly embed it into the compound, making sure it's smooth and straight.

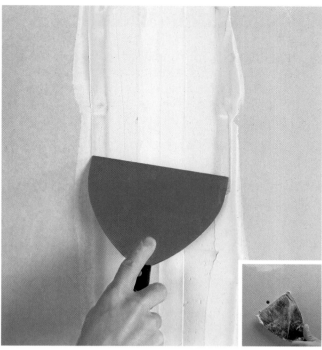

4 Smooth the tape with the taping knife. Apply enough pressure to force compound from underneath the tape, leaving the tape flat and with a thin layer underneath. Cover all exposed screw heads with the first of three coats of compound (inset). Let compound dry overnight.

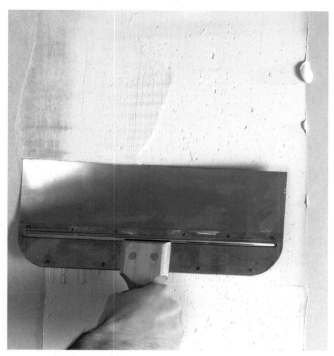

5 Second-coat the seams with a thin, even layer of compound, using a 12" knife. Feather the sides of the compound first, holding the blade almost flat and applying pressure to the outside of the blade so that the blade just skims over the center of the seam.

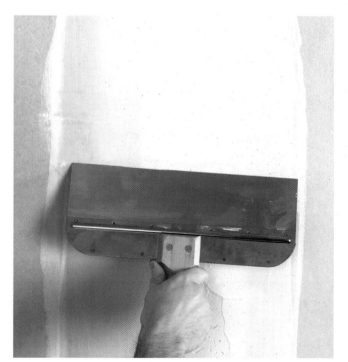

6 After feathering both sides, make a pass down the center of the seam, leaving the seam smooth and even, the edges feathered out to nothing. Completely cover the joint tape. Let second coat dry, then apply a third coat, using the 12" knife. After the third coat dries completely, sand the compound lightly with a drywall sander or a 150-grit sanding sponge.

Tip: Finish any inside corners using paper-faced metal inside corner bead to produce straight, durable corners with little fuss. Embed the bead into a thin layer of compound, then smooth the paper with a taping knife. Apply two finish coats to the corner, then sand the compound smooth.

Patching Exterior Walls

Many remodeling projects involve patching or repairing exterior wall surfaces, and the key to a successful job is to follow the original work. This will help you determine the best installation method and make sure the patch blends in with the surrounding area.

To patch siding, use a staggered pattern so that vertical end joints are not aligned between rows. If you've installed a window or door into an existing opening, you may have to remove some siding pieces before patching in new ones to maintain the staggered installation.

Wood siding generally is easy to match with new material from a lumberyard. Vinyl and metal siding can be more difficult to match, so contact the siding manufacturer before making any changes to your existing surfaces. It's also important that you have the right trim pieces to make sure the patch looks good and creates a weatherproof barrier.

Windows and doors with nailing flanges (see pages 92 to 93) must be covered with wood or metal molding, usually purchased separately. After the window is installed, hold trim pieces in place, then mark an outline around the trim onto the siding. Trim the siding to fit.

Everything You Need
Tools: circular saw, flat pry bar, aviation snips, trowel, scratching tool, whisk broom.
Materials: exterior-wall sheathing, building paper, siding, 6d siding nails, paintable silicone caulk, stucco mix, tint (optional), self-furring metal lath, spray bottle.

Tips for Installing Vinyl Siding

Cut vinyl siding using a circular saw, metal snips, or a utility knife. Outfit a circular saw with a plywood blade (fine-toothed), and install the blade backward so the teeth point down. Make the cuts slowly, using standard cutting techniques. NOTE: Do not cut any material other than vinyl siding with the saw blade installed backward. When cutting siding with a utility knife, score the panels using a framing square as a guide, then snap along the scored line.

Attach siding panels so they can expand and contract with temperature changes. Lock the bottom edge underneath the nailing strip of the panel below, using a zip tool (see page 59) if necessary. Hold the panel flat to the sheathing without stretching it upward and nail through the centers of the nailing-strip slots, leaving about 1/32" between the nail head and the panel. Fasten the middle of the panel first, and space the nails following manufacturer's instructions.

How to Patch Wood Lap Siding

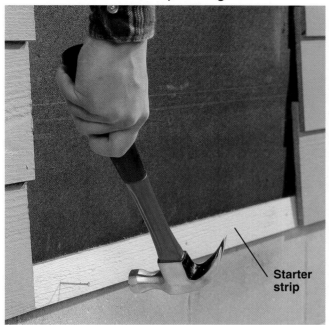

1 Cover the patch area with sheathing and building paper, if not already present. If the bottom row of siding is missing, nail a starter strip cut from a piece of siding along the bottom of the patch area, using 6d siding nails. Leave a ¼" gap at each joint in the starter strip to allow for expansion.

Starter strip

2 Use a flat pry bar to remove lengths of lap siding on both sides of patch area, creating a staggered pattern. When new siding is installed, the end joints will be offset for a less conspicuous appearance.

3 Cut the bottom piece of lap siding to span the entire opening, and lay it over the starter strip. Allow a ¼" expansion gap between board ends. Attach the siding with pairs of 6d siding nails driven at each stud location.

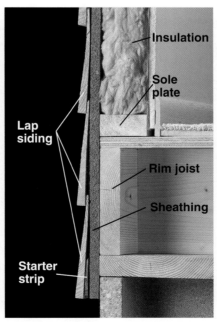

Insulation
Sole plate
Lap siding
Rim joist
Sheathing
Starter strip

4 Cut and install succeeding rows of siding, nailing only near the top of the siding at stud locations. Work upward from the bottom to create the proper overlap.

5 Fill joints between the siding pieces with paintable silicone caulk. Repaint the entire wall surface as soon as the caulk dries to protect the new siding against weather.

Tips for Patching Stucco

For small jobs, use premixed stucco, available at building centers. For best results, apply the stucco in two or three layers, letting each layer dry completely between applications. Premixed stucco also can be used on larger areas, but it is more expensive than mixing your own ingredients.

For large jobs, combine dry stucco mix with water, following the manufacturer's directions, or use the ingredients lists shown here. A stucco finish typically contains two or three layers, depending on the application (see below). The mixtures for the base and brown coats should be just moist enough to hold their shape when squeezed (inset). A finish-coat mix requires slightly more water than other coats. If you need to color the finish coat, mix test batches first, adding measured amounts of tint to each batch. Let the test batches dry for at least an hour to get an accurate indication of the final color.

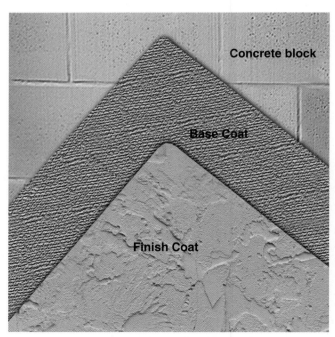

Concrete block
Base Coat
Finish Coat

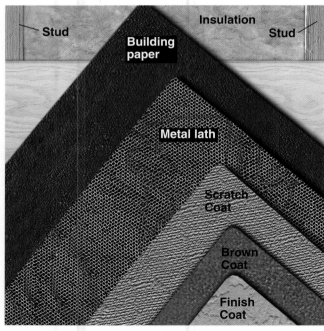

Stud
Insulation
Stud
Building paper
Metal lath
Scratch Coat
Brown Coat
Finish Coat

When applying stucco over brick or block (left), use two coats: a ⅜"-thick base coat and a ¼"-thick finish coat. Do not apply stucco directly over painted concrete block. **On wood-frame construction or an insulation-board surface (right),** first cover the area with building paper and metal lath. Then apply three coats of stucco: a scratch coat (⅜" to ½" thick), a brown coat (⅜" thick), and a finish coat (⅛" thick). Both the base coat on masonry walls and the scratch coat on wood-frame walls should be "scratched" after they are applied. This involves etching horizontal grooves into the partially set stucco using a scratching tool. You can make your own scratching tool by driving a row of 1½" wire nails through a piece of 1 × 2. The grooves provide a gripping surface for the next stucco layer.

How to Patch Stucco

1 Cover the patch area with sheathing and building paper, if not already present. Cut self-furring metal lath, using aviation snips, and attach it to the sheathing with 1½" galvanized roofing nails, driven into the wall studs every 6". Overlap pieces of lath by 2". NOTE: If patch area extends to the base of the wall, install a metal stop bead at the bottom of the wall.

2 Mix a batch of stucco for the scratch coat (page 74). Apply a ⅜"-thick layer of stucco over the lath, using a trowel. Press firmly to fill any voids, and cover the lath completely. Let the stucco dry until it will hold the impression of a thumbprint, then use a scratching tool to make shallow grooves across the entire surface. Let the stucco set for two days, dampening it every few hours with fine spray to help it cure evenly.

3 Mix a batch of stucco for the brown coat (page 74), and apply it in a ⅜"-thick layer or until the patch area is within ¼" to ⅛" of the surrounding surface. Let the coat cure for two days, dampening it every few hours.

4 Mix a stucco finish coat (page 74). Dampen the wall, then apply the finish coat to match the surrounding stucco. The texture for the finish coat above was dashed on with a flick of a whisk broom, then flattened with a trowel. Keep the finish coat damp for a week while it cures. Let the stucco dry for several more days if you plan to paint it.

Replacing Windows & Doors

Planning Window Installations

Windows and skylights are a room's main source of natural light, but they perform other essential functions, as well. A window's design and its treatment can add personality and charm to a room, while its shape and placement allow you to direct light where it's needed. By breaking up walls and ceilings, windows and skylights can expand a room's perceived boundaries, making it appear larger.

The right windows also help ensure your comfort in all seasons by letting you control the flow of warmth, light, and fresh air into your home. When choosing windows, it's important to consider your needs for privacy and energy efficiency, as well as the visual effect that the windows will have on the exterior of your home.

The brainstorming part of planning for window installations is the time to consider how various window design options might alter or enhance the room. Since different kinds of windows offer different benefits, the first step in choosing the right windows is determining and prioritizing your design needs.

There are many benefits to be gained by replacing windows: adding more sunlight to make a room seem larger, ventilating the room, improving a view, eliminating drafts, reducing heating and cooling costs, gaining an egress for a bedroom, and defining a space.

When installing windows, consider the sizes, positions, and proportions of the windows carefully, so that they fit in with the other architectural elements of your home. For example, it's best to align the tops of all the windows in a straight line (typically 80" above the floor, level with the doors). Even if the windows are different heights, positioning the tops along the same line will give both the interior and the exterior of your home a sense of order.

When adding or enlarging windows, be sure to consider any state and local code restrictions.

Windows are your home's eyes to the outside world. They provide natural light, open readily, and serve as a barricade to insects, intruders, and natural elements. They are also one of the more expensive elements of your home, which is good reason to choose them wisely—they can last 40 years or more.

By installing a bay window in place of a double casement window, the owners of this home brightened their living room and created a sweeping view of a pastoral scene. Bay windows make any room seem larger and brighter, and add visual interest to the exterior of the home.

Removing a small double-hung window and installing two double casement windows was the first step in turning this dark bedroom into a bright space for sitting and relaxing. Casement-style windows were chosen because they provide an unobstructed view and good ventilation.

Upgrade old, leaky windows with new, energy-efficient sash-replacement kits. Kits are available in a variety of styles to match your existing windows or to add a new decorative accent to your home. Most kits offer natural or painted interior surfaces and a choice of outdoor surface finishes.

Installing New Window Sashes

If you're looking to replace or improve old single- or double-hung windows, consider using sash-replacement kits. They can give you energy-efficient, maintenance-free windows without changing the outward appearance of your home or breaking your budget.

Unlike prime window replacement, which changes the entire window and frame, or pocket window replacement, in which a complete window unit is set into the existing frame, sash replacement uses the original window jambs, eliminating the need to alter exterior or interior walls or trim. Installing a sash-replacement kit involves little more than removing the old window stops and sashes and installing new vinyl jamb liners and wood or vinyl sashes. And all of the work can be done from inside your home.

Most sash-replacement kits offer tilt features and other contemporary conveniences. Kits are available in vinyl, aluminum, or wood construction, with various options for color and glazing, energy efficiency, security features, and noise reduction.

Nearly all major window manufacturers offer sash-replacement kits designed to fit their own windows. You can also order custom kits that are sized to your specific window dimensions. A good fit is essential to the performance of your new windows. Review the tips shown on page 81 for measuring your existing windows, and follow the manufacturer's instructions for the best fit.

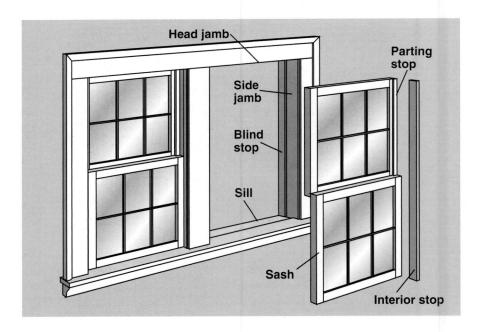

Everything You Need

Tools: sill-bevel gauge, flat pry bar, scissors, screwdriver, nail set.

Materials: sash-replacement kit, 1" galvanized roofing nails, fiberglass insulation, finish nails, wood-finishing materials.

Tips for Measuring for Sash-replacement Kits

Head jamb

Measure the width of the existing window at the top, middle, and bottom of the frame. Use the smallest measurement, then reduce the figure by ⅜". Measure the height of the existing window from the head jamb to the point where the outside edge of the bottom sash meets the sill. Reduce the figure by ⅜". NOTE: Manufacturers' specifications for window sizing may vary.

Sill-bevel gauge

Use a sill-bevel gauge to determine the bevel of the existing windowsill. This helps ensure the sash kit will fit properly. Also make sure that the sill, side, and head jambs are straight, level, and plumb. Measure the frame diagonally to check for square (if the diagonal measurements are equal, the frame is square). If the frame is not square, check with the sash-kit manufacturer: Most window kits can accommodate some deviation in frame dimensions.

How to Install a Sash-replacement Kit

1 Carefully remove the interior stops from the side jambs, using a putty knife or pry bar. Save the stops for reinstallation.

2 With the bottom sash down, cut the cord holding the sash balancing weight on each side of the sash. Let the weights and cords fall into the weight pockets.

(continued next page)

Photos this page courtesy of Marvin Windows and Doors

How to Install a Sash-replacement Kit (continued)

3 Lift out the bottom sash. Remove the parting stops from the head and side jambs. (The parting stops are the strips of wood that separate the top and bottom sash.) Cut the sash cords for the top sash; then lift out the top sash. Remove the sash-cord pulleys. If possible, pull the weights from the weight pockets at the bottom of the side jambs, then fill the weight pockets with fiberglass insulation. Repair any parts of the jambs that are rotted or damaged.

4 Position the jamb-liner brackets, and fasten them to the jambs with 1" galvanized roofing nails. Place one bracket approximately 4" from head jamb, and one 4" from the sill. Leave 1/16" clearance between the blind stop and the jamb-liner bracket. Install any remaining brackets, spacing them evenly along the jambs.

5 Position any gaskets or weatherstripping provided for the jamb liners. Carefully position each liner against its brackets and snap it into place. When both liners are installed, set the new parting stop into the groove of the existing head jamb, and fasten it with small finish nails. Install a vinyl sash stop in the interior track at the top of each liner, to prevent the bottom sash from being opened too far.

6 Set the sash control mechanism, using a slotted screwdriver. Gripping the screwdriver firmly, slide down the mechanism until it is about 9" above the sill, then turn the screwdriver to lock the mechanism and prevent it from springing upward. The control mechanisms are spring-loaded—do not let them go until they are locked in place. Set the mechanism in each of the four sash channels.

7 Install top sash into the jamb liners. Set the cam pivot on one side of the sash into the outside channel. Tilt the sash, and set the cam pivot on the other side of the sash. Make sure both pivots are set above the sash control mechanisms. Holding the sash level, tilt it up, depress the jamb liners on both sides and set the sash in the vertical position in the jamb liners. Once the sash is in position, slide it down until the cam pivots contact the locking terminal assemblies.

8 Install the bottom sash into the jamb liners, setting it into the inside sash channels. When the bottom sash is set in the vertical position, slide it down until it engages the control mechanisms. Open and close both sashes to make sure they operate properly.

9 Reinstall the stops that you removed in step 1. Fasten them with finish nails, using the old nail holes, or drill new pilot holes for the nails.

10 Check the tilt operation of the bottom sash to make sure the stops do not interfere. Remove the labels, and clean the windows. Paint or varnish the new sash as desired.

Header

Angled stud

Jambs

Shims

Insulation

Double rough sill

Cripple studs

Jack stud

King stud

Framing & Installing Windows

Many windows must be custom-ordered several weeks in advance. To save time, you can complete the interior framing before the window unit arrives, but be sure you have the exact dimensions of the window unit before building the frame. Do not remove the outside wall surface until you have the window and accessories and are ready to install them.

Follow the manufacturer's specifications for rough opening size when framing for a window. The listed opening usually is 1" wider and ½" taller than the actual dimensions of the window unit. The following pages show techniques for wood-frame houses with platform framing.

If your house has balloon framing (page 31), use the method shown on page 158 to install a header. Consult a professional to install a window on the second story of a balloon-framed house.

If your house has masonry walls, or if you are installing polymer-coated windows, you may want to attach your window using masonry clips instead of nails.

If your home's exterior has siding or is stucco, see pages 58 to 63 for tips on removing these surfaces and making the opening.

Everything You Need

Tools: tape measure, pencil, combination square, hammer, level, circular saw, handsaw, pry bar, nippers, drill, reciprocating saw, stapler, nail set, caulk gun.

Materials: 10d common nails, 5d galvanized roofing nails, shims, 2 × lumber, ⅛" plywood, building paper, drip edge, 10d galvanized casing nails, 8d casing nails, fiberglass insulation, paintable silicone caulk.

How to Frame a Window Opening

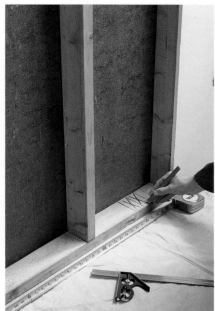

1 Prepare the project site and remove the interior wall surfaces (pages 54 to 57). Measure and mark the rough opening width on the sole plate. Mark the locations of the jack studs and king studs on the sole plate. Where practical, use the existing studs as king studs.

2 Measure and cut the king studs, as needed, to fit between the sole plate and the top plate. Position the king studs and toenail them to the sole plate with 10d nails.

3 Check the king studs with a level to make sure they are plumb, then toenail them to the top plate with 10d nails.

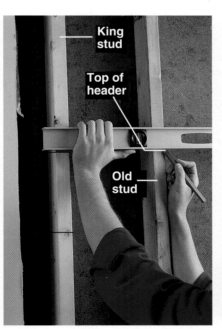

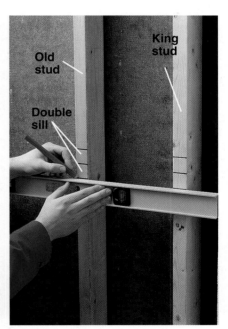

4 Measuring from the floor, mark the top of the rough opening on one of the king studs. This line represents the bottom of the window header. For most windows, the recommended rough opening is ½" taller than the height of the window frame.

5 Measure and mark where the top of the window header will fit against the king stud. The header size depends on the distance between the king studs (page 32). Use a carpenter's level to extend the lines across the old studs to the opposite king stud.

6 Measure down from header line and mark the double rough sill on the king stud. Use a carpenter's level to extend the lines across the old studs to the opposite king stud. Make temporary supports (pages 66 to 69) if removing more than one stud.

(continued next page)

7 Set a circular saw to its maximum blade depth, then cut through the old studs along the lines marking the bottom of the rough sill and along the lines marking the top of the header. Do not cut the king studs. On each stud, make an additional cut about 3" above the sill cut. Finish the cuts with a handsaw.

8 Knock out the 3" stud sections, then tear out the old studs inside the rough opening, using a pry bar. Clip away any exposed nails, using nippers. The remaining sections of the cut studs will serve as cripple studs for the window.

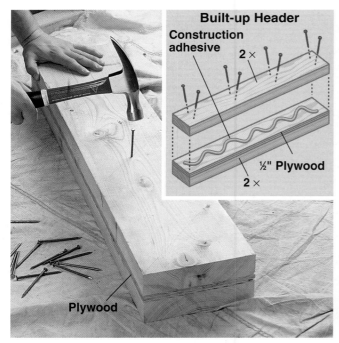

9 Build a header to fit between the king studs on top of the jack studs, using two pieces of 2 × lumber sandwiched around ½" plywood.

10 Cut two jack studs to reach from the top of the sole plate to the bottom header lines on the king studs. Nail the jack studs to the king studs with 10d nails driven every 12". NOTE: On a balloon-framed house the jack studs will reach to the sill plate.

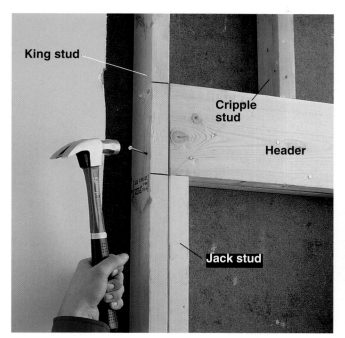

11 Position the header on the jack studs, using a hammer if necessary. Attach the header to the king studs, jack studs, and cripple studs, using 10d nails.

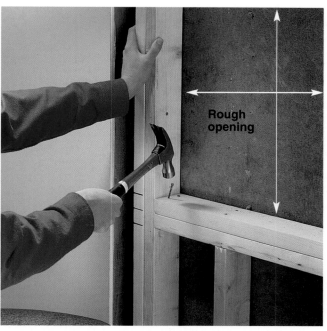

12 Build the rough sill to reach between the jack studs by nailing a pair of 2 × 4s together. Position the rough sill on the cripple studs, and nail it to the jack studs and cripple studs with 10d nails.

Tips for Framing a Round-top Window

Create a template to help you mark the rough opening on the sheathing. Scribe the outline of the curved frame on cardboard, allowing an extra ½" for adjustments within the rough opening. A ¼ × 1¼" metal washer makes a good spacer for scribing the outline. Cut out the template along the scribed line.

Tape the template to the sheathing, with the top flush against the header. Use the template as a guide for attaching diagonal framing members across the top corners of the framed opening. The diagonal members should just touch the template. Outline the template on the sheathing as a guide for cutting the exterior wall surface (pages 58 to 63).

How to Install a Window

1 Remove the exterior wall surface as directed on pages 58 to 63, then test-fit the window, centering it in the rough opening. Support the window with wood blocks and shims placed under the side jambs and mullion post. Check to make sure the window is plumb and level, and adjust the shims, if necessary.

2 Trace the outline of the brick molding on the wood siding. Remove the window after finishing the outline. NOTE: If you have vinyl or metal siding, you should have enlarged the outline to make room for the extra J-channel moldings required by these sidings.

3 Cut the siding along the outline just down to the sheathing. For a round-top window, use a reciprocating saw held at a low angle. For straight cuts, use a circular saw adjusted so the blade cuts through only the siding. Use a sharp chisel to complete the cuts at the corners (page 161).

4 Cut 8"-wide strips of building paper and slide them between the siding and sheathing around the entire window opening. Bend the paper around the framing members and staple it in place. Work from the bottom up, so each piece overlaps the piece below.

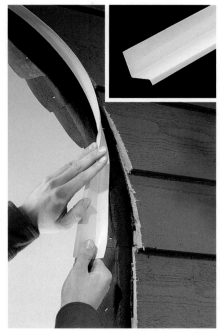

5 Cut a length of drip edge to fit over the top of the window, then slide it between the siding and building paper. For round-top windows, use flexible vinyl drip edge; for rectangular windows, use rigid metal drip edge (inset).

6 Insert the window in the opening, and push the brick molding tight against the sheathing.

7 Check to make sure the window is level.

8 If the window is perfectly level, nail both bottom corners of the brick molding with 10d galvanized casing nails. If the window is not perfectly level, nail only at the higher of the two bottom corners.

9 If necessary, have a helper adjust the shim under the low corner of the window from the inside, until the window is level.

10 From outside, drive 10d galvanized casing nails through the brick molding and into the framing members near the remaining corners of the window.

(continued next page)

11 Place pairs of shims together to form flat shims. From inside, insert shims into the gaps between the jambs and framing members, spaced every 12". On round-top windows, also shim between the angled braces and curved jamb.

12 Adjust the shims so they are snug, but not so tight that they cause the jambs to bow. On multiple-unit windows, make sure the shims under the mullion posts are tight.

13 Use a straightedge to check the side jambs to make sure they do not bow. If necessary, adjust the shims until the jambs are flat. Open and close the window to make sure it works properly.

14 At each shim location, drill a pilot hole, then drive an 8d casing nail through the jamb and shims. Be careful not to damage the window. Drive the nail heads below the wood surface with a nail set.

15 Fill the gaps between the window jambs and the framing members with loosely packed fiberglass insulation. Wear work gloves when handling insulation.

16 Trim the shims flush with the framing members, using a handsaw.

17 From outside, drive 10d galvanized casing nails, spaced every 12", through the brick moldings and into the framing members. Drive all nail heads below the wood surface with a nail set.

18 Apply paintable silicone caulk around the entire window unit. Fill nail holes with caulk. See pages 174 to 177 to trim the interior of the window.

Installation Variation: Masonry Clips

Tip: Use metal masonry clips when the brick molding on a window cannot be nailed because it rests against a masonry or brick surface. The masonry clips hook into precut grooves in the window jambs (above, left), and are attached to the jambs with screws. After the window unit is positioned in the rough opening, the masonry clips are bent around the framing members and anchored with screws (above, right). NOTE: Masonry clips also can be used in ordinary lap siding installations if you want to avoid making nail holes in the smooth surface of the brick moldings. For example, windows that are precoated with polymer-based paint can be installed with masonry clips so that the brick moldings are not punctured with nails.

How to Install a Window with a Nailing Flange

1 Test-fit the window in the rough opening, centering it side-to-side in the opening. On the interior side, level and plumb the window, using shims at the sill to make any necessary adjustments. Do not allow shims to cause the sill or jambs to bow or impede the window's operation. Mark the position of the shims on the wall.

2 On the exterior side, measure out from the window on all sides and mark the wood siding at the width of the brick molding to be installed. Remove the window, and connect the marks, using a straightedge. Cut along the outline using a circular saw (page 161). NOTE: See pages 58 to 63 for removing different types of exterior wall surfaces.

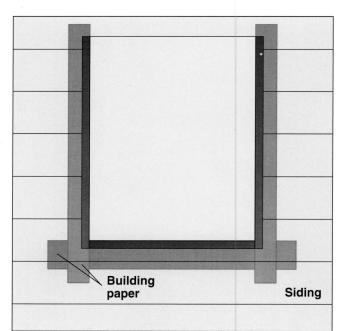

Building paper

Siding

3 Cut an 8"-wide strip of building paper for the sill, long enough to extend several inches past the sides of the rough opening. Slide paper between siding and sheathing, wrapping it over the inside of the rough opening, and staple it in place. Also install building paper along the sides of the rough opening, overlapping the paper at the sill by a few inches, and tucking the top edge under existing paper at header.

4 Apply a heavy bead of silicone caulk around the perimeter of the exterior rough opening. Set the window in position, then reshim it so it is level and plumb, as in step 1. On the exterior side, make sure the space between siding and window frame is equal to the width of the brick molding on all sides of the window. Tack window to the header at one end of the top nailing flange, using a 5d galvanized roofing nail.

5 Make final adjustments to ensure the window is level and plumb, then nail the window in place with 5d galvanized roofing nails, beginning at the header. Follow the nailing pattern specified by the manufacturer. Check to make sure the window is fully operable and that the interior trim will not impede its operation before fastening at the sides and sill.

6 Cut an 8"-wide strip of building paper and install it at the header, so it is tucked beneath the existing building paper and covering the nailing flange at the top of the window. Make sure it also overlaps the building paper at the sides by a few inches. Staple the paper in place.

Aluminum drip edge

7 Install aluminum drip edge along the length of the cutout. Apply construction adhesive to the drip edge, then slide it under the siding at the top of the window. Cut each brick molding piece to size, mitering the ends at 45°. Position brick molding between window jamb and siding. Drill pilot holes through the brick molding, and into the framing members.

8 Attach the brick molding with 8d galvanized casing nails, then set the heads with a nail set. Caulk the joint between brick molding and siding. On the interior side, loosely pack fiberglass insulation in the spaces between the window frame and framing members. See pages 174 to 177 to trim the interior of the window.

Window frames have full-length king studs, as well as jack studs that support the header. The sill defines the bottom of the rough opening.

Framing a Window in a Gable Wall

Although most windows in a home are located in load-bearing exterior walls, standard attic windows are commonly located in gable walls, which often are non–load-bearing. Installing a window in a non–load-bearing gable wall is fairly simple and doesn't require a temporary support for the framing. Some gable walls, however, are load-bearing: A common sign is a heavy structural ridge beam that supports the rafters from underneath, rather than merely at the rafter ends. Hire a contractor to build window frames in load-bearing gable walls. If you aren't certain what type of wall you have, consult a professional.

A common problem with framing in a gable wall is that the positions of the floor joists may make it difficult to attach new studs to the wall's sole plate. One solution is to install an extra-long header and sill between two existing studs, positioning them at the precise heights for the rough opening. You can then adjust the width of the rough opening by installing vertical studs between the header and sill.

Everything You Need

Tools: circular saw, handsaw, plumb bob, T-bevel, 4-ft. level, combination square, reciprocating saw.

Materials: framed window or door unit; 2 × 4 lumber; 16d, 10d, and 8d common nails; ½"-thick plywood; construction adhesive.

How to Frame a Window in a Gable Wall

1 Determine the rough opening width by measuring the window unit and adding 1". Add 3" to that dimension to get the distance between the king studs. Mark the locations of the king studs onto the sole plate of the gable wall.

2 Using a plumb bob, transfer the king-stud marks from the sole plate to the sloping top plates of the gable wall.

3 Cut the king studs to length, angle-cutting the top ends so they meet flush with the top plates. Fasten each king stud in place by toenailing the ends with three 8d nails.

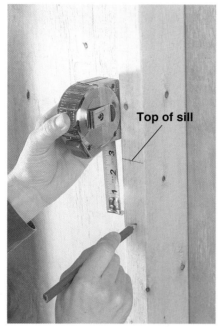

4 Find the height of the rough opening by measuring the height of the window unit and adding ½". Measure up from where the finished floor height will be, and mark the top of the sill. Make a second mark for the bottom of the sill, 3" down from the top mark.

5 Measure up from the top sill mark, and mark the height of the rough opening (bottom of header). Make another mark 3½" up, to indicate the top of the header. Using a level, transfer all of these marks to the other king stud and to all intermediate studs.

6 Draw level cutting lines across the intermediate studs at the marks for the bottom of the sill and top of the header. Cut along the lines with a reciprocating saw, then remove the cutout portions. The remaining stud sections will serve as cripple studs.

7 Cut the jack studs to reach from the sole plate to the bottom header marks on the king studs. Nail the jack studs to the inside faces of the king studs using 10d common nails driven every 16".

8 Build a built-up header with 2 × 4s and plywood (page 86). Size it to fit snugly between king studs. Set header on top of jack studs. Nail through king studs into header with 16d nails, then toenail jack studs and cripple studs to header, using 8d nails.

9 Build sill to fit snugly between jack studs by nailing together two 2 × 4s. Position sill at the top sill markings, and toenail it to the jack studs. Toenail cripple studs to sill. See pages 58 to 63 to remove the exterior wall surface and pages 88 to 93 to install the window.

Installing a Garden Window

Although often found in kitchens, a garden window is an attractive option for nearly any room in your home. Projecting out from the wall 16" to 24", garden windows add space to a room, making it feel larger. The glass roof and box-like design make them ideal growing environments for plants or display areas for collectibles. Garden windows also typically include front- or side-opening windows. These allow for ventilation and are usually available in either awning or casement style.

Home stores often stock garden windows in several common sizes. However, it may be difficult to locate a stock window that will fit in your existing window rough opening. In cases like this you must rebuild the rough opening to the proper size. It may be worth the added expense to custom-order your garden window to fit into the existing rough opening.

The large amount of glass in a garden window has a direct effect on the window's energy efficiency. When purchasing a garden window, as a minimum, look for double-pane glass with low-emissivity (low-E) coatings. More expensive super-efficient types of glass are available for severely cold climates.

Installation methods for garden windows vary by manufacturer. Some units include a nailing flange that attaches to the framing and holds the window against the house. Other models hang on a separate mounting frame that attaches to the outside of the house. In this project, the garden window has a built-in mounting sleeve that slides into the rough opening and is attached directly to the rough framing.

Photo courtesy of Kolbe & Kolbe Millwork Company, Inc.

Everything You Need

Tools: tape measure, hammer, level, framing square, circular saw, wood chisel, stapler, drill and bits, caulking gun, utility knife.

Materials: garden window kit, wood strips, 2 × 4s, shims, exterior trim, building paper, 3" screws, drip edge, construction adhesive, 4d siding nails, 8d galvanized casing nails, interior trim, paintable silicone caulk.

How to Install a Garden Window

1 Prepare the project site and remove the interior and exterior trim, then remove the existing window (pages 64 to 65).

2 Check the rough opening measurements to verify the correct window sizing. The rough opening should be about ½" larger than the window height and width. If necessary, attach wood strips to the rough framing as spacers to bring the opening to the required size.

3 Use a level to check that the sill of the rough opening is level and the side jambs are plumb. Use a framing square to make sure each corner is square. The rough framing must be in good condition in order to support the weight of the garden window. If the framing is severely deteriorated or out of plumb or square, you may need to reframe the rough opening (pages 84 to 87).

4 Insert the garden window into the opening, pressing it tight against the framing. Support the unit with notched 2 × 4s under the bottom edge of the window until it has been fastened securely to the framing.

(continued next page)

5 The inside edge of the window sleeve should be flush with the interior wall surface. Check the sill of the garden window for level. Shim beneath the lower side of the sill, if necessary, to make it level.

6 Once the garden window is in place and level, hold a piece of window trim in place along the exterior of the window and trace the outline onto the siding. Remove the window. Cut the siding down to the sheathing using a circular saw (page 161). See pages 58 to 63 for help with removing different types of siding.

7 Install strips of building paper between siding and sheathing. Wrap them around the framing and staple them in place. On the sides, work from the bottom up, so each piece overlaps the piece below. Reposition the window and reshim. Make sure the space between the window and the siding is equal to the width of the trim on all sides.

8 Drill countersunk pilot holes every 12" to 16" through the window sleeve into the rough header, jack studs, and sill.

9 Insert shims between the window sleeve and rough frame at each hole location along the top and sides to prevent bowing of the window frame. Fasten the window to the framing, using 3" screws. Continue checking for level, plumb, and square as the screws are tightened.

10 Locate and mark the studs nearest the edges of the window, using a stud finder. Cut two pieces of siding to fit behind the brackets and tack them in place over the marked studs with 4d siding nails. Position the support brackets with the shorter side against the siding and the longer side beneath the window. Fasten the brackets to the window and the studs, using the included screws.

Drip edge

11 Cut a piece of drip edge to length, apply construction adhesive to its top flange, and slide it under the siding above the window. Cut each trim piece to size. Position the trim and attach it using 8d galvanized casing nails driven through pilot holes. Seal the edges of the trim with a bead of paintable silicone caulk, approximately ⅜" wide.

12 Cut all protruding shims flush with the framing, using a utility knife or handsaw. Insulate or caulk gaps between the window sleeve and the wall. Finish the installation by reinstalling the existing interior trim or installing new trim (pages 174 to 177).

Installing a Bay Window

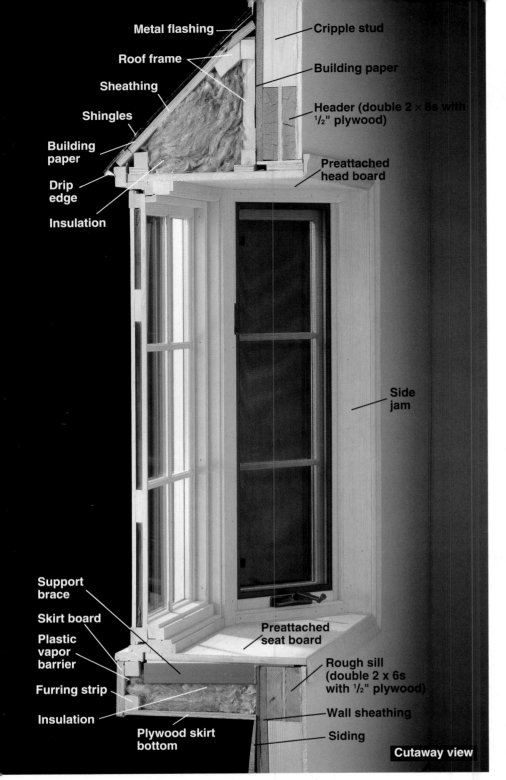

Metal flashing
Roof frame
Sheathing
Shingles
Building paper
Drip edge
Insulation
Cripple stud
Building paper
Header (double 2 × 8s with ½" plywood)
Preattached head board
Side jam
Support brace
Skirt board
Plastic vapor barrier
Furring strip
Insulation
Plywood skirt bottom
Preattached seat board
Rough sill (double 2 x 6s with ½" plywood)
Wall sheathing
Siding

Cutaway view

Modern bay windows are pre-assembled for easy installation, but it still will take several days to complete an installation. Bay windows are large and heavy, and installing them requires special techniques. Have at least one helper to assist you, and try to schedule the work when there's little chance of rain. Using prebuilt bay window accessories will speed your work (see page 101).

A large bay window can weigh several hundred pounds, so it must be anchored securely to framing members in the wall and supported by braces attached to framing members below the window. Some window manufacturers include cable-support hardware that can be used instead of metal support braces.

Before purchasing a bay window unit, check with the local building department regarding the code requirements. Many local codes require large windows and low bay windows with window seats to be glazed with tempered glass for safety.

Everything You Need

Tools: straightedge, circular saw, wood chisel, pry bar, drill, level, nail set, stapler, aviation snips, roofing knife, caulk gun, utility knife, T-bevel.

Materials: bay window unit, prebuilt roof frame kit, metal support brackets, 2 × lumber, 16d galvanized common nails, 16d and 8d galvanized casing nails, 3" and 2" galvanized utility screws, 16d casing nails, tapered wood shims, building paper, fiberglass insulation, 6-mil polyethylene sheeting, drip edge, 1" roofing nails, step flashing, shingles, top flashing, roofing cement, 2 × 2 lumber, 5½" skirt boards, window trim, ¾" exterior-grade plywood, paintable silicone caulk.

Tips for Installing a Bay Window

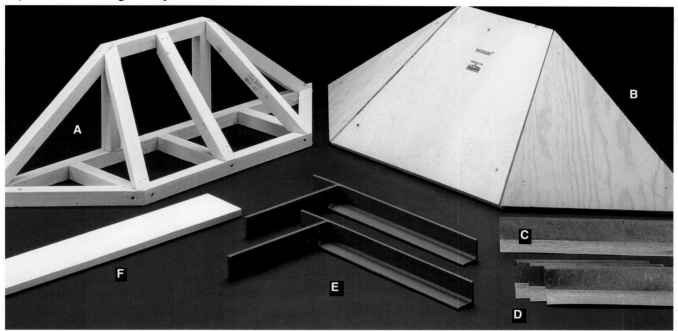

Use prebuilt accessories to ease installation of a bay window. Roof frames (A) come complete with sheathing (B), metal top flashing (C), and step flashing (D), and can be special-ordered at most home centers. You will have to specify the exact size of your window unit and the angle (pitch) you want for the roof. You can cover the roof inexpensively with building paper and shingles or order a copper or aluminum shell. Metal support braces (E) and skirt boards (F) can be ordered at your home center if not included with window unit. Use two braces for bay windows up to 5 ft. wide and three braces for larger windows. Skirt boards are clad with aluminum or vinyl and can be cut to fit with a circular saw or miter saw.

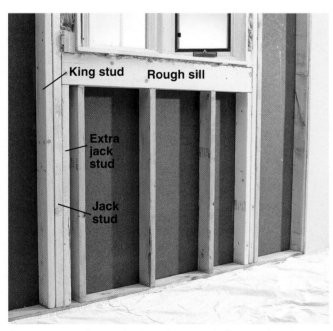

Construct a bay window frame similar to that for a standard window (see pages 84 to 87) but use a built-up sill made from two 2 × 6s sandwiched around ½" plywood (page 86). Install extra jack studs under the sill ends to help carry the window's weight.

Build an enclosure above the bay window if the roof soffit overhangs the window. Build a 2 × 2 frame (top) to match the angles of the bay window, and attach the frame securely to the wall and overhanging soffit. Install a vapor barrier and insulation (page 105), then finish the enclosure so it matches the siding (bottom).

(continued next page)

How to Install a Bay Window

1 Prepare the project site and remove interior wall surfaces (pages 52 to 57), then frame the rough opening. Remove the exterior wall surfaces as directed on pages 58 to 63. Mark for removal a section of siding directly below rough opening. The width of the marked area should equal that of the window unit and the height should equal that of the skirt board.

2 Set the blade on a circular saw just deep enough to cut through the siding, then cut along the outline. Stop just short of the corners to avoid damaging the siding outside the outline. Use a sharp chisel to complete the corner cuts. Remove the cut siding inside the outline.

3 Position the support braces along the rough sill within widest part of the bay window and above cripple stud locations. Add cripple studs to match the support brace locations, if necessary. Draw outlines of the braces on the top of the sill. Use a chisel or circular saw to notch the sill to a depth equal to the thickness of the top arm of the support braces.

4 Slide the support braces down between the siding and the sheathing. Pry the siding material away from the sheathing slightly to make room for the braces, if necessary. NOTE: On stucco, you will need to chisel notches in the masonry surface to fit the support braces.

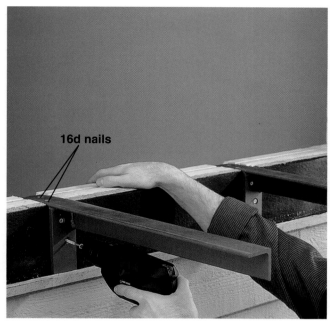

5 Attach the braces to the rough sill with galvanized 16d common nails. Drive 3" utility screws through the front of the braces and into the rough sill to prevent twisting.

6 Lift the bay window onto the support braces and slide it into the rough opening. Center the unit within the opening.

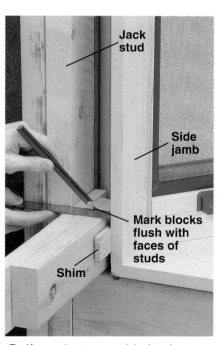

7 Check the window unit to make sure it is level. If necessary, drive shims under the low side to level the window. Temporarily brace the outside bottom edge of the unit with 2 × 4s to keep it from moving on the braces.

8 Set the roof frame on top of the window, with the sheathing loosely tacked in place. Trace the outline of the window and roof unit onto the siding. Leave a gap of about ½" around the roof unit to allow room for flashing and shingles.

9 If gap between side jambs and jack studs is more than 1" wide, mark and cut wood blocks to bridge the gap (smaller gaps require no blocks). Leave a small space for inserting wood shims. Remove the window, then attach blocks every 12" along studs.

(continued next page)

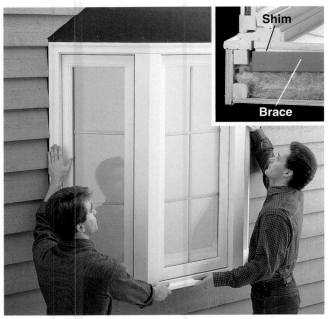

10 Cut the siding just down to the sheathing along the outline, using a circular saw. Stop just short of corners, then use a wood chisel to complete the corner cuts (page 161). Remove the cut siding. Pry the remaining siding slightly away from the sheathing around the roof outline to allow for easy installation of the metal flashing. Cover the exposed sheathing with 8"-wide strips of building paper (step 4, page 88).

11 Set the bay window unit back on the braces, and slide it back into the rough opening until the brick moldings are tight against the sheathing. Insert wood shims between the outside end of the metal braces and the seat board (inset). Check the unit to make sure it is level, and adjust the shims, if necessary.

12 Anchor the window by drilling pilot holes and driving 16d casing nails through the brick molding and into the framing members. Space nails every 12", and use a nail set to drive the nail heads below the surface of the wood.

13 Drive wood shims into the spaces between the side jambs and the blocking or jack studs and between the headboard and header, spacing the shims every 12". Fill the spaces around the window with loosely packed fiberglass insulation. At each shim location, drive 16d casing nails through the jambs and shims and into the framing members. Cut off the shims flush with the framing members, using a handsaw or utility knife. Use a nail set to drive the nail heads below the surface. If necessary, drill pilot holes to prevent splitting the wood.

14 Staple sheet plastic over the top of the window unit to serve as a vapor barrier. Trim the edges of the plastic around the top of the window, using a utility knife.

15 Remove the sheathing pieces from the roof frame, then position the frame on top of the window unit. Attach the roof frame to the window and to the wall at stud locations, using 3" utility screws.

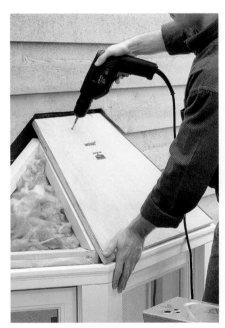

16 Fill the empty space inside the roof frame with loosely packed fiberglass insulation. Screw the sheathing back onto the roof frame, using 2" utility screws.

17 Staple asphalt building paper over the roof sheathing. Make sure each piece of building paper overlaps the one below by at least 5".

18 Cut drip edges with aviation snips, then attach them around the edge of the roof sheathing, using roofing nails.

(continued next page)

19 Cut and fit a piece of step flashing on each side of the roof frame. Adjust the flashing so it overhangs the drip edge by ¼". Flashings help guard against moisture damage.

20 Trim the end of the flashing to the same angle as the drip edge. Nail the flashing to the sheathing with roofing nails.

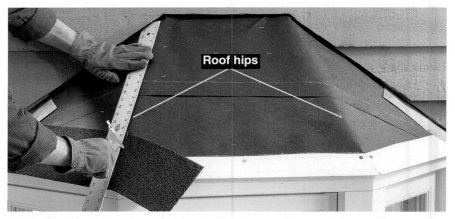

21 Cut 6"-wide strips of shingles for the starter row. Use roofing nails to attach the starter row shingles so they overhang the drip edge by about ½". Cut the shingles along the roof hips with a straightedge and roofing knife.

22 Nail a full row of shingles over the starter row, aligning the bottom edges with the bottom edge of the starter row. Make sure shingle notches are not aligned.

23 Install another piece of step flashing on each side of the roof, overlapping the first piece of flashing by about 5".

24 Cut and install another row of full shingles. The bottom edges should overlap the tops of the notches on the previous row by ½". Attach the shingles with roofing nails driven just above the notches.

25 Continue installing alternate rows of step flashing and shingles to the top of the roof. Bend the last pieces of step flashing to fit over the roof hips.

26 When the roof sheathing is covered with shingles, install the top flashing. Cut and bend the ends over the roof hips, and attach it with roofing nails. Attach the remaining rows of shingles over the top flashing.

27 Find the height of the final rows of shingles by measuring from the top of the roof to a point ½" below the top of the notches on the last installed shingle. Trim the shingles to fit.

28 Attach the final row of shingles with a thick bead of roofing cement—not nails. Press firmly to ensure a good bond.

29 Make ridge caps by cutting shingles into 1-ft.-long sections. Use a roofing knife to trim off the top corners of each piece, so the ridge caps will be narrower at the top than at the bottom.

30 Install the ridge caps over the roof hips, beginning at the bottom of the roof. Trim the bottom ridge caps to match the edges of the roof. Keep the same amount of overlap with each layer.

(continued next page)

31 At the top of the roof hips, use a roofing knife to cut the shingles to fit flush with the wall. Attach the shingles with roofing cement—do not use any nails.

32 Staple sheet plastic over the bottom of the window unit to serve as a vapor barrier. Trim the plastic around the bottom of the window.

33 Cut and attach a 2 × 2 skirt frame around the bottom of the bay window, using 3" galvanized utility screws. Set the skirt frame back about 1" from the edges of the window.

34 Cut skirt boards to match the shape of the bay window bottom, mitering the ends to ensure a tight fit. Test-fit the skirt board pieces to make sure they match the bay window bottom.

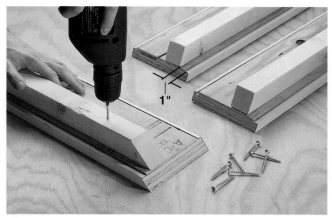

35 Cut a 2 × 2 furring strip for each skirt board. Miter the ends to the same angles as the skirt boards. Attach the furring strips to the back of the skirt boards, 1" from the bottom edges, using 2" galvanized utility screws.

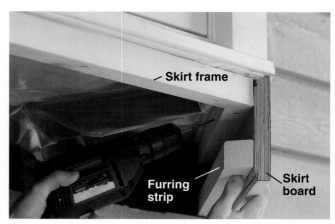

36 Attach the skirt board pieces to the skirt frame. Drill ⅛" pilot holes every 6" through the back of the skirt frame and into the skirt boards, then attach the skirt boards with 2" galvanized utility screws.

37 Measure the space inside the skirt boards, using a T-bevel to duplicate the angles. Cut a skirt bottom from ¾" exterior-grade plywood to fit this space.

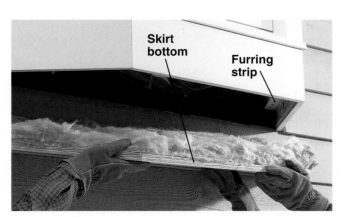

38 Lay fiberglass insulation on the skirt bottom. Position the skirt bottom against the furring strips and attach it by driving 2" galvanized utility screws every 6" through the bottom and into the furring strips.

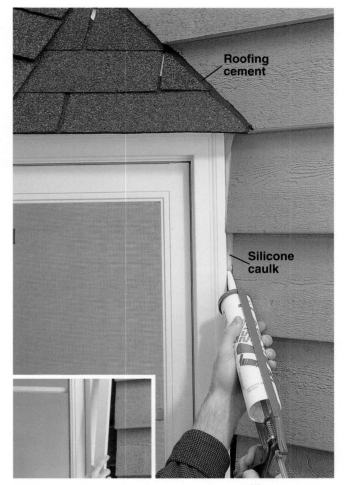

39 Install any additional trim pieces (inset) specified by your window manufacturer, using 8d galvanized casing nails. Seal roof edges with roofing cement, and seal around the rest of the window with paintable silicone caulk. See pages 70 to 71 to finish the walls, and pages 174 to 177 to trim the interior of the window.

Installing a Glass Block Window

Glass block is a durable material that transmits light while reducing visibility, making it a perfect material for creating unique windows. Glass block windows are energy-efficient and work particularly well as accent windows, or in rooms where privacy is desired, such as bathrooms.

Glass block is available in a wide variety of sizes, shapes, and patterns. It can be found, along with other necessary installation products, at specialty distributors or home centers.

Building with glass block is much like building with mortared brick, with two important differences. First, glass block must be supported by another structure and cannot function in a load-bearing capacity. Second, glass block cannot be cut, so take extra time to make sure the layout is accurate.

When installing a glass block window, the size of the rough opening is based on the size and number of blocks you are using. It is much easier to make an existing opening smaller to accommodate the glass block rather than make it larger, which requires reframing the rough opening. To determine the rough opening width, multiply the nominal width of the glass block by the number of blocks horizontally, and add ¼". For the height, multiply the nominal height by the number of blocks vertically and add ¼".

Because of its weight, a glass block window requires a solid base. The framing members of the rough opening will need to

Photo courtesy of Pittsburgh Corning Corporation

be reinforced. Contact your local building department for requirements in your area.

Use ¼" plastic T-spacers between blocks to ensure consistent mortar joints and to support the weight of the block to prevent mortar from squeezing out before it sets. (T-spacers can be modified into L or flat shapes for use at corners and along the channel.) For best results, use premixed glass block mortar. This high-strength mortar is a little drier than regular brick mortar, because glass doesn't wick water out of the mortar as brick does.

Because there are many applications for glass block, and installation techniques may vary,

ask a glass block retailer or manufacturer about the best products and methods for your specific project.

Everything You Need

Tools: tape measure, circular saw, hammer, utility knife, tin snips, drill, mixing box, trowel, 4-ft. level, rubber mallet, jointing tool, sponge, nail set, paintbrush, caulk gun.

Materials: 2 × 4 lumber, 16d common nails, glass block perimeter channels, 1" galvanized flat-head screws, glass block mortar, glass blocks, ¼" T-spacers, expansion strips, silicone caulk, construction adhesive, mortar sealant.

How to Install a Glass Block Window

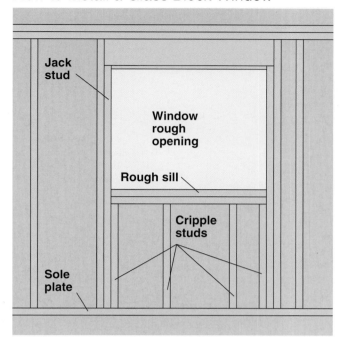

1 Measure the size of the rough opening and determine the size of the glass block window you will install (opposite page). Reinforce the rough opening framing by doubling the rough sill and installing additional cripple studs. Cut all pieces to size and fasten with 16d common nails.

2 Cut perimeter channel to length for the sill and side jambs, mitering the ends at 45°. Align front edge of channel flush with front edge of exterior wall sheathing. Drill pilot holes every 12" through the channels (if not provided), and fasten the channels in place with 1" galvanized flat-head screws. NOTE: Paint screw heads white to help conceal them.

3 For the header, cut a channel to length, mitering the ends at 45°, then cut it in half lengthwise, using a utility knife. Align one half of the channel flush with the exterior face of the sheathing, and fasten in place with 1" galvanized flat-head screws.

4 Set two blocks into the sill channel, one against each jamb—do not place mortar between blocks and channels. Place a ¼" flat spacer against the first block. Mix glass block mortar and liberally butter the leading edge of another block, then push it tight against the first block. Make sure the joint is filled with mortar.

(continued next page)

5 Lay the remainder of the first course, building from both jambs toward the center. Use flat spacers between blocks to maintain proper spacing. Plumb and level each block as you work, then also check the entire course for level. Tap blocks into place using the rubber handle of the trowel—do not use metal tools with glass block. Butter both sides of the final block in the course to install it.

6 At the top of the course, fill any depression at the top of each mortar joint with mortar and insert a ¼" T-spacer, then lay a ⅜" bed of mortar for the next course. Lay the blocks for each course, using T-spacers to maintain proper spacing. Check each block for level and plumb as you work.

7 Test the mortar as you work. When it can resist light finger pressure, remove the T-spacers (inset) and pack mortar into the voids, then tool the joints with a jointing tool. Remove excess mortar with a damp sponge, or a nylon or natural-bristle brush.

8 To ease block placement in the final course, trim the outer tabs off one side of the T-spacers, using tin snips. Install the blocks of the final course. After the final block is installed, work in any mortar that has been forced out of the joints.

Expansion strip

9 Cut an expansion strip for the header 1½" wide and to length. Slide it between the top course of block and the header of the rough opening. Apply a bead of construction adhesive to the top edge of the remaining half of the header channel, and slide it between the expansion strip and header.

10 Clean glass block thoroughly with wet sponge, rinsing often. Allow surface to dry, then remove cloudy residue with clean, dry cloth. Caulk between glass block and channels, and between channels and framing members before installing trim on exterior (pages 88 to 91). After brick molding is installed, allow mortar to cure for two weeks. Apply sealant.

Variation: Glass Block Window Kits

Some glass block window kits do not require mortar. Instead, the blocks are set into the perimeter channels and the joints are created using plastic spacer strips. Silicone caulk is then used to seal the joints.

Photo courtesy of Pittsburgh Corning Corporation

Preassembled glass block windows are simple to install. These vinyl-clad units have a nailing flange around the frame, which allows them to be hung using the same installation techniques as for standard windows with a nailing flange (pages 92 to 93).

113

Header

Bucks

Basement window openings must have support above to carry the weight of the house. An opening in masonry is usually fitted with wood bucks to serve as a rough window frame.

Egress windows in basements require large wells that meet code specifications (117). The prefabricated window well shown here has a stepped side that serves as stairs for emergency escape. Spaces behind the steps can hold plants to dress up the view from the window.

Photo courtesy of The Bilco Company

Enlarging a Basement Window Opening

Whether the goal is to add more natural light or to provide emergency egress, enlarging a window opening for a new window is a common project for basement remodels. The actual installation of the window is the same as for any other window (pages 88 to 91 and page 177). However, it's not always a do-it-yourself job. There are many factors to consider, and depending on your basement configuration and the size of window you want, it may be best to hire a professional to do some or all of the work.

The first, and most important, consideration is ensuring there will be adequate support for your house once the window opening is expanded or created. If you're not changing the width of the opening, the means for support should already be in place. Increasing the opening's width, however, will require a new wood header or a steel lintel to span the top of the opening and carry the weight from above.

The second consideration is the window well, which must be dug before a window can be expanded. Digging a window well can be a fairly extensive project; page 117 gives you an idea of what's involved.

After preparing the well comes the task of cutting into the foundation wall. With concrete block, this is a messy job but surprisingly easy. If your foundation walls are poured concrete, you'll need to have a professional cut the opening. For many window types, the rough opening in the masonry must be wrapped with dimensional lumber to provide a frame for fastening the window. The lumber pieces—called bucks—are usually 2 × 10s or 2 × 12s and should cover the width of the block. To prevent rotting from moisture, use pressure-treated lumber for the window bucks.

How to Enlarge a Window Opening in a Concrete Block Wall

1 Remove the old window unit and frame, then mark the rough opening on both the interior and exterior surfaces of the wall, using a level as a guide.

2 Score the cutting lines, using a masonry chisel and hand maul. Be sure to wear eye protection and work gloves.

3 Cut along the scored lines with a circular saw and masonry blade. Make several passes with the saw, gradually deepening the cut until the saw blade is at maximum depth.

4 Break both the inside and outside mortar lines on all sides of the center block in the top row of the area being removed.

(continued next page)

5 Strike the face of the center block with a masonry hammer until the block either comes loose or breaks into pieces.

6 Chip out large pieces, then break the mortar around the remaining blocks. Chip out the remaining blocks using the chisel and maul.

7 Create a smooth surface by filling the hollow areas in the cut blocks with broken pieces of concrete block, then troweling in fresh concrete. Make sure all of the surfaces are flat. Let the concrete dry overnight.

8 Cut pressure-treated 2 × lumber to frame the opening. If necessary, rip-cut the bucks to width so they are flush with the block on both sides. Apply construction adhesive to the bucks and set them in place.

9 Anchor the bucks by drilling pilot holes with a masonry bit, then driving self-tapping masonry screws into the blocks, spaced every 10". Seal joints between the bucks and the masonry with silicone caulk—on both sides of wall.

Window Wells

Window wells for standard basement windows are usually small steel shells that let in very little natural light. If your basement project includes expanding existing window openings or adding new ones, you'll need wells that make the most of the new windows. If you're adding an egress window (page 28) for a bedroom or as a secondary fire escape, the window well must be built to strict building code specifications. There are also some general considerations for wells, such as appearance, size, and drainage.

Window wells can be made of a variety of different materials. Prefabricated wells include the standard corrugated steel type that you can buy at home centers and specialty units made of polyethylene. For a custom-built well, you can use concrete block, landscaping timbers, or boulders.

Sizing for a window well depends on several factors. First, the well must extend far enough from the foundation to accommodate the window's operation. For example, casement windows need more room than sliders. Second, the size of the well affects how much light reaches the window. While a bigger well lets in more light than a smaller one, it also creates a larger hole that children or pets can fall into if it is uncovered, and a large well collects more water. As general minimums, a window well should be about 6" wider than the window opening, and should extend at least 18" from the foundation wall. And all wells should extend 8" below the windowsill and 4" above grade.

The minimum dimensions for an egress-window well will be determined by your local building code. Typically, wells for egress windows must be at least 9 sq. ft. overall, measure at least 36" in width, and extend 36" from the foundation wall. Wells more than 44" deep must have a permanently attached ladder or a step system that doesn't interfere with the window's operation.

Providing adequate drainage for your window wells is particularly important if you plan to leave them uncovered. All wells should have a layer of gravel that is at least 6" deep and stops 3" below the window frame. Uncovered wells, however, may need a drain pipe or a continuous layer of gravel that leads to the footing drain or other perimeter drain system.

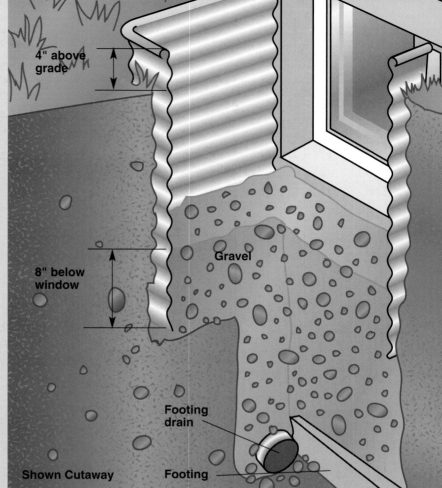

4" above grade

8" below window

Gravel

Footing drain

Shown Cutaway

Footing

Window wells should extend 8" below the window frame and 4" above the ground. Wells for egress windows must be at least 36" wide and project 36" from the foundation, and those deeper than 44" must have a ladder or other means of escape. To keep water from pooling near the window, well bases should have a 6" layer of gravel. More extensive drainage can be provided by gravel that passes water down to a footing drain or by a well drain leading to daylight.

Photo courtesy of The Bilco Company

Plastic well covers keep rain, snow, and debris from entering your well. Covers on egress-window wells must be hinged or easily removable from inside the well.

Installing a Tubular Skylight

Any interior room can be brightened with a tubular skylight. Tubular skylights are quite energy-efficient and are relatively easy to install, with no complicated framing involved.

The design of tubular skylights varies among manufacturers, with some using solid plastic reflecting tubes and others using flexible tubing. Various diameters are also available. Measure the distance between the framing members in your attic before purchasing your skylight, to be sure it will fit.

This project shows the installation of a tubular skylight on a sloped, asphalt-shingled roof. Consult the dealer or manufacturer for installation procedures on other roof types.

Photo courtesy of Sun Tunnel Systems, Inc.

Everything You Need

Tools: pencil, drill, tape measure, wallboard saw, reciprocating saw or jig saw, pry bar, screwdriver, hammer, wire cutters, utility knife, chalk.

Materials: tubular skylight kit, stiff wire, 2" roofing nails or flashing screws, roofing cement.

How to Install a Tubular Skylight

1 Drill a pilot hole through the ceiling at the approximate location for your skylight. Push a stiff wire up into the attic to help locate the hole. In the attic, make sure the space around the hole is clear of any insulation. Drill a second hole through the ceiling at the centerpoint between two joists.

2 Center the ceiling ring frame over the hole and trace around it with a pencil. Carefully cut along the pencil line with a wallboard saw or reciprocating saw. Save the wallboard ceiling cutout to use as your roof-hole pattern. Attach the ceiling frame ring around the hole with the included screws.

3 In the attic, choose the most direct route for the tubing to reach the roof. Find the center between the appropriate rafters and drive a nail up through the roof sheathing and shingles.

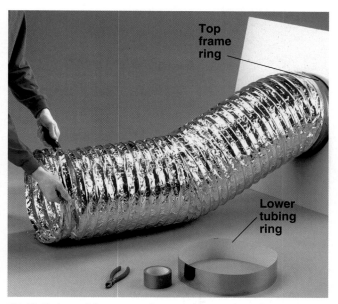

4 Use the wallboard ceiling cutout, centered over the nail hole, as a template for the roof opening. Trace the cutout onto the roof with chalk. Drill a starter hole to insert the reciprocating saw blade, then cut out the hole in the roof. Pry up the lower portion of the shingles above the hole. Remove any staples or nails around the hole edge.

5 Pull the tubing over the top frame ring. Bend the frame tabs out through the tubing, keeping two or three rings of the tubing wire above the tabs. Wrap the junction three times around with included PVC tape. Then, in the attic, measure from the roof to the ceiling. Stretch out the tubing and cut it to length with a utility knife and wire cutters. Pull the loose end of tubing over the lower ring and wrap it three times with PVC tape.

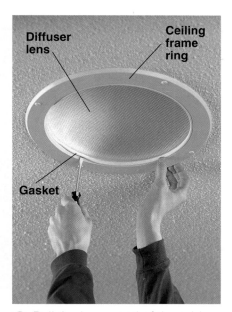

6 Lower the tubing through the roof hole and slide the flashing into place with the upper portion of the flashing underneath the existing shingles. This is easier with two people, one on the roof and one in the attic.

7 Secure the flashing to the roof with 2" roofing nails or flashing screws. Seal under the shingles and over all nail heads with roofing cement. Attach the skylight dome and venting to the frame with the included screws.

8 Pull the lower end of the tubing down through the ceiling hole. Attach the lower tubing ring to the ceiling frame ring and fasten it with screws. Attach the gasket to the diffuser lens and work the gasket around the perimeter of the ceiling frame. Repack any insulation around the tubing in the attic.

Everything You Need

Tools: 4-ft. level, circular saw, drill, combination square, reciprocating saw, pry bar, chalk line, stapler, caulk gun, utility knife, tin snips, plumb bob, jig saw, wallboard tools.

Materials: 2 x lumber; 16d and 10d common nails; 1 x 4; building paper; roofing cement; skylight flashing; 2", 1¼", and ¾" roofing nails; finish nails; fiberglass insulation; ½" wallboard; twine; wallboard screws; 6-mil polyethylene sheeting; finishing materials.

Installing a Standard Skylight

Depending on the model you choose and where you place it, a skylight can offer warmth in the winter, cooling ventilation in the summer, and a view of the sky or the treetops around your house during any season. And, of course, skylights provide natural light.

Because a skylight lets in so much light, the sizing and placement of the unit are important considerations. A skylight that's too big can quickly overheat a space, especially in an attic. The same is true of using too many skylights in any one room. For that reason it's often best to position a skylight away from the day's brightest sun. You may want an operable skylight that opens and closes to vent warm air.

When a skylight is installed above an unfinished attic space, a special skylight shaft must be constructed to channel light directly to the room below. To install a skylight shaft, see pages 126 to 129.

Installing a skylight above finished space involves other considerations. First, the ceiling surface must be removed to expose the

rafters. To remove wall and ceiling surfaces, see pages 54 to 59.

A skylight frame is similar to a standard window frame (page 33). It has a header and sill, like a window frame, but has king rafters, rather than king studs. Skylight frames also have trimmers that define the sides of the rough opening. Refer to the manufacturer's instructions to determine what size to make the opening for the skylight you select.

With standard rafter-frame roof construction, you can safely cut into one or two rafters as long as you permanently support the cut rafters, as shown in the following steps. If your skylight requires alteration of more than two rafters or if your roofing is made with unusually heavy material, such as clay tile or slate, consult an architect or engineer before starting the project.

Today's good-quality skylight units are unlikely to leak, but a skylight is only as leakproof as its installation. Follow the manufacturer's instructions, and install the flashing meticulously, as it will last a lot longer than any sealant.

How to Install a Skylight

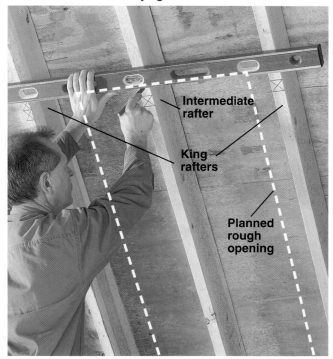

1 Use the first rafter on each side of the planned rough opening as a king rafter. Measure and mark where the double header and sill will fit against the king rafters. Then, use a level as a straightedge to extend the marks across the intermediate rafter.

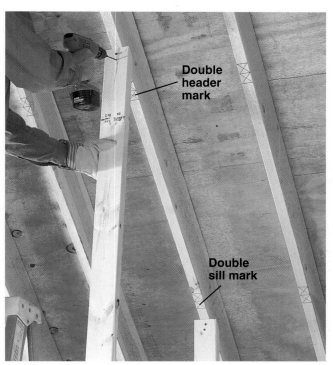

2 Brace the intermediate rafter by installing two 2 × 4s between the rafter and the attic floor. Position the braces just above the header marks and just below the sill marks. Secure them temporarily to the rafter and subfloor (or joists) with screws.

3 Reinforce each king rafter by attaching a full-length "sister" rafter against its outside face. Cut sister rafters from the same size of lumber as existing rafters, matching lengths and end cuts exactly. Work each one into position, flush against the outside face of the king rafters, then nail the sisters to the kings with pairs of 10d common nails, spaced 12" apart.

4 Use a combination square to transfer the sill and header marks across the face of the intermediate rafter, then cut along the outermost lines with a reciprocating saw. Do not cut into the roof sheathing. Carefully remove the cutout section with a pry bar. The remaining rafter portions will serve as cripple rafters.

(continued next page)

5 Build a double header and double sill to fit snugly between the king rafters, using 2 × lumber that is the same size as the rafters. Nail the header pieces together using pairs of 10d nails, spaced 6" apart.

6 Install the header and sill, anchoring them to the king rafters and cripple rafters with 16d common nails. Make sure the ends of the header and sill are aligned with the appropriate marks on the king rafters.

7 If your skylight unit is narrower than the opening between the king studs, measure and make marks for the trimmers: They should be centered in the opening and spaced according to the manufacturer's specifications. Cut the trimmers from the same 2 × lumber used for the rest of the frame, and nail them in place with 10d common nails. Remove the 2 × 4 braces.

8 Mark the opening for the roof cutout by driving a screw through the sheathing at each corner of the frame. Then, tack a couple of scrap boards across the opening to prevent the roof cutout from falling and causing damage below.

9 From the roof, measure between the screws to make sure the rough opening dimensions are accurate. Snap chalk lines between the screws to mark the rough opening, then remove the screws.

10 Tack a straight 1 × 4 to the roof, aligned with the inside edge of one chalk line. Make sure the nail heads are flush with the surface of the board.

11 Cut through the shingles and sheathing along the chalk line, using a circular saw and an old blade or a remodeling blade. Rest the saw foot on the 1 × 4, and use the edge of the board as a guide. Reposition the 1 × 4, and cut along the remaining lines. Remove the cutout roof section.

12 Remove the shingles around the rough opening with a flat pry bar, exposing at least 9" of building paper on all sides of the opening. Remove whole shingles, rather than cutting them.

(continued next page)

13 Cut strips of building paper and slide them between the shingles and existing building paper. Wrap the paper so that it covers the faces of the framing members, and staple it in place.

14 Spread a 5"-wide layer of roofing cement around the roof opening. Set the skylight into the opening so that the nailing flange rests on the roof. Adjust unit so that it sits squarely in opening.

15 Nail through the flange and into sheathing and framing members with 2" galvanized roofing nails spaced every 6". NOTE: If skylight uses L-shaped brackets instead of a nailing flange, follow manufacturer's instructions.

16 Patch in shingles up to the bottom edge of skylight unit. Attach the shingles with 1¼" roofing nails driven just below the adhesive strip. If necessary, cut shingles with a utility knife so they fit against bottom of the skylight.

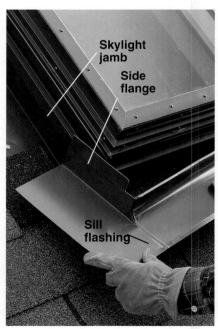

17 Spread roofing cement on the bottom edge of the sill flashing, then fit flashing around bottom of unit. Attach flashing by driving ¾" galvanized roofing nails through the vertical side flange (near the top of the flashing) and into the skylight jambs.

18 Spread roofing cement on the bottom of a piece of step flashing, then slide flashing under drip edge on one side of the skylight. Step flashing should overlap sill flashing by 5". Press the step flashing down to bond it. Repeat on opposite side of skylight.

124

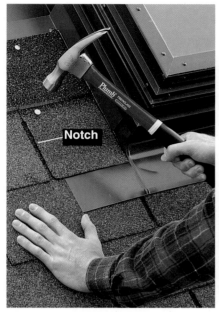

19 Patch in the next row of shingles on each side of the skylight, following the existing shingle pattern. Drive a 1¼" roofing nail through each shingle and the step flashing and into the sheathing. Drive additional nails just above the notches in the singles.

20 Continue applying alternate rows of step flashing and shingles, using roofing cement and roofing nails. Each piece of flashing should overlap the preceding piece by 5".

21 At the top of the skylight, cut and bend the last piece of step flashing on each side, so the vertical flange wraps around the corner of the skylight. Patch in the next row of shingles.

22 Spread roofing cement on bottom of head flashing, to bond it to the roof. Place flashing against top of skylight so vertical flange fits under drip edge and horizontal flange fits under shingles above skylight.

23 Fill in the remaining shingles, cutting them to fit, if necessary. Attach the shingles with roofing nails driven just above the notches.

24 Apply a continuous bead of roofing cement along the joint between the singles and the skylight. Finish the interior of the framed opening as desired.

How to Build a Skylight Shaft

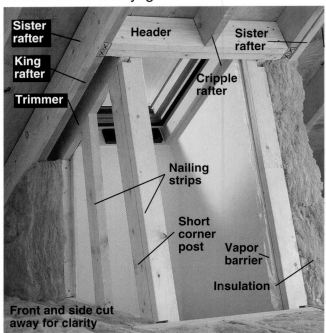

Sister rafter
Header
Sister rafter
King rafter
Cripple rafter
Trimmer
Nailing strips
Short corner post
Vapor barrier
Insulation

Front and side cut away for clarity

A skylight shaft is made with 2 × 4 lumber and wall-board, and includes a vapor barrier and fiberglass insulation. You can build a straight shaft with four vertical sides or an angled shaft that has a longer frame at ceiling level and one or more sides set at an angle. Since the ceiling opening is larger, an angled shaft lets in more direct light than a straight shaft.

1 Remove any insulation in the area where the skylight will be located; turn off and reroute electrical circuits as necessary. Use a plumb bob as a guide to mark reference points on the ceiling surface, directly below the inside corners of the skylight frame.

Plumb mark

2 If you are installing a straight shaft, use the plumb marks made in step 1 to define the corners of the ceiling opening; drive a finish nail through the ceiling surface at each mark. If you are installing an angled shaft, measure out from the plumb marks and make new marks that define the corners of the ceiling opening; drive finish nails at the new marks.

3 From the room below, mark cutting lines, then remove the ceiling surface (pages 54 to 57).

4 Use the nearest joists on either side of the ceiling opening to serve as king joists. Measure and mark where the double header and double sill will fit against the king joists, and where the outside edge of the header and sill will cross any intermediate joists.

5 If you will be removing a section of an intermediate joist, reinforce the king joists by nailing full-length "sister" joists to the outside faces of the king joists, using 10d nails.

6 Install temporary supports below the project area to support the intermediate rafter on both sides of the opening (pages 66 to 69). Use a combination square to extend cutting lines down the sides of the intermediate joist, then cut out the joist section with a reciprocating saw. Pry loose the cutout portion of the joist, being careful not to damage the ceiling surface.

7 Build a double header and double sill to span the distance between the king joists, using 2 × dimensional lumber the same size as the joists.

(continued next page)

8 Install the double header and double sill, anchoring them to the king joists and cripple joists with 10d nails. The inside edges of the header and sill should be aligned with the edge of the ceiling cutout.

9 Complete the ceiling opening by cutting and attaching trimmers, if required, along the sides of the ceiling cutout between the header and sill. Toenail the trimmers to the header and sill with 10d nails.

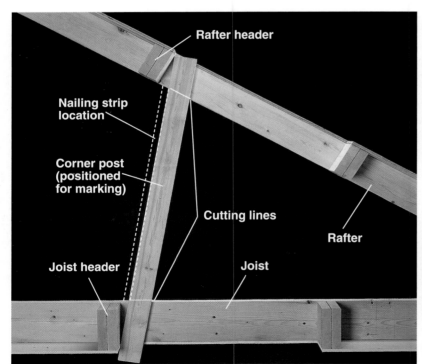

10 Install 2 × 4 corner posts for the skylight shaft. To measure for the posts, begin with a 2 × 4 that is long enough to reach from the top to the bottom of the shaft. Hold the 2 × 4 against the inside of the framed openings, so it is flush with the top of the rafter header and the bottom of the joist header (left photo). Mark cutting lines where the 2 × 4 meets the top of the joist or trimmer, and the bottom of the rafter or trimmer (right photo). Cut along the lines, then toenail the posts to the top and bottom of the frame with 10d nails.

11 Attach a 2 × 4 nailing strip to the outside edge of each corner post to provide a nailing surface for attaching the wallboard. Notch the ends of the nailing strips to fit around the trimmers; a perfect fit is not necessary.

12 Install additional 2 × 4 nailing strips between the corner posts if the distances between posts are more than 24". Miter the top ends of the nailing strips to fit against the rafter trimmers.

13 Wrap the skylight shaft with fiberglass insulation. Secure the insulation by wrapping twine around the shaft and insulation.

14 From inside the shaft, staple a plastic vapor barrier of 6-mil polyethylene sheeting over the insulation.

15 Finish the inside of the shaft with wallboard (pages 70 to 71). **Tip:** To reflect light, paint the shaft interior with a light-colored, semi-gloss paint.

Planning Door Installations

Choosing the right door requires some thought and evaluation. A door should complement the architectural style of a home, as well as meet the specific needs of its location.

Exterior doors, for instance, provide security and a barrier to the elements. You can immediately reduce heat loss by replacing an old entry door. Exterior doors link indoor and outdoor living areas and can improve your view, such as with French and patio doors. Exterior doors also make your home more inviting to guests and more secure against intruders.

Interior doors define boundaries and offer privacy. They can significantly enhance the look and feel of a room. You can make more efficient use of floor space simply by changing the location of interior doors.

When planning your project, keep in mind that exterior entry doors should be at least 36" wide, and they are usually 1¾" thick. Interior passage doors between rooms must be at least 30" wide, and they are usually 1⅜" thick. However, for greater accessibility, all interior doors should be a minimum of 32" wide (pages 34 to 37). Double-entry doors, such as patio or French, may be 60", 64", or 72" wide. The standard height for any door is 80".

The material that you choose is just as important as the style. Entry doors may be solid wood, or steel or fiberglass shells filled with insulation. Interior doors may be hollow-core, or they may be solid-core, which is effective for soundproofing a room. French and patio doors incorporate glass panels in their design.

The basic steps for framing a rough opening for an interior prehung door are the same for closet doors. However, for large closet openings, such as for double bifold or bypass doors, use a built-up header: two 2 × 4s set on edge and nailed together with a strip of ½"-thick plywood in between (page 86). This provides additional strength to support the weight of the doors.

Replacing an old entry door (left) with a new steel door (right) keeps out winter chills while creating a warm welcome for guests, increasing the home's curb appeal.

Improve traffic flow by relocating a door or a doorway. In this small room, the doorways were located in the center of facing walls, causing the foot traffic path to consume most of the usable space. By shifting one of them to open into an adjacent hall, the owners turned this wasted space into a functional office.

Wall studs

Top plate

Cripple stud

Header

King stud

Jack stud

Sole plate

Framing an Opening for an Interior Door

Framing a door opening requires straight, dry lumber, so the door unit fits evenly into the rough opening and won't bind later on. For best results, use a prehung door unit and buy the unit before framing the door opening.

Although unmounted doors are widely available, installing them is a complicated job that is best left to a professional. Prehung interior doors are by far the most common. Most are 32" wide, but other sizes are available.

Sliding, or bypass, doors and folding doors are popular for closets. Pocket doors, which slide into an enclosure in the wall, are practical in narrow hallways and other cramped spaces.

When replacing an existing door, choosing a new unit the same size as the old door makes your work easier, because you can use framing members already in place.

Finish the wallboard (pages 70 to 71) before installing the door.

Everything You Need

Tools: tape measure, framing square, hammer, handsaw.

Materials: 2 x 4 lumber, prehung door unit, bypass or folding door kit and doors, or pocket door and kit, 8d common nails.

How to Frame an Opening for a Prehung Door

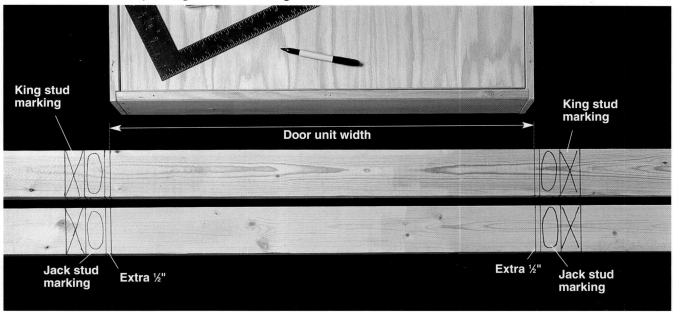

King stud marking

Door unit width

King stud marking

Jack stud marking **Extra ½"**

Extra ½" **Jack stud marking**

1 Mark the rough opening on the top and sole plates. Measured between the insides of jack studs, it should be about 1" wider than the actual width of the door to allow for adjustments during installation.

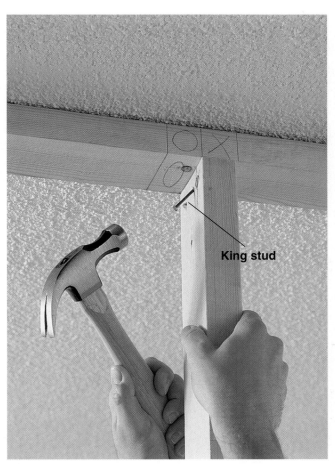

King stud

2 Measure and cut the king studs and position them at the markings (X). Toenail the joints by driving nails through the king stud and into the header at a 45° angle.

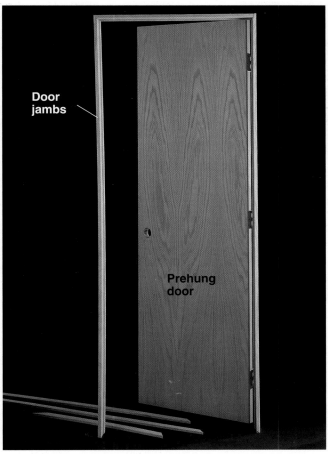

Door jambs

Prehung door

Tip: A prehung door greatly simplifies installation for standard-size openings. Prehung doors are sold with temporary braces in place that support the door jambs during shipping. The braces are removed for installation.

(continued next page)

How to Frame an Opening for a Prehung Door (continued)

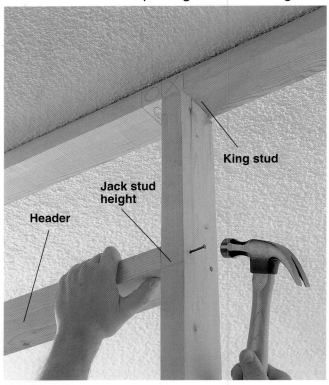

3 Mark the height of the jack stud on each king stud. The height of a jack stud for a standard door is 83½", or ½" taller than the door. Endnail the header to the king stud above the mark for the jack stud.

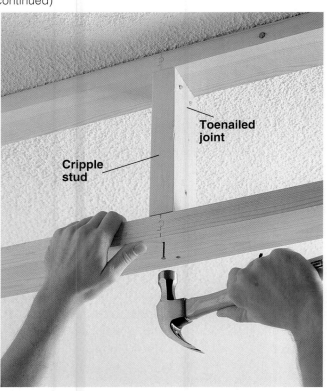

4 Install a cripple stud above the header, halfway between king studs. Toenail cripple stud to top plate, and endnail through bottom of header into the cripple stud. Install any additional cripple studs needed to maintain stud spacing of the rest of wall.

5 Position the jack studs against the insides of the king studs. Endnail through the top of the header down into the jack studs.

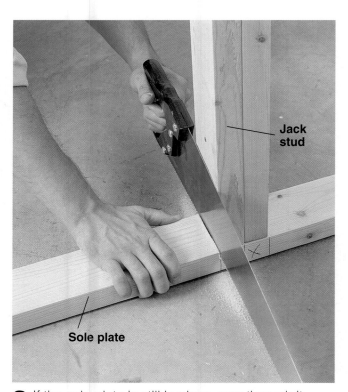

6 If the sole plate is still in place, saw through it along the inside edges of the jack studs. Remove the cut portion of the plate.

134

Tips for Framing Openings for Sliding & Folding Doors

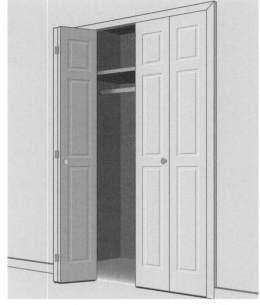

The same basic framing techniques are used, whether you're planning to install a sliding, bifold, pocket, or prehung interior door (pages 133 to 134). The different door styles require different frame openings. Purchase the doors and hardware in advance, and consult the manufacturer's instructions for the exact dimensions of the rough opening for the door you select.

Most bifold doors are designed to fit in an 80"-high finished opening. Wood bifold doors have the advantage of allowing you to trim the doors, if necessary, to fit openings that are slightly shorter.

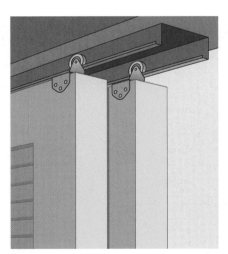

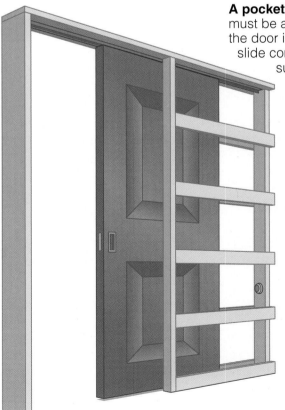

A pocket door's rough opening must be about twice the width of the door itself to allow the door to slide completely into the enclosure in the finished wall.

One style of enclosure is formed by nailing a pocket door cage (available at home centers) to the framing, then adding wallboard and trim. See pages 142 to 145 for instructions on installing pocket doors, and information on the variety of styles available.

Standard bypass-door openings are 4, 5, 6, or 8 ft. The finished width should be 1" narrower than the combined width of the doors to provide a 1" overlap when the doors are closed. For long closets that require three or more doors, subtract another 1" from the width of the finished opening for each door. Check the hardware installation instructions for the required height of the opening.

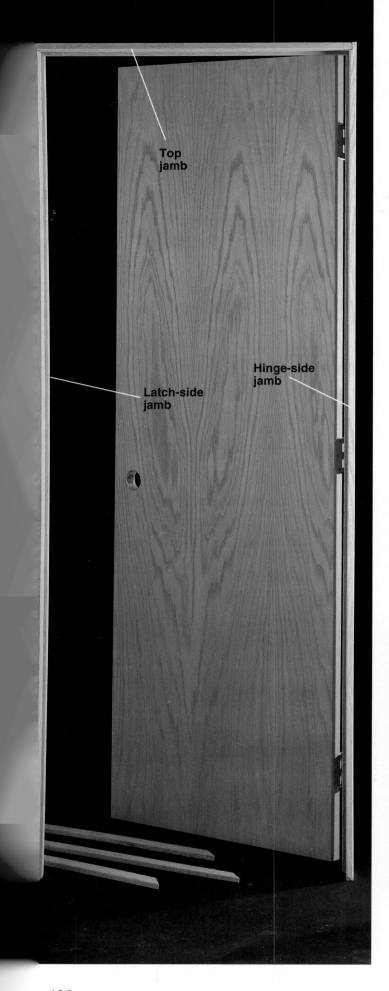

Top jamb

Latch-side jamb

Hinge-side jamb

Installing a Prehung Interior Door

Prehung doors come as single units with the door already hung on hinges attached to a factory-built frame. To secure the unit during shipping, most prehung doors are braced or nailed shut with a couple of duplex nails driven through the jambs and into the door edge. These nails must be removed before you install the door.

The key to installing doors is to plumb and fasten the hinge-side jamb first. After that's in place, you can position the top and latch-side jambs by checking the reveal—the gap between the closed door and the jamb.

Standard prehung doors have 4½"-wide jambs and are sized to fit walls with 2 × 4 construction and ½" wallboard. If you have thicker walls, you can special-order doors to match, or you can add jamb extensions to standard-size doors.

Everything You Need

Tools: 4-ft. level, nail set, handsaw.

Materials: prehung door unit, wood shims, 8d casing nails.

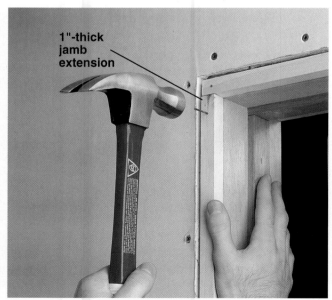

1"-thick jamb extension

If your walls are built with 2 × 6 studs, extend the jambs by attaching 1"-thick wood strips to the jamb edges on both sides. Use glue and 4d casing nails to attach these extensions to the jambs.

How to Install a Prehung Interior Door

1 Set the door unit into the framed opening so the jamb edges are flush with the wall surfaces and the unit is centered from side to side. Using a level, adjust the unit so the hinge-side jamb is plumb.

2 Starting near top hinge, insert pairs of shims driven from opposite directions into gap between framing and jamb, sliding shims in until they are snug. Check jamb to make sure it remains plumb and does not bow inward. Install shims near each hinge and the top and bottom of the jamb.

3 Anchor the hinge-side jamb with 8d casing nails driven through the jamb and shims and into the framing. Drive nails only at the shim locations.

 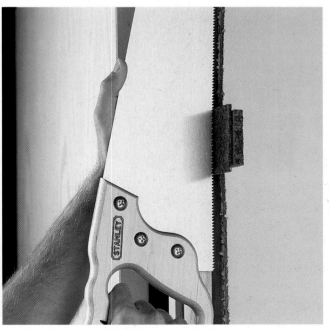

Reveal

4 Insert pairs of shims into the gap between the framing members and the top jamb and latch-side jamb, aligning them roughly with the hinge-side shims. With the door closed, adjust the shims so the reveal is consistent. Drive casing nails through the jambs and shims and into the framing members.

5 Set all nails below the surface of the wood with a nail set, then cut off the shims flush with the wall surface, using a handsaw or utility knife. Hold the saw vertically to prevent damage to the door jamb or wall. See pages 174 to 177 to install the door casing.

Framing & Installing French Doors

Traditionally, French doors open onto the patio or lush garden of a backyard. But you can create stylish entrances inside your home by bringing French doors to formal dining rooms, sitting rooms or dens, and master suites.

French doors are made up of two separate doors, hinged on opposing jambs of a doorway. The doors swing out from the center of the doorway and into or out from a room. Like most

doors, French doors are typically sold in prehung units, but are also available separately. They are generally available only in wood, with a variety of designs and styles to choose from.

Before purchasing a prehung French door unit, determine the size of doors you will need. If you are planning to install the doors in an existing doorway, measure the dimensions of the rough opening, from the unfin-

ished framing members, then order the unit to size—the manufacturer or distributor will help you select the proper unit.

You can also pick the prehung unit first, then alter an existing opening to accommodate it (as shown in this project). In this case, build the rough opening a little larger than the actual dimensions of the doors to accommodate the jambs. Prehung units typically require adding 1" to the width and ½" to the height.

If the doorway will be in a load-bearing wall, you will need to make temporary supports (pages 66 to 69), and install an appropriately sized header. Sizing the header (depth) is critical: it's based on the length of the header, the material it's made from, and the weight of the load it must support. For actual requirements, consult your local building department.

When installing French doors, it is important to have consistent reveals between the two doors and between the top of the doors and the head jamb. This allows the doors to close properly and prevents the hinges from binding.

Everything You Need

Tools: tape measure, circular saw, 4-ft. level, hammer, handsaw, drill, utility knife, nail set.

Materials: prehung French door unit, 2 × 4 and 2 × 6 lumber, ½" plywood, 10d & 16d common nails, wood shims, 8d finish nails.

How to Frame & Install French Doors

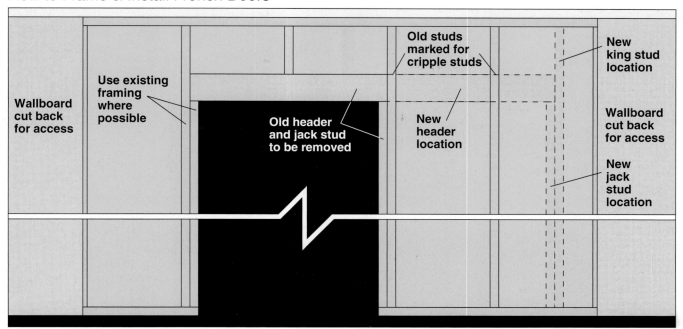

Wallboard cut back for access

Use existing framing where possible

Old header and jack stud to be removed

Old studs marked for cripple studs

New header location

New king stud location

Wallboard cut back for access

New jack stud location

1 Shut off power and water to the area. Remove the wall surfaces from both sides of the wall (pages 52 to 57), leaving one stud bay open on each side of the new rough opening. Also remove or reroute any wiring, plumbing, or ductwork. Lay out the new rough opening, marking the locations of all new jack and king studs on both the top and bottom plates. Where practical, use existing framing members. To install a new king stud, cut a stud to size and align with the layout marks, toenail to the bottom plate with 10d common nails, check for plumb, then toenail to the top plate to secure. Finally, mark both the bottom and top of the new header on one king stud, then use a level to extend the lines across the intermediate studs to the opposite king stud. If using existing framing, measure and mark from the existing jack stud.

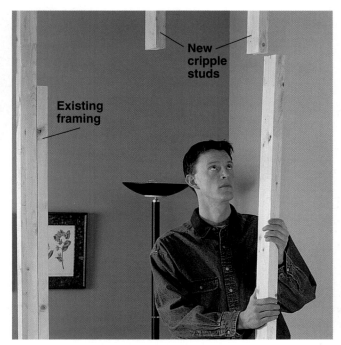

New cripple studs

Existing framing

2 Cut the intermediate studs at the reference marks for the top of the header, using a reciprocating saw. Pry the studs away from the sole plates and remove—the remaining top pieces will be used as cripple studs.

3 To install a jack stud, cut the stud to fit between the sole plate and the bottom of the header, as marked on the king stud. Align it at the mark against the king stud, then fasten it in place with 10d common nails driven every 12".

(continued next page)

4 Build the header to size (page 32; and page 86, step 9) and install, fastening it to the jack studs, king studs, and cripple studs, using 16d common nails. Use a handsaw to cut through the bottom plate so it's flush with the inside faces of the jack studs. Remove the cutout portion.

5 Finish the walls (for wallboard installation, see pages 70 to 71) before installing the doors, then set the prehung door unit into the framed opening so the jamb edges are flush with the finished wall surfaces and the unit is centered from side to side.

6 Using a level, adjust the unit to plumb one of the side jambs. Starting near the top of the door, insert pairs of shims driven from opposite directions into the gap between the framing and the jamb, sliding the shims until they are snug. Check the jamb to make sure it remains plumb and does not bow inward.

7 Working down along the jamb, install shims near each hinge and near the floor. Make sure the jamb is plumb, then anchor it with 8d finish nails driven through the jamb and shims and into the framing. Leave the nail heads partially protruding so the jamb can be readjusted later if necessary.

8 Install shims at the other side jamb, aligning them roughly with the shims of the first jamb. With the doors closed, adjust the shims so the reveal between the doors is even and the tops of the doors are aligned.

9 Shim the gap between the header and the head jamb to create a consistent reveal along the top when the doors are closed. Insert pairs of shims every 12". Drive 8d finish nails through the jambs and shims and into the framing members.

10 Drive all the nails fully, then set them below the surface of the wood with a nail set. Cut off the shims flush with the wall surface, using a handsaw or utility knife. Hold the saw vertically to prevent damage to the door jamb or wall. Install the door casing (pages 174 to 177).

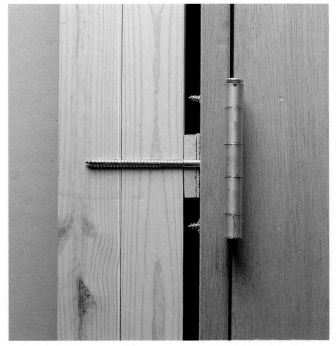

Option: Replace the center mounting screw on each hinge with a 3" wood screw to provide extra support for door hinges and jambs. These long screws extend through the side jambs and deep into the framing members. Be careful not to overtighten screws—overtightening will cause the jambs to bow.

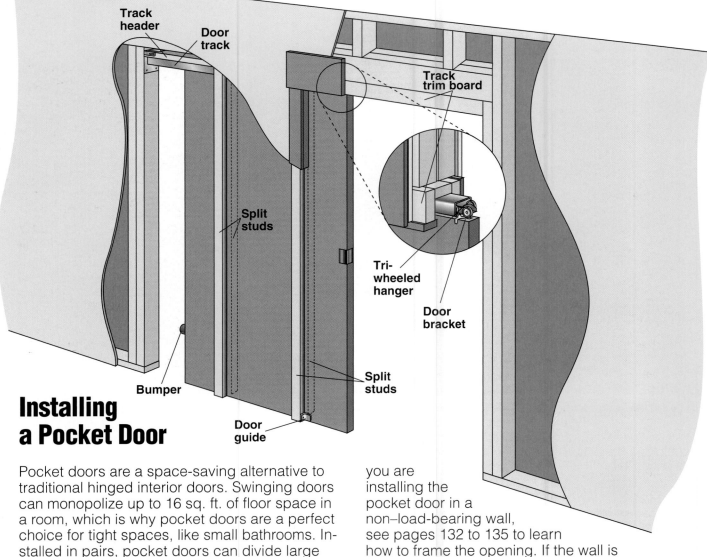

Track header

Door track

Track trim board

Split studs

Tri-wheeled hanger

Door bracket

Bumper

Door guide

Split studs

Installing a Pocket Door

Pocket doors are a space-saving alternative to traditional hinged interior doors. Swinging doors can monopolize up to 16 sq. ft. of floor space in a room, which is why pocket doors are a perfect choice for tight spaces, like small bathrooms. Installed in pairs, pocket doors can divide large rooms into more intimate spaces and can still be opened to use the entire area.

Pocket door hardware kits generally are universal and can be adapted for almost any interior door. In this project, the frame kit includes an adjustable track, steel-clad split studs, and all the required hanging hardware. The latch hardware, jambs, and the door itself are all sold separately. Pocket door frames can also be purchased as preassembled units that can be easily installed into a rough opening.

Framing and installing a pocket door is not difficult in new construction or a major remodel. But retrofitting a pocket door in place of a standard door, or installing one in a wall without an existing door, is a major project that involves removing the wall material, framing the new opening, installing and hanging the door, and refinishing the wall. Hidden utilities, such as wiring, plumbing, and heating ducts, must be rerouted if encountered.

The rough opening for a pocket door is at least twice the width of a standard door opening. If you are installing the pocket door in a non–load-bearing wall, see pages 132 to 135 to learn how to frame the opening. If the wall is load bearing, you will need to install an appropriately sized header (page 86).

Because pocket doors are easy to open and close and require no threshold, they offer increased accessibility for wheelchair or walker users, provided the handles are easy to use (page 145). If you are installing a pocket door for this purpose, be aware that standard latch hardware may be difficult to use for some individuals. Page 147 includes some handle variations for easier accessibility.

Everything You Need

Tools: tape measure, circular saw, hammer, nail set, screwdriver, level, drill, handsaw, hacksaw, wallboard tools.

Materials: 2 × 4 lumber, 16d, 8d & 6d common nails, pocket door frame kit, door, 1¼" wallboard screws, wallboard materials, manufactured pocket door jambs (or build jambs from 1x material), 8d & 6d finish nails, 1½" wood screws, door casing.

How to Install a Pocket Door

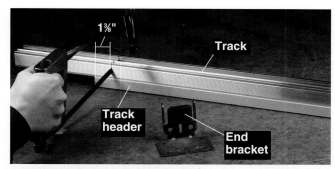

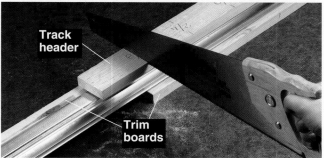

1 Prepare the project area and frame the rough opening to the manufacturer's recommended dimensions (pages 132 to 135). Measuring from the floor, mark each jack stud at the height of the door plus ¾" to 1½" (depending on the door clearance above the floor) for the overhead door track. Drive a nail into each jack stud, centered on the mark. Leave about ⅛" of the nail protruding.

2 Remove the adjustable end bracket from the overhead door track. Cut the wooden track header at the mark that matches your door size. Turn the track over and cut the metal track 1⅜" shorter than the wooden track header, using a hacksaw (top). Replace the end bracket. Cut the side trim boards along the marks corresponding to your door size, being careful not to cut the metal track (bottom).

3 Set end brackets of track on the nails in the jack studs. Adjust track to level and set the nails. Then drive 8d common nails through remaining holes in end brackets.

4 Snap chalk lines on the floor across the opening, even with the sides of the rough opening. Tap floor plate spacers into bottom ends of pairs of steel-clad split studs. Butt one split stud pair against the door track trim board, check it for plumb, and fasten it to the track header using 6d common nails (left). Center the other split stud pair in the "pocket" and fasten it to the track header. Plumb the split studs again and attach them to floor with 8d common nails or 2" screws driven through spacer plates (right).

(continued next page)

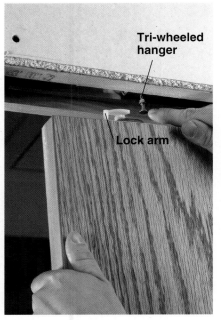

5 Install wallboard over the pocket to the edge of the opening. You may want to leave the wallboard off one side of the wall to allow for door adjustment. Do not finish wallboard until the door has been completely installed and adjusted. Use 1¼" wallboard screws, which will not protrude into the pocket.

6 Paint or stain the door as desired. When the door has dried, attach two door brackets to the top of the door, using included screws driven through pilot holes. Install the rubber bumper to the rear edge of the door with its included screw.

7 Slide two tri-wheeled hangers into the overhead door track. Set the door in the frame, aligning the hangers with the door brackets. Then raise the door and press each hanger into the door bracket until it snaps into place. Close the lock arm over the hanger.

8 Cut the strike-side jamb to length and width. Fasten it to the jack stud, using 8d finish nails, shimming jamb to plumb as necessary. Close door and adjust the hanger nuts to fine-tune the door height so the door is parallel with the jamb from top to bottom.

9 Measure and cut the split jambs to size. Fasten each split jamb to front edge of split stud, using 8d finish nails. Maintain ³⁄₁₆" clearance on both sides of door. If necessary, shim between the bumper and door until the door is flush with the jambs when open.

10 Measure and cut the split head jambs to size. Use 1½" wood screws driven through countersunk pilot holes to attach the head jamb on the side that has access to the lock arm of the hangers, to allow for easy removal of the door. Attach the other head jamb using 6d finish nails. Maintain ¾₁₆" clearance on each side of the door.

11 Install the included door guides on both sides of the door near the floor at the mouth of the pocket. Install the latch hardware according to the manufacturer's directions. Finish the wallboard and install casing around the door (pages 174 to 177). Fill all nail holes, then paint or stain the jambs and casing as desired.

Improving Pocket Door Accessibility

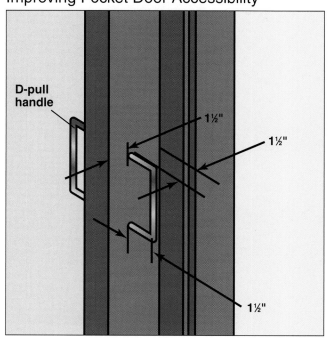

D-pull handle

1½"

1½"

1½"

1½"

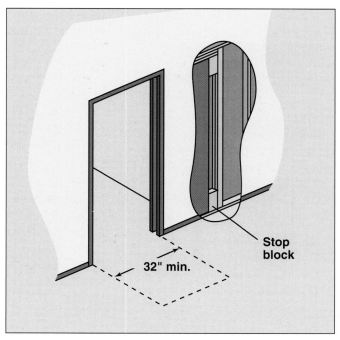

32" min.

Stop block

D-pull handles are easier to use than standard recessed hardware. Choose pulls that project at least 1½" from the door. Mount the pulls 1½" from the edge of the door to provide room for fingers when the door is closed (left). Install a stop block at the back of the frame (right), so the door stops 1½" short of the D-pull to provide room for fingers when the door is open. Because this design reduces the width of the door opening by 3", you must use a 36"-wide door to maintain the recommended doorway width of 32".

Mounting Bifold Doors

Bifold doors provide easy access to a room or area without requiring much clearance for opening. They are a convenient addition to closets, as well as a clever way to conceal a utility room or washing machine and clothes dryer.

Most home centers stock kits that include two pairs of pre-hinged doors, a head track, and all the necessary hardware and fasteners. Typically, the doors in these kits have predrilled holes for the pivot and guide posts. Hardware kits are also sold separately for custom projects.

A variety of door styles are available, some featuring louvered panels or glass panes. Most doors are designed to fit a standard 80" opening, but if the floor is carpeted or tiled, you may need to trim them. Make minor adjustments using a plane, and larger alterations with a circular saw and straightedge (pages 228 to 229).

To operate properly, bifold doors must be hung level and plumb in the opening. Before installation begins, make sure the opening has square corners, a level header, and straight jambs.

Allow a minimum clearance gap of ⅛" between the doors at the center, hinges, and jambs to prevent binding.

Installing bifold doors is an easy task, though just as there are many door styles, there are also many types of mounting hardware. Make sure to read and follow the manufacturer's instructions for the product you

Photo courtesy of Craftmaster Manufacturing, Inc.

Everything You Need

Tools: tape measure, circular saw, drill, plane, screwdriver, hacksaw.

Materials: prehinged bifold doors, head track, mounting hardware, pan-head screws, flat-head screws.

use. Most models operate by means of a two-post system: pivot posts on each jamb-side door and a top guide post on each lead door. The top posts fit in the track at the header, while the pivot post fits into an anchor bracket at the foot of each jamb, providing a pivot point.

After the doors are installed, the top and bottom pivots can be adjusted to align the doors. Adjustments to door height typically require turning the bottom pivot clockwise to lower the door and counterclockwise to raise it. To align the doors vertically, loosen the screw in the top guide post and slide it left or right. Some jamb brackets also allow the bottom pivot post to be repositioned along the length of the bracket for additional vertical adjustment.

Photo courtesy of Madawaska Doors, Inc.

A variety of designer bifold doors are available for installation between rooms. They provide the same attractive appearance as French doors (pages 138 to 141) but require much less floor space.

How to Mount Bifold Doors

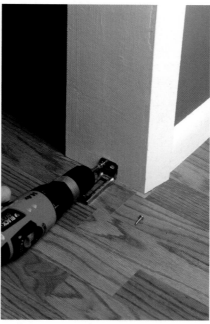

1 Cut the head track to the width of the opening, using a hacksaw. Insert the roller mounts into the track, then position the track in the opening. Fasten it to the header, using pan-head screws.

2 Measure and mark each side jamb at the floor for the anchor bracket, so the center of the bracket aligns exactly with the center of the head track. Fasten the brackets in place with flat-head screws.

3 Check the height of the doors in the opening, and trim if necessary (opposite page). Insert a pivot post into predrilled holes at the top and bottom of the two jamb-side doors, at the jamb side of each door. Make sure the pivot posts fit snugly.

4 Insert a guide post into the predrilled holes at the top of both lead doors. Make sure the guide posts fit snugly.

5 Fold one pair of doors closed and lift into position, inserting the pivot and guide posts into the head track. Slip the bottom pivot post into the anchor bracket. Repeat for the other pair of doors.

6 Close the doors and check for equal spacing along the side jambs and down the center. To align the doors, adjust the top and bottom pivots following the manufacturer's directions.

Installing a Storm Door

Install a storm door to improve the appearance and weather resistance of an old entry door, or to protect a newly installed door against weathering. In all climates, adding a storm door can extend the life of an entry door.

When buying a storm door, look for models that have a solid inner core and seamless outer shell construction. Carefully note the dimensions of your door opening, measuring from the inside edges of the entry door's brick molding. Choose a storm door that opens from the same side as your entry door.

Everything You Need

Tools: tape measure, pencil, plumb bob, hacksaw, hammer, drill and bits, screwdrivers.

Materials: storm door unit, wood spacer strips, 4d casing nails.

Adjustable sweeps help make storm doors weathertight. Before installing the door, attach the sweep to the bottom of the door. After the door is mounted, adjust the height of the sweep so it brushes the top of the sill lightly when the door is closed.

How to Cut a Storm Door Frame to Fit a Door Opening

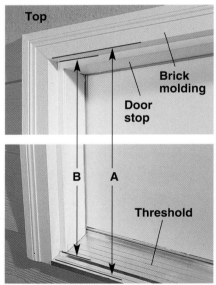

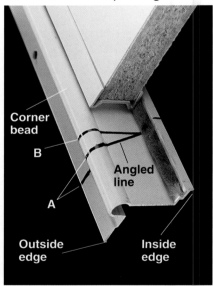

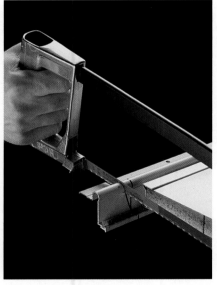

1 Because entry door thresholds are slanted, the bottom of the storm door frame needs to be cut to match the threshold angle. Measure from the threshold to the top of the door opening along the corner of the brick molding (A), then measure along the front edge of entry door stop (B).

2 Subtract ⅛" from measurements A and B to allow for small adjustments when the door is installed. Measuring from the top of the storm door frame, mark the adjusted points A and B on the corner bead. Draw a line from point A to the outside edge of the frame and from point B to the inside edge. Draw an angled line from point A on corner bead to point B on the inside edge.

3 Use a hacksaw to cut down through the bottom of the storm door frame, following the angled line. Make sure to hold the hacksaw at the same slant as the angled line to ensure that the cut will be smooth and straight.

How to Fit & Install a Storm Door

Brick molding

Push hinge side tight

1 Position the storm door in the opening and push the frame tight against the brick molding on the hinge side of the storm door, then draw a reference line on the brick molding, following the edge of the storm door frame.

Push latch side tight

2 Push the storm door frame tight against the brick molding on the latch side, then measure the gap between the reference line and the hinge side of the door frame. If the distance is greater than ⅜", spacer strips must be installed to ensure the door will fit snugly.

3 To install spacers, remove the door, then nail thin strips of wood to the inside of the brick molding at storm door hinge locations. The thickness of the wood strips should be ⅛" less than the gap measured in step 2.

4 Replace the storm door and push it tight against the brick molding on the hinge side. Drill pilot holes through the hinge-side frame of the storm door and into the brick molding spaced every 12". Attach the frame with mounting screws.

5 Remove any spacer clips holding the frame to the storm door. With the storm door closed, drill pilot holes and attach the latch-side frame to the brick molding. Use a coin to keep an even gap between the storm door and the storm door frame.

6 Center the top piece of the storm door frame on top of the frame sides. Drill pilot holes and screw the top piece to the brick molding. Adjust the bottom sweep, then attach the locks and latch hardware as directed by the manufacturer.

Installing an Attic Access Ladder

When positioning your attic access, make sure there is enough clearance for the ladder to swing down unobstructed, as well as adequate landing space. In the attic, make sure the space is clear of wiring, pipes, or other obstructions. To ease framing and installation, orient the door opening parallel to the ceiling joists, if possible.

Pull-down attic ladders provide instant access to your attic space, making it easy to store and retrieve items without squeezing through a tight access panel. You can replace an existing access panel with a ladder kit, or install the ladder in a more convenient location.

When purchasing an access ladder, consider the amount of use it will get. A basic wooden ladder system may be sufficient for occasional use a few times a year. More frequent use may call for a more sturdy model, such as an aluminum ladder, or disappearing staircase.

It's important that the ladder you install is the proper size for your ceiling height. Never install one that is shorter than your ceiling height. Compare units for weight load, incline angle and quality of materials when choosing the right ladder for your home. Although most attic ladders are installed the same way, always follow the manufacturer's directions.

Everything You Need

Tools: tape measure, framing square, pencil, wallboard saw, reciprocating saw, drill and bits, hammer, hacksaw.

Materials: attic access ladder kit, stiff wire, 2 × lumber (for framing and temporary supports), 3" deck screws, 2" and 1¼" wallboard screws, casing, 1 × 4 lumber (for temporary ledgers).

Tip: Before purchasing an attic access ladder, examine your home's framing in the attic. If your roof is framed with trusses, make sure to purchase a ladder unit that will fit between the trusses; never cut or alter the trusses.

Tip: Standard rafter and joist framing allows you the option to cut one of the joists to install a wider ladder unit. If you have to cut a joist, build temporary supports to support the joist during the project, then frame in permanent headers to carry the cut joist ends (pages 66 to 69).

Tips for Purchasing Attic Access Ladders

Temporary support clips come with some ladder units. They hold the unit in place while you fasten it to the framing. Consult the manufacturer's directions if your unit includes these supports.

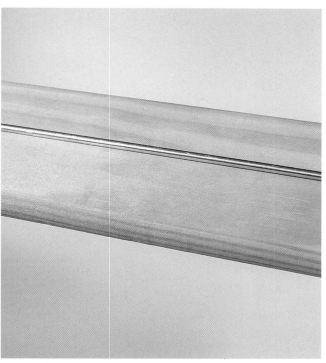

Metal truss rods beneath the treads of wooden ladders provide additional strength. Compare the weight load ratings of ladders before you purchase. The minimum capacity you should buy is 250 pounds.

Fully insulated attic access doors will help prevent heat loss and reduce energy costs.

Designer ladders such as this concertina model can make attic access not only practical but stylish. Because of its compact size this ladder also requires less ceiling space.

Photo courtesy of Architectural Stairs, Inc.

(continued next page)

How to Install an Attic Access Ladder

1 Mark the approximate location for the attic access door on the room ceiling. Drill a hole at one of the corners and push the end of a stiff wire up into the attic. In the attic, locate the wire and clear away insulation in the area. Using dimensions provided by the manufacturer, mark the rough opening across the framing members, using one of the existing joists as one side of the frame. Add 3" (the width of two 2 ×s) to the rough opening length dimension to allow for the headers.

2 If the width of your ladder unit requires that you cut a joist, build temporary supports in the room below to support each end of the cut joist to prevent damage to your ceiling (pages 66 to 69). Use a reciprocating saw to cut through the joist at both end marks, then remove the cut piece. CAUTION: Do not stand on the cut joist.

3 Cut two headers to fit between the joists using 2 x lumber the same size as your ceiling joists. Position the headers perpendicular to the joists, butting them against the cut joists. Make sure the corners are square and attach the headers with three 3" deck screws into each joist.

4 Cut a piece of 2 x lumber to the length of the rough opening to form the other side of the frame. Square the corners and attach the side piece to each header with three 3" deck screws.

5 Cut the rough opening in the ceiling, using a wallboard saw. Use the rough opening frame to guide your saw blade.

6 Fasten the edges of the wallboard to the rough opening frame using 1¼" wallboard screws spaced every 8". Prepare the ladder's temporary support clips according to the manufacturer's directions.

7 If your ladder does not include support clips, attach 1 × 4 boards at both ends of the opening, slightly overlaping the edges, to act as ledgers to support the unit while fastening.

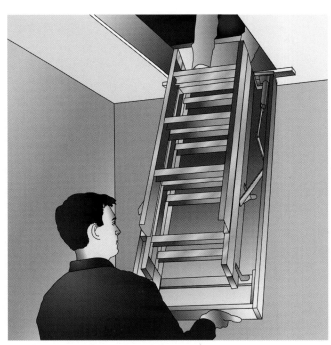

8 With a helper, lift the unit through the opening and rest it on the ledgers. Make sure the unit is square in the frame and the door is flush with the ceiling surface. Shim the unit as needed. NOTE: Do not stand on the unit until it is firmly attached to the framing.

9 Attach ladder unit to rough framing with 10d nails or 2" screws driven through holes in the corner brackets and hinge plates. Continue fastening unit to frame, driving screws or nails through each side of the ladder frame into the rough frame. Remove temporary ledgers or support clips when complete.

(continued next page)

11 Fully extend the ladder and test-fit the adjustable feet on the rails. Adjust the feet so there are no gaps in the hinges and the feet are flush with the floor. Drill through the rails using a recommended size bit and attach the adjustable feet with included nuts, washers, and bolts.

10 Open the ladder, keeping the lower section folded back. With the tape measure along the top of the rail, measure the distance from the end of the middle section to the floor (A) on each rail. Subtract 3" and mark the distances on the right and left rails of the third section. Use a square to mark a cutting line across the rails. Place a support under the lower section and trim along the cutting line with a hacksaw. (For wooden ladders see manufacturer's directions.)

12 Install casing around the edges to cover the gap between the ceiling wallboard and the ladder frame (pages 174 to 177). Leave a ⅜" clearance between the door panel and the casing.

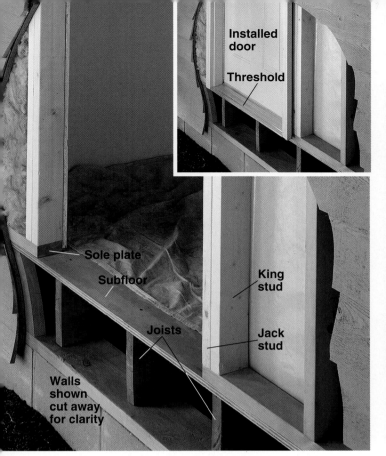

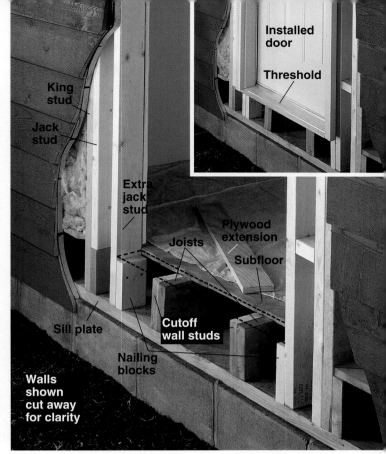

A new door opening in a platform-framed house (page 30) has studs that rest on a sole plate running across the top of the subfloor. The sole plate is cut away between the jack studs so the threshold for the new door can rest directly on the subfloor.

A new door opening in a balloon-framed house (page 31) has studs extending past the subfloor to rest on the sill plate. Jack studs rest either on the sill plate or on top of the joists. To provide a surface for the door threshold, install nailing blocks, and extend subfloor out to the ends of the joists, using plywood.

Framing an Opening for an Entry Door

The rough opening for a new exterior door should be framed after the interior preparation work is done (pages 52 to 57), but before the exterior wall surfaces are removed (pages 58 to 63). The methods for framing the opening will vary, depending on what type of construction your house was built with (see photos, above).

Make sure the rough opening is 1" wider and ½" taller than the dimensions of the door you plan to install, including the jambs, to allow space for adjustment during installation.

Because exterior walls are always load-bearing, the framing for an exterior door requires a larger header than those used for interior partition walls.

Local building codes will specify a minimum size for the door header based on the size of your rough opening, but you'll learn how to estimate header size on page 32.

Always build temporary supports to hold up the ceiling if your project requires that you cut or remove more than one stud in a load-bearing wall (pages 66 to 69).

When you finish framing, measure across the top, middle, and bottom of the door opening to make sure it is uniform from the top to the bottom. If there are major differences in the opening size, adjust the studs so the opening is uniform.

Everything You Need

Tools: tape measure, pencil, level, plumb bob, reciprocating saw, circular saw, handsaw, hammer, pry bar, nippers.

Materials: 2 × lumber, ⅜" plywood, 10d nails.

(continued next page)

How to Frame an Exterior Door Opening (Platform Framing)

1 Prepare the project site and remove the interior wall surfaces (pages 52 to 57).

2 Measure and mark the rough opening width on the sole plate. Mark the locations of the jack studs and king studs on the sole plate. (Where practical, use existing studs as king studs.)

3 If king studs need to be added, measure and cut them to fit between the sole plate and top plate. Position the king studs and toenail them to the sole plate with 10d nails.

4 Check the king studs with a level to make sure they are plumb, then toenail them to the top plate with 10d nails.

5 Measuring from the floor, mark the rough opening height on one king stud. For most doors, the recommended rough opening is ½" taller than the height of the door unit. This line marks the bottom of the door header.

6 Determine the size of the header needed (pages 32 to 33), and measure and mark where the top of it will fit against a king stud. Use a level to extend the lines across the intermediate studs to the opposite king stud.

7 Cut two jack studs to reach from the top of the sole plate to the rough opening marks on the king studs. Nail the jack studs to the king studs with 10d nails driven every 12". Make temporary supports (pages 66 to 69) if you are removing more than one stud.

8 Use a circular saw set to maximum blade depth to cut through the old studs that will be removed. The remaining stud sections will be used as cripple studs for the door frame. NOTE: Do not cut king studs. Make additional cuts 3" below the first cuts, then finish the cuts with a handsaw.

9 Knock out the 3" stud sections, then tear out the rest of the studs with a pry bar. Clip away any exposed nails, using nippers.

10 Build a header to fit between the king studs on top of the jack studs. Use two pieces of 2 × lumber sandwiched around ½" plywood (page 86). Attach header to the jack studs, king studs, and cripple studs, using 10d nails.

11 Use a reciprocating saw to cut through the sole plate next to each jack stud, then remove the sole plate with a pry bar. Cut off any exposed nails or anchors, using nippers.

How to Frame an Exterior Door Opening (Balloon Framing)

1 Remove the interior wall surfaces (pages 52 to 57). Select two existing studs to use as king studs. The distance between selected studs must be at least 3" wider than the planned rough opening. Measuring from the floor, mark the rough opening height on a king stud.

2 Determine the header size (pages 32 to 33) and measure and mark where the top of it will fit against a king stud. Use a level to extend the line across the studs to the opposite king stud.

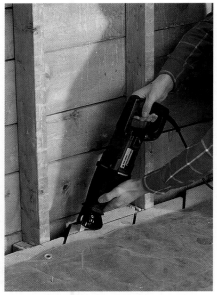

3 Use a reciprocating saw to cut open the subfloor between the studs, and remove any fire blocking in the stud cavities. This allows access to the sill plate when installing the jack studs. If you will be removing more than one wall stud, make temporary supports (pages 66 to 69).

4 Use a circular saw to cut studs along the lines marking the top header. NOTE: Do not cut king studs. Make two additional cuts on each stud, 3" below the first cut and 6" above the floor. Finish the cuts with a handsaw, then knock out the 3" sections with a hammer. Remove studs with a pry bar.

5 Cut two jack studs to reach from the top of the sill plate to the rough opening mark on the king studs. Nail the jack studs to the king studs with 10d nails driven every 12".

6 Build a header to fit between the king studs on top of the jack studs, using two pieces of 2 × lumber sandwiched around ½" plywood (page 86). Attach header to the jack studs, king studs, and cripple studs, using 10d nails.

7 Measure and mark the rough opening width on the header. Use a plumb bob to mark the rough opening on the sill plate (inset).

8 Cut and install additional jack studs, as necessary, to frame the sides of the rough opening. Toenail the jack studs to the header and the sill plate, using 10d nails. NOTE: You may have to go to the basement to do this.

9 Install horizontal 2 × 4 blocking between the studs on each side of the rough opening, using 10d nails. Blocking should be installed at the lockset location and at the hinge locations on the new door.

10 Remove the exterior wall surface as directed on pages 58 to 63.

11 Cut off the ends of the exposed studs flush with the tops of the floor joists, using a reciprocating saw or handsaw.

12 Install 2 × 4 nailing blocks next to the jack studs and joists, flush with the tops of the floor joists. Replace any fire-blocking that was removed. Patch the subfloor area between the jack studs with plywood to form a flat, level surface for the door threshold.

Installing an Entry Door

Prehung entry doors come in many styles, but all are installed using the same basic methods. Because entry doors are very heavy—some large units weigh several hundred pounds—make sure you have help before beginning installation.

To speed your work, do the indoor surface removal (pages 52 to 57) and framing work (pages 155 to 159) in advance. Before installing the door, make sure you have all the necessary hardware. Protect the door against the weather by painting or staining it and by adding a storm door (pages 148 to 149).

Everything You Need

Tools: metal snips, hammer, level, pencil, circular saw, wood chisel, nail set, caulk gun, stapler, drill and bits, handsaw.

Materials: building paper, drip edge, wood shims, fiberglass insulation, 10d galvanized casing nails, silicone caulk, entry door kit.

How to Install an Entry Door

1 Remove the door unit from its packing. Do not remove the retaining brackets that hold the door closed. Remove exterior surface material inside the framed opening as directed on pages 58 to 63.

2 Test-fit the door unit, centering it in the rough opening. Check to make sure door is plumb. If necessary, shim under the lower side of the door jamb until the door is plumb and level.

Brick molding

3 Trace an outline of brick molding on siding. NOTE: If you have vinyl or metal siding, see pages 58 to 59 for advice on removing the siding. Remove the door unit after finishing the outline.

4 Cut the siding along the outline, just down to the sheathing, using a circular saw (pages 60 to 61). Stop just short of the corners to prevent damage to the siding that will remain.

5 Finish the cuts at the corners with a sharp wood chisel.

6 Cut 8"-wide strips of building paper and slide them between the siding and sheathing at the top and sides of the opening. Each piece overlaps the piece below it. Bend paper around the framing members and staple it in place.

Drip edge

7 To provide an added moisture barrier, cut a piece of drip edge to fit the width of the rough opening, then slide it between the siding and the building paper at the top of the opening. Do not nail the drip edge.

8 Apply several thick beads of silicone caulk to the subfloor at the bottom of the door opening. Also apply silicone caulk over the building paper on the front edges of the jack studs and header.

(continued next page)

How to Install an Entry Door (continued)

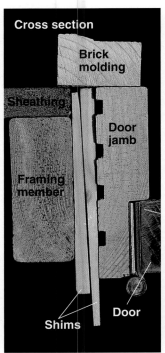

Cross section

Brick molding

Sheathing

Framing member

Door jamb

Door

Shims

9 Center the door unit in the rough opening, and push the brick molding tight against the sheathing. Have a helper hold the door unit steady until it is nailed in place.

10 From inside, place pairs of hardwood wedge shims together to form flat shims (left), and insert shims into the gaps between the door jambs and framing members. Insert shims at the lockset and hinge locations and every 12" thereafter (right).

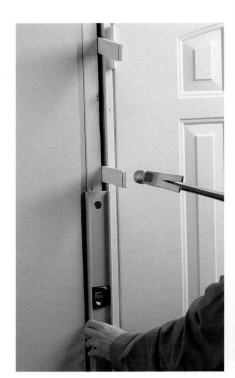

11 Adjust the shims, if necessary, until the door unit is plumb and level.

12 From outside, drive 10d casing nails through the door jambs and into the framing members at each shim location. Use a nail set to drive the nail heads below the surface of the wood.

13 Remove the retaining brackets installed by the manufacturer, then open and close the door to make sure that it works properly.

14 Remove two of the screws on the top hinge and replace them with long anchor screws (usually included with the unit). These anchor screws will penetrate into the framing members to strengthen the installation.

15 Anchor brick molding to the framing members with 10d galvanized casing nails driven every 12". Use a nail set to drive the nail heads below the surface of the wood.

16 Adjust the door threshold to create a tight seal, following manufacturer's recommendations.

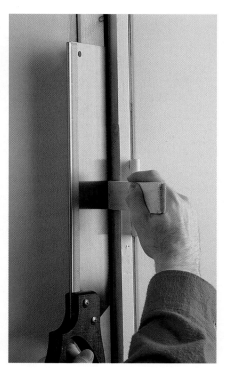

17 Cut off the shims flush with the framing members, using a handsaw. Fill the gaps between the jambs and the framing members with loosely packed fiberglass insulation.

18 Apply paintable silicone caulk around the entire door unit and fill the nail holes with latex caulk. Finish the door and install the lockset as directed by the manufacturer.

Installing a Patio Door

For easy installation, buy a patio door with the door panels already mounted in a preassembled frame. Try to avoid patio doors sold with frame kits that require complicated assembly.

Because patio doors have very long bottom sills and top jambs, they are susceptible to bowing and warping. To avoid these problems, be very careful to install the patio door so it is level and plumb and to anchor the unit securely to framing members. Yearly caulking and touch-up painting helps prevent moisture from warping the jambs.

Everything You Need

Tools: pencil, hammer, circular saw, handsaw, wood chisel, stapler, caulk gun, level, pry bar, cordless screwdriver, drill and bits, nail set.

Materials: shims, drip edge, building paper, silicone and latex caulk,10d casing nails, 3" wood screws, sill nosing, fiberglass insulation, patio door kit.

© Brad Daniels (above)

Screen doors, if not included with the unit, can be ordered from most patio door manufacturers. Screen doors have spring-mounted rollers that fit into a narrow track on the outside of the patio door threshold.

Tips for Installing Sliding Doors

Remove heavy glass panels if you must install the door without help. Reinstall the panels after the frame has been placed in the rough opening and nailed at opposite corners. To remove and install the panels, remove the stop rail, found on the top jamb of the door unit.

Adjust the bottom rollers after installation is complete. Remove the coverplate on the adjusting screw, found on the inside edge of the bottom rail. Turn the screw in small increments until the door rolls smoothly along the track without binding when it is opened and closed.

Tips for Installing French-style Patio Doors

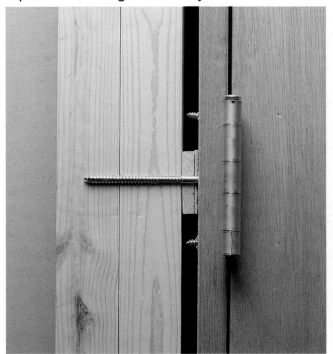

Provide extra support for door hinges by replacing the center mounting screw on each hinge with a 3" wood screw. These long screws extend through the side jambs and deep into the framing members.

Keep a uniform ⅛" gap between the door, side jambs, and top jamb to ensure that the door will swing freely without binding. Check this gap frequently as you shim around the door unit.

How to Install a Patio Door

1 Prepare the work area and remove the interior wall surfaces (pages 52 to 57), then frame the rough opening for the patio door (pages 155 to 159). Remove the exterior surfaces inside the framed opening (pages 58 to 63).

2 Test-fit the door unit, centering it in the rough opening. Check to make sure door is plumb. If necessary, shim under the lower side jamb until the door is plumb and level. Have a helper hold the door in place while you adjust it.

3 Trace the outline of the brick molding onto the siding, then remove the door unit. NOTE: If you have vinyl or metal siding, see pages 58 to 59 for advice on removing the siding.

4 Cut the siding along the outline, just down to the sheathing, using a circular saw. Stop just short of the corners to prevent damage to the remaining siding. Finish the cuts at the corners with a sharp wood chisel.

5 To provide an added moisture barrier, cut a piece of drip edge to fit the width of the rough opening, then slide it between the siding and the existing building paper at the top of the opening. Do not nail the drip edge.

6 Cut 8"-wide strips of building paper and slide them between siding and sheathing. Bend paper around framing members and staple it in place. Each piece overlaps the piece below it.

7 Apply several thick beads of silicone caulk to the subfloor at the bottom of the door opening.

8 Apply silicone caulk around the front edge of the framing members, where the siding meets the building paper.

9 Center the patio door unit in the rough opening so the brick molding is tight against the sheathing. Have a helper hold the door unit from outside until it is shimmed and nailed in place.

10 Check the door threshold to make sure it is level. If necessary, shim under the lower side jamb until the patio door unit is level.

(continued next page)

11 If there are gaps between the threshold and subfloor, insert shims coated with caulk into the gaps, spaced every 6". Shims should be snug, but not so tight that they cause the threshold to bow. Clear off excess caulk immediately.

12 Place pairs of hardwood wedge shims together to form flat shims. Insert the shims every 12" into the gaps between the side jambs and the jack studs. For sliding doors, shim behind the strike plate for the door latch.

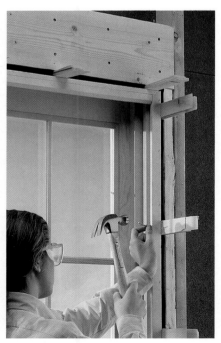

13 Insert shims every 12" into the gap between the top jamb and the header.

14 From outside, drive 10d casing nails, spaced every 12", through the brick molding and into the framing members. Use a nail set to drive the nail heads below the surface of the wood.

15 From inside, drive 10d casing nails through the door jambs and into the framing members at each shim location. Use a nail set to drive the nail heads below the surface of the wood.

16 Remove one of the screws and cut the shims flush with the stop block found in the center of the threshold. Replace the screw with a 3" wood screw driven into the subfloor as an anchor.

17 Cut off the shims flush with the face of the framing members, using a handsaw. Fill gaps around the door jambs and beneath the threshold with loosely packed fiberglass insulation.

18 Reinforce and seal the edge of the threshold by installing sill nosing under the threshold and against the wall. Drill pilot holes and attach the sill nosing with 10d casing nails.

19 Make sure the drip edge is tight against the top brick molding, then apply paintable silicone caulk along the top of the drip edge and along the outside edge of the side brick moldings. Fill all exterior nail holes with caulk.

20 Caulk completely around the sill nosing, using your finger to press the caulk into any cracks. As soon as the caulk is dry, paint the sill nosing. Finish the door and install the lockset as directed by the manufacturer. See pages 174 to 177 to trim the interior of the door.

Finishing Windows & Doors

Final Details

After your windows and doors are in place and you've made sure they operate properly, install the interior trim, or casing, to complete the project. A good lumberyard or home center will have a variety of casing in several wood species as well as manufactured materials. Some wood trim is expensive; you may want to save your trim from the original unit to reuse with the new unit. Be sure to practice your cutting and fitting techniques on scrap materials before you begin the project.

Most window and door units do not come with casing; it's up to you to select a molding that looks good with the window and door, and matches or complements other trim in the room. A good remodeling project looks like an original part of the home design, not like an afterthought.

Don't be afraid to get creative with window and door trim. You can paint or stain the casing to match the color of your cabinetry or wall trim. You'll also find casings and brick moldings in many different profiles. For added personal touches, use details such as corner blocks.

Because exteriors are exposed to the elements, protect these surfaces by doing the outdoor finishing work first. Patched siding and new trim should be caulked and painted as soon as possible to seal them against the weather.

Other finishing projects for your home may include installing a door closer, a keyless entry deadbolt, and a garage door opener.

Finally, keep security in mind when considering a window or door project. Installing a peephole, adding a heavy-duty latch guard, installing a deadbolt lock, and using auxiliary locks on sliding windows are just a few ways to help keep your windows and doors secure against intruders.

Tips for Finishing Windows & Doors

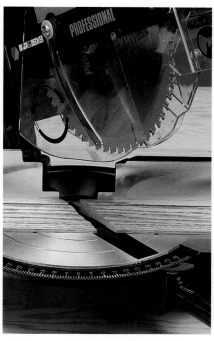

On window and door casings, mark a line across the front face of the piece as a reference for the cutting direction. Then lay the casing flat on the saw table and set the blade to 45°. If you have a compound saw, set the bevel adjustment to 0°. Make sure to keep your hand at a safe distance from the blade.

Check for square. Any gap between the blade of a combination square and the workpiece means the corner is not a true 90°, and should be trimmed for better fit.

Specialty tools and supplies for painting include: work light (A), paint pan (B), paint remover (C), primer/sealer (D), tapered sash brush (E), trim brush (F), scraper (G), sandpaper (H), paint rollers (I).

The doors of your kitchen cabinets can be easily painted; be sure to paint both sides. Begin with the inner surfaces, then paint the recessed panels, the horizontal rails, and finally the vertical stiles.

Trimming Windows & Doors

Window and door casings provide an attractive border around windows and doors. They also cover the gaps between window and door jambs and the surfaces of surrounding walls.

Install window and door casings with a consistent reveal between the inside edges of the jambs and casings.

In order to fit casings properly, the jambs and wall surfaces must lie in the same plane. If one of them protrudes, the casings will not lie flush. To solve this problem, you may need to use a block plane to shave the protruding jamb. Or, you may need to attach an extension to build up the jamb to match the plane of the wall.

Wallboard screws rely on the strength of untorn face paper to support the wallboard. If the paper around the screws is damaged, drive additional screws nearby where the paper is still intact.

Everything You Need

Tools: tape measure, drill, pencil, nail set, hammer or pneumatic nailer, level, combination square, straight-edge, miter saw.

Materials: casing material, baseboard molding and corner blocks (optional), 4d and 6d finish nails, wood putty.

Photo courtesy of Andersen Windows, Inc.

How to Install Mitered Casing on Windows & Doors

1 On each jamb, mark a reveal line ⅛" from the inside edge. The casings will be installed flush with these lines.

2 Place a length of casing along one side jamb, flush with the reveal line. At the top and bottom of the molding, mark the points where horizontal and vertical reveal lines meet. (When working with doors, mark the molding at the top only.)

3 Make 45° miter cuts on the ends of the moldings. Measure and cut the other vertical molding piece, using the same method.

4 Drill pilot holes spaced every 12" to prevent splitting, and attach the vertical casings with 4d finish nails driven through the casings and into the jambs. Drive 6d finish nails into the framing members near the outside edge of the casings.

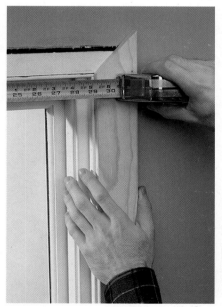

5 Measure the distance between the side casings, and cut top and bottom casings to fit, with ends mitered at 45°. If window or door unit is not perfectly square, make test cuts on scrap pieces to find the correct angle of the joints. Drill pilot holes and attach with 4d and 6d finish nails.

6 Locknail the corner joints by drilling pilot holes and driving 4d finish nails through each corner, as shown. Drive all nail heads below the wood surface, using a nail set, then fill the nail holes with wood putty.

How to Install Butted Door Casings

1 On each jamb, mark a reveal line ⅛" from the inside edge. The casings will be installed flush with these lines.

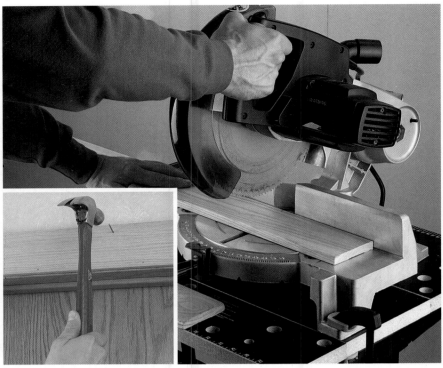

2 Cut the head casing to length. Mark the centerpoint of the head casing and the centerpoint of the head jamb. Align the casing with the head jamb reveal line, matching the centerpoints so that the head casing extends evenly beyond both side jambs. Nail the casing to the wall at stud locations and at the jamb (inset).

3 Hold the side casings against the head casing and mark them for cutting, then cut the side casings to fit.

4 Align the side casings with the side jamb reveal lines, then nail the casings to the jambs and framing members. Set the nails, using a nail set. Fill the nail holes with wood putty.

Options for Installing Window & Door Casing

Combine mitered and butted casings. Form miter joints at the top of the window, then square-cut the bottoms of the side casings. Cut the sill casing to extend 1" beyond the side casings. Hand-sand the ends with 150-grit sandpaper, removing any rough edges. Mark the sill casing 1" from each end, then invert it so the thick end is up. Attach the sill casing to the wall with finish nails so the pencil marks are aligned with the edges of the side casings.

Dress up door casings by adding a piece of ornate baseboard molding or a plinth block. Nail the molding to the jambs with 2" finish nails so the beveled edge is aligned with reveal lines for the casings.

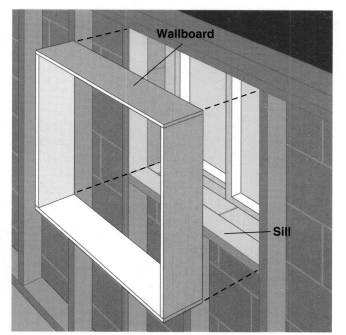

Add corner blocks, also known as rosettes, at the ends of the head casing. Attach the corner blocks once the side and head casings are in place. Set the nails, using a nail set, after all pieces are installed.

The frame around a basement window acts like casing. It is flush with the edges of the masonry on all sides. Install a sill at the base of the window opening, and add a header, if you wish. Fill the space between framing members and masonry with fiberglass insulation or non-expanding foam insulation. Install wallboard so it butts against the window frame.

177

Installing Stool & Apron Window Trim

Stool and apron trim brings a traditional look to a window, and is most commonly used with double-hung styles. The stool serves as an interior sill; the apron (or the bottom casing) conceals the gap between the stool and the finished wall.

In many cases, such as with 2 × 6 walls, jamb extensions made from 1 × finish-grade lumber need to be installed to bring the window jambs flush with the finished wall. Many window manufacturers also sell jamb extensions for their windows.

The stool is usually made from 1 × finish-grade lumber, cut to fit the rough opening, with "horns" at each end extending along the wall for the side casings to butt against. The horns extend beyond the outer edge of the casing by the same amount that the front edge of the stool extends past the face of the casing, usually under 1".

If the edge of the stool is rounded, beveled, or otherwise decoratively routed, you can create a more finished appearance by returning the ends of the stool to hide the end grain. A pair of miter cuts at the rough horn will create the perfect cap piece for wrapping the grain of the front edge of the stool around the horn. The same can be done for an apron cut from a molded casing.

As with any trim project, tight joints are the secret to a successful stool and apron trim job. Take your time to ensure all the pieces fit tightly. Also, use a pneumatic nailer—you don't want to spend all that time shimming the jambs perfectly only to knock them out of position with one bad swing of a hammer.

Tip: "Back-cut" the ends of casing pieces where needed to help create tight joints, using a sharp utility knife.

Everything You Need

Tools: tape measure, straightedge, circular saw or jig saw, handsaw, plane or rasp, drill, hammer, pneumatic nailer (optional).

Materials: 1 × finish lumber; casing; wood shims; 4d, 6d, and 8d finish nails.

How to Install Stool & Apron Window Trim

1 Cut the stool to length, with several inches at each end for creating the horn returns. With the stool centered at the window and tight against the wallboard, shim it to its finished height. At each corner, measure the distance between the window frame and the stool, then mark that dimension on the stool.

2 Open a compass so it touches the wall and the tip of the rough opening mark on the stool, then scribe the plane of the wall onto the stool to complete the cutting line for the horn.

3 Cut out the notches for the horn, using a jig saw or a sharp handsaw. Test-fit the stool, making any minor adjustments with a plane or a rasp to fit it tightly to the window and the walls.

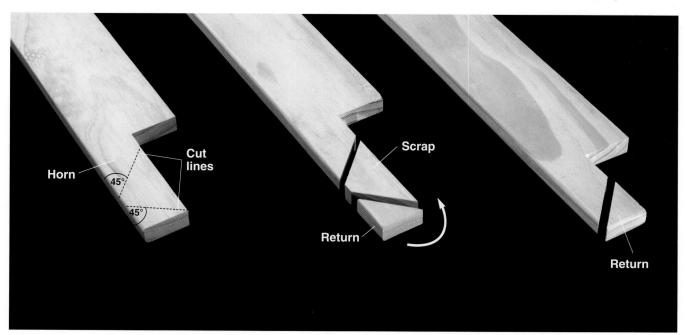

Horn   45°   45°   **Cut lines**

Scrap

Return

Return

4 To create a return at the horn of the stool, miter-cut the return pieces at 45° angles. Mark the stool at its overall length and cut it to size with 45° miter cuts. Glue the return to the mitered end of the horn so the grain wraps around the corner. NOTE: Use this same technique to create the returns on the apron (step 13, page 181), but make the cuts with the apron held on-edge, rather than flat.

(continued next page)

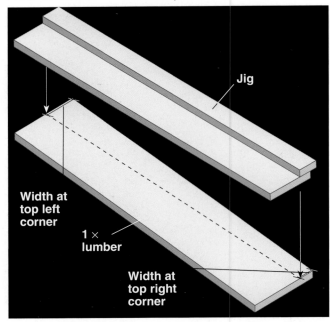

Width at top left corner

1 × lumber

Jig

Width at top right corner

5 Where extensions are needed, cut the head extension to its finished length—the distance between the window side jambs plus the thickness of both side extensions (typically 1 × stock). For the width, measure the distance between the window jamb and the finished wall at each corner, then mark the measurements on the ends of the extension. Use a straightedge to draw a reference line connecting the points. Build a simple cutting jig, as shown.

6 Clamp the jig on the reference line, then rip the extension to width, using a circular saw; keep the baseplate tight against the jig and move the saw smoothly through the board. Reposition the clamp when you near the end of the cut. Cut both side extensions to length and width, using the same technique as for the head extension (step 5).

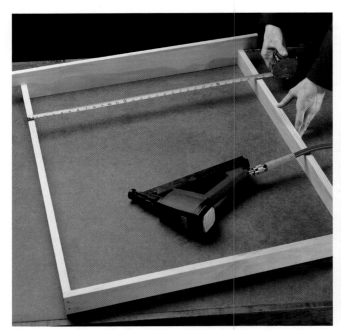

7 Build a box frame with the extensions and stool, using 6d finish nails and a pneumatic nailer. Measure to make sure the box has the same dimensions as the window jambs. Drive nails through the top of the head extension into the side extensions, and through the bottom of the stool into side extensions.

8 Apply wood glue to back edge of frame, then position it against front edge of window jambs. Use wood shims to adjust frame, making sure pieces are flush with window jambs. Fasten frame at each shim location, using 8d finish nails driven through pilot holes. Loosely pack insulation between framing members and extensions.

9 On the edge of each extension, mark a ¼" reveal at the corners, the middle, and the stool. Place a length of casing along the head extension, aligned with the reveal marks at the corners. Mark where the reveal marks intersect, then make 45° miter cuts at each point. Reposition the casing at the head extension and attach, using 4d finish nails at the extensions, and 6d finish nails at the framing members.

10 Cut the side casings to rough length, leaving the ends slightly long for final trimming. Miter one end at 45°. With the pointed end on the stool, mark the height of the side casing at the top edge of the head casing.

11 To get a tight fit for side casings, align one side of a T-bevel with the reveal, mark the side extension and position the other side flush against the horn. Transfer angle from T-bevel to end of casing, and cut casing to length.

12 Test-fit the casings, making any final adjustments with a plane or rasp. Fasten the casing with 4d finish nails at the extensions, and 6d finish nails at the framing members.

13 Cut apron to length, leaving a few inches at each end for creating the returns (step 4, page 179). Position the apron tight against the bottom edge of the stool, then attach it, using 6d finish nails driven every 12".

Applying Window Film

Window film has come a long way from the heat-sensitive shrink-wrap it once was. The latest generation of films adhere directly to the glass surface and are nearly invisible. Some of the benefits window film provides are:

• Heat Control—reduces solar heat gain and heat loss through the windows.

• UV Blocking—reduces the sun's harmful ultra-violet rays, significantly decreasing fading of fabrics, carpet, and furnishings.

• Privacy—reduces visibility into your home. Available in a wide variety of tints, from opaque reflective films that block views to softer tints that simply reduce window glare.

• Safety & Security—resists penetration and holds broken glass together, reducing the risk of injury and providing added security.

• Decoration—replicates etched, frosted, and other window styles.

Window film is available in standard widths, typically ranging from 24" to 48", and is cut to the dimensions of the glass surface. When ordering window film, order at least 10% more than your estimate to allow for errors.

Before cleaning the windows for the application, carefully read the manufacturer's instructions—some prohibit the use of household cleaners that contain ammonia or vinegar, which can dissolve the film's adhesive. Many manufacturers sell cleaning solutions that are safe to use with their products. Also, most films cannot be used on plastic, Plexiglas, etched, frosted, leaded, scratched, or cracked glass.

When applying the film, handle it carefully; scratches, creases, and tears cannot be repaired. Make sure to keep both the window and film well lubricated with plenty of soapy water during the installation.

After the film is applied, allow the adhesive to cure for a week, then clean the windows with a cleaning solution specified by the manufacturer.

Window film kits generally include: rolls of window film, a squeegee, cleaning solution, film removal solution, a scraper, and a utility knife.

To cover large windows, overlap two pieces of film vertically (step 2), then use a straightedge and razor blade to cut through the center of both layers of film. Carefully remove the two waste pieces and adjust the film pieces to create a tight seam. Rewet the film and slowly, firmly squeegee from top to bottom.

Everything You Need

Tools: spray bottle, straightedge, razor blades, rubber squeegee, paper towels.

Materials: soapy water, window film.

How to Apply Window Film

1 Clean the window thoroughly, using soapy water and a clean rubber squeegee. Use a razor blade or scraper to remove paint or debris. Unroll the film on a clean, flat surface, then cut the film 1" larger than the window dimensions. NOTE: For small or irregular windows, pretrim the film to the final dimensions, including the 1/16" perimeter gap (step 4).

2 Remove the liner from the film, exposing the adhesive side. Spray both the adhesive side of the film and the window with soapy water. Make sure the window is completely wet. At the top of the window, smooth the film onto the glass and slide it into position so it covers the entire glass surface.

3 Spray the film with soapy water, then start 2" from the top, and make one pass with the squeegee from left to right, working water and air out from under film. Lightly squeegee the rest of the film downward, leaving the 2" perimeter unsmoothed. Keep the film wet and push bubbles to the nearest film edge, then squeegee the 2" perimeter area out to the edges.

4 Use a razor blade and 1/16"-thick guide to trim the film around the edges. Wet the film and squeegee again, pressing firmly to remove all the water to ensure the adhesive will cure clearly. Start at the top of the window and work from the center to the left, then from the center to the right, to the bottom of the window. The film will begin to adhere within 30 minutes.

Refinishing an Interior Door

Although refinishing woodwork and doors may seem like an overwhelming project, the right techniques can greatly simplify the job. A combination of heat and chemical stripping is the key to making the job easier. Use a heat gun and scraper to remove most of the old paint, and take off the rest by chemically stripping and scraping the wood.

You may need to do some experimenting to find a combination of stains that produce a uniform color.

Everything You Need

Tools: screwdriver, hammer, sander, heat gun, sawhorses, staple gun, paintbrush, broad scrapers, specialty scraper, drill.

Materials: plastic sheeting, abrasive pad, mineral spirits, stainable wood putty, semi-paste chemical stripper, 150- and 220-grit sandpaper, rags, wood stain, varnish or tung oil.

1 Remove the door and mask off the work area by attaching plastic to the door jambs to keep fumes and dust out of the rest of the house. Remove hinges and other door hardware, as well as receptacle and cover plates close to the work area.

2 With a heat gun and broad scraper, remove the old paint. Scrape off loose, flaky paint before heat stripping (paint flakes can be ignited by a heat gun). Always use extra care near the edges of the woodwork to prevent damage to the wood and adjoining walls.

3 Brush a heavy layer of semi-paste chemical stripper onto the woodwork contours and edges. (A heat gun can scorch these more delicate surfaces.) If the chemical stripper is not clinging well to vertical surfaces, try adding cornstarch to thicken it.

4 You may need a specialty scraper to scrape the contours in the door header and other trim areas. After removing most of the paint from these areas, apply a thin layer of stripper to all woodwork, then scrub with an abrasive pad to remove the remaining finish materials.

5 Remove all door hardware, then strip off the old finish using heat stripping, chemical stripping, and scraping.

6 Clean the woodwork and door by scrubbing all the wood surfaces with an abrasive pad dipped in mineral spirits. This removes the wax residue left by the chemical stripper, as well as traces of the old varnish.

7 Prepare for the finish by using stainable wood putty to fill any holes and gouges in the door and the woodwork. Then, after sanding, you can tint the putty with stain so it matches the color of the surrounding wood.

8 Sand the woodwork and door using a sander with 150-grit sandpaper to even out the wood surfaces, then finish-sand with 220-grit sandpaper, using a variety of grips and sanding blocks to prepare the surface.

9 Stain the wood, then apply a topcoat. Tung oil is a good choice because it is easy to apply and is a very effective product for vertical surfaces. Three coats will give you a hard, durable finish that is not overly glossy.

10 After chemically stripping and cleaning the hardware, drill new pilot holes, and reattach it. Then mount the hinges on the door jamb, and hang the door. Last, remount all receptacle and switch cover plates.

Painting Windows & Doors

Start by painting the inside portions of trim and working out toward the walls. On windows, for instance, first paint the edges close to the glass, then the surrounding face trim.

Doors should be painted quickly because of the large surface. To avoid overlap marks, always paint from dry surfaces back into wet paint. On baseboards, begin at the top edge and work down to the flooring. Plastic floor guards or a wide broadknife can help shield carpet and wood flooring from paint drips.

Alkyds and latex enamels may require two coats. Always sand lightly between coats and wipe with a tack cloth so that the second coat bonds properly.

Everything You Need

Tools: screwdriver, hammer, paintbrushes, putty knife, sawhorses, broadknife.

Materials: gloss enamel paint, wood sealer, sanding paper.

Painting double-hung windows is easier if you are able to remove them from their frames. Newer, spring-mounted windows are released by pushing against the frame (arrow).

Mount the window easel-style by inserting 2 nails into the legs of a wooden stepladder. Or, lay window flat on a bench or sawhorses. NOTE: Do not paint sides or bottom of sashes.

How to Paint a Window

1 Using a tapered sash brush, begin by painting the wood next to the glass. Use the narrow edge of the brush, and overlap paint onto the glass to create a weatherseal.

2 Clean excess paint off glass with a putty knife wrapped in a clean cloth. Rewrap the knife often so that you always wipe with clean fabric. Leave ¹⁄₁₆" paint overlap from sash onto glass.

Case molding

Sash

Sill

Apron

3 Paint the flat portions of sashes first, then the case moldings, sill, and apron. Use slow brush strokes, and avoid getting paint between the sash and the frame.

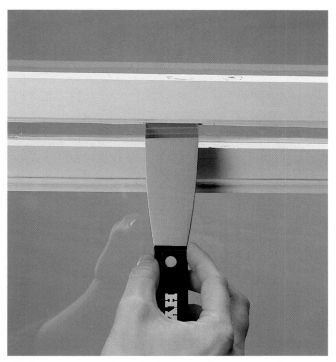

4 If you must paint windows in place, move the painted windows up and down several times during the drying period to keep them from sticking. Use a putty knife to avoid touching painted surfaces.

How to Paint a Door

1 Remove door by driving the lower hinge pin out with a screwdriver and hammer. Have a helper hold the door in place. Drive out the upper hinge pin.

2 Place the door flat on sawhorses to paint. On paneled doors, paint in the following order: recessed panels (1), horizontal rails (2), and vertical stiles (3).

3 Let the door dry. If a second coat of paint is needed, sand lightly and wipe the door with a tack cloth before repainting.

4 Seal the unpainted edges of the door with clear wood sealer to prevent moisture from entering the wood. Water can cause wood to warp and swell.

Tips for Painting Trim

Protect walls and floor surfaces with a wide broadknife, or with a plastic shielding tool.

Wipe paint off of broadknife or shielding tool each time it is moved.

Paint both sides of cabinet doors. This provides an even moisture seal and prevents warping.

Paint deeply patterned surfaces with a stiff-bristled brush, like this stenciling brush. Use small circular strokes to penetrate recesses.

Installing a Door Closer

The basic function of a door closer is to close and latch the door with a smooth, controlled motion after the door has been released. Many local building codes require door closers on fire doors between the garage and the residence. Closers can also help protect children from the dangers of basements, laundry rooms, or workshops.

Most door closers have adjustment screws for door speed and closing power, which allow you to adjust the closing action to your needs. Some applications call for the door to close quickly and then slow down to avoid slamming. For other doors, you may want the door to close slowly, then speed up at the end to ensure that it latches.

Everything You Need

Tools: tape measure, pencil, screwdriver, drill and bits.

Materials: door closer.

How to Install a Door Closer

1 Assemble the arm and closer according to manufacturer's directions. Mark and drill pilot holes into the pull side of the door and frame, using template or dimensions provided by manufacturer.

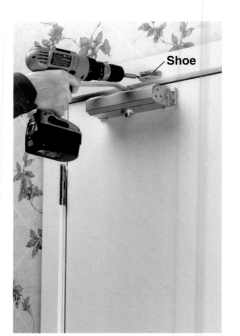

Shoe

2 Position the closer on the door, making sure the closing-speed adjustment valves are facing the hinges. Attach the closer to the door with included screws. Then attach the shoe to the door frame.

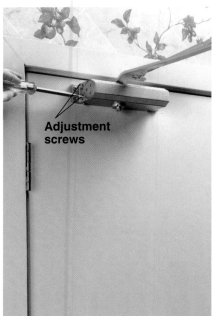

Adjustment screws

3 Adjust the length of the forearm so it forms a right angle with the door. Connect the arm to the shoe with its included screw. Adjust the door speed and closing power according to the manufacturer's directions.

Installation Variations

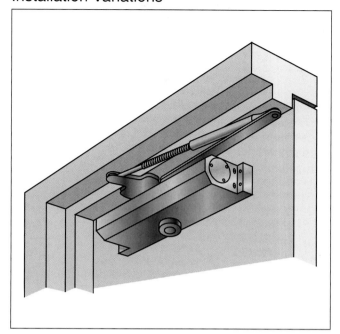

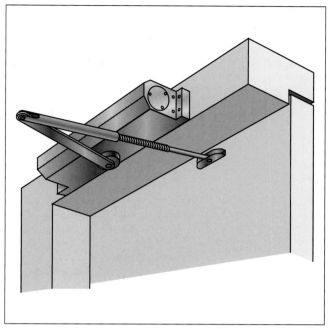

Parallel arm method: This method allows the closer arm to tuck against the jamb and out of the room space. Install the closer on the push side of the door using the included optional mounting bracket. Consult the manufacturer's directions for parallel arm installation methods. NOTE: Adjustment screws should face away from the hinges when using this method.

Top jamb method: Mount the closer to the frame above the door on the push side of the door and attach the shoe to the door. Consult the manufacturer's directions for top jamb installation methods.

Door Closer Options

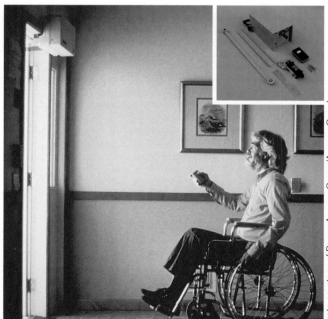

Hinge-pin closers use an adjustable spring to pull doors shut. To install, simply replace the pin in the existing door hinge with the hinge-pin closer. Check the hinge-pin closer for door weight ratings—heavy doors may require more than one closer.

Remote control door openers allow access for wheelchair users or those who lack the strength to open heavy doors. Some of these remote systems are quite complex and should be installed by a professional.

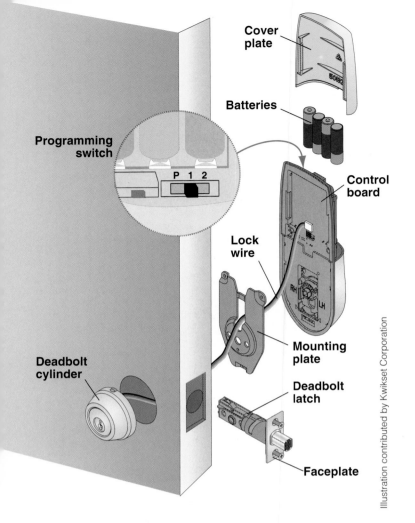

Cover plate

Batteries

Programming switch

P 1 2

Control board

Lock wire

Mounting plate

Deadbolt cylinder

Deadbolt latch

RH LH

Faceplate

Illustration contributed by Kwikset Corporation

Installing a Keyless Entry Deadbolt

Keyless entry provides home security with the push of a button. These systems generally work with either a small keychain remote or a programmable keypad. It is a great addition if you have children who must come home to an empty house after school. After you teach your children the keypad code, you won't have to worry about lost or stolen keys.

If you are replacing an old deadbolt with a keyless entry system, don't assume that the new lock will fit the existing holes. If the door and jamb holes are slightly misaligned the lock will not work properly. Consult the manufacturer's directions for measurement requirements, and make sure the holes in the door and jamb are properly sized and aligned.

Everything You Need

Tools: awl, drill with ⅛" bit, hole saw, spade bits, utility knife, hammer, chisel, flat-head and Phillips screwdrivers.

Materials: keyless entry deadbolt kit, nail, 3" wood screws.

How to Install a Keyless Entry Deadbolt

1 Tape the template supplied with your lock to the door in the desired location, usually about 5½" above the existing lockset. Mark the center positions for the cylinder and deadbolt holes with an awl (inset). Then, drill pilot holes at the marked points entirely through the door face and 2" deep into the door edge.

2 Use a drill and hole saw of the recommended size to bore the cylinder hole. To avoid splintering the wood, drill through one side until the pilot bit comes through, then finish drilling the hole from the other side.

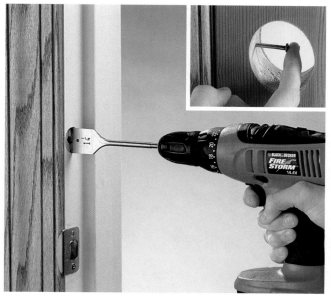

3 Mark the center of the strike box onto the door-jamb by closing the door and pressing a nail from inside the cylinder hole through the pilot hole in the door edge until it marks the door jamb (inset). Use the recommended spade bit to bore a 1"-deep hole into the jamb. Bore the deadbolt latch hole through the door edge and into the cylinder hole, using the recommended spade bit.

4 Insert the deadbolt latch into the edge hole and hold it in place temporarily with the included screws. Score around the faceplate with a utility knife (inset). Then, remove the latch and use a hammer and chisel to carefully remove material until the faceplate fits flush with the door. Attach the faceplate to the door with the included screws.

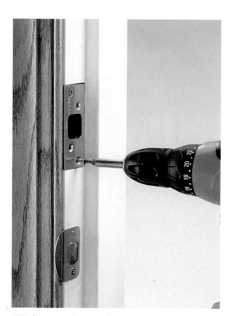

5 Insert the strike box into the door jamb, and make sure the deadbolt is precisely aligned with the strike plate. Mark and chisel out a recess so the strike plate is flush with the jamb. Drill pilot holes and install the strike plate with 3" wood screws.

6 Fit the exterior portion of the lock into the cylinder hole, sliding the cylinder tailpiece through the proper hole on the deadbolt. Route the lock wire underneath the deadbolt, making sure it is free of any moving parts. Fit the wire through the proper hole on the interior mounting plate and attach the plate to the deadbolt with the included screws.

7 Follow the manufacturer's instructions to align your lock control for a left- or right-hand door. Plug the lock wire into the receiving wire on the interior control board. With the bolt extended and the knob in the vertical position, slide the board into place and attach it with the included screws. Install the batteries and follow the manufacturer's instructions to program the remote and entry codes.

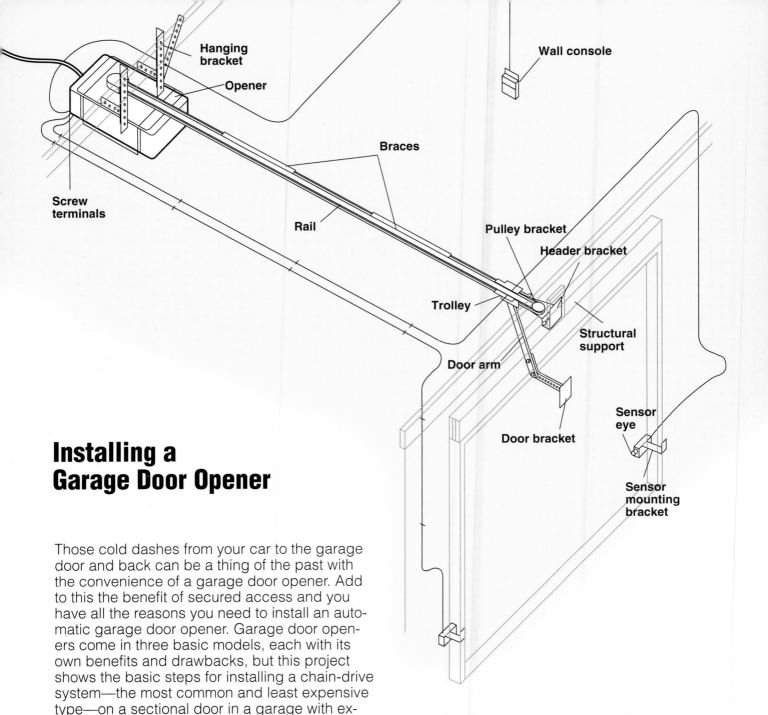

Hanging bracket

Opener

Wall console

Braces

Screw terminals

Rail

Pulley bracket

Header bracket

Trolley

Structural support

Door arm

Door bracket

Sensor eye

Sensor mounting bracket

Installing a Garage Door Opener

Those cold dashes from your car to the garage door and back can be a thing of the past with the convenience of a garage door opener. Add to this the benefit of secured access and you have all the reasons you need to install an automatic garage door opener. Garage door openers come in three basic models, each with its own benefits and drawbacks, but this project shows the basic steps for installing a chain-drive system—the most common and least expensive type—on a sectional door in a garage with exposed joists. If you have a one-piece door, a lightweight metal or glass-paneled door, or a garage with a finished ceiling, consult the manufacturer's directions for alternative installation procedures.

Before you begin, read all the manufacturer's instructions and the list of safety tips on page 195. Then, make sure your garage door is properly balanced and moves smoothly. Open and close the door to see if it sticks or binds at any point. Release the door in the half-open position. It should stay in place, supported by its own springs. If your door is not balanced or sticks at any point, call a garage door service professional before installing the opener.

Most garage door openers plug into a standard grounded receptacle located near the unit. Some local codes may require openers to be hard-wired into circuits. Consult the manufacturer's directions for hard-wiring procedures.

Everything You Need

Tools: stepladder, tape measure, screwdriver, pliers, wire cutters, pencil, hammer, adjustable wrench, ½" and 7/16" sockets and ratchet wrench, drill and bits.

Materials: garage door opener kit, 2 × lumber (for door header, if necessary).

Garage Door Safety Tips

Whether you're adding an opener to a new or old garage door, these tips will help make it a safe part of your home. (Also see pages 241 to 243 for information on repairing garage doors.)

• Before beginning the installation, be sure the garage door manually opens and closes properly.

• If you have a one-piece door, with or without a track, read all additional manufacturer's installation information.

• The gap between the bottom of the garage door and the floor must not exceed ¼". If it does, the safety reversal system may not work properly.

• If the garage has a finished ceiling, attach a sturdy metal bracket to structural supports before installing the opener. This bracket and hardware are not usually provided with the garage door opener kit.

• Install the wall-mounted garage door control within sight of the garage door, out of reach of children (at a minimum height of 5 ft.), and away from all moving parts of the door.

• Use the emergency release handle to disengage the trolley only when the garage door is closed. Never use the handle to pull the door open or closed.

• Never use an extension cord or two-wire adapter to power the opener. Do not change the opener plug in any way to make it fit an outlet. Be sure the opener is grounded.

• When an obstruction breaks the light beam while the door is closing, most door models stop and reverse to full open position, and the opener lights flash 10 times. If no bulbs are installed, you will hear 10 clicks.

• To avoid any damage to vehicles entering or leaving the garage, be sure the door provides adequate clearance when open fully.

• Garage doors may include tempered glass, laminate glass, or clear-plastic panels—all safe window options.

Wood garage doors can accommodate a variety of openers. A modern convenience is added without altering the door's traditional look.

Steel garage doors are lighter than wood doors, but they still may be too heavy to lift without an opener, especially double-wides.

(continued next page)

How to Install a Garage Door Opener

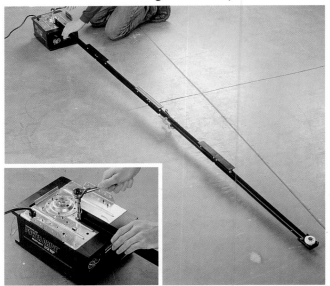

1 Start by aligning the rail pieces in proper order and securing them with the included braces and bolts. Screw the pulley bracket to the door end of the rail and slide the trolley onto the rail. Make sure the pulley and all rail pieces are properly aligned and that the trolley runs smoothly without hitting any hardware along the rail. Remove the two screws from the top of the opener, then attach the rail to the opener using these screws (inset).

2 The drive chain/cable should be packaged in its own dispensing carton. Attach the cable loop to the front of the trolley using the included linking hardware. Wrap the cable around the pulley, then wrap the remaining chain around the drive sprocket on the opener. Finally, attach it to the other side of the trolley with linking hardware. Make sure chain is not twisted, then attach the cover over the drive sprocket. Tighten the chain by adjusting the nuts on the trolley until the chain is ½" above the base of the rail.

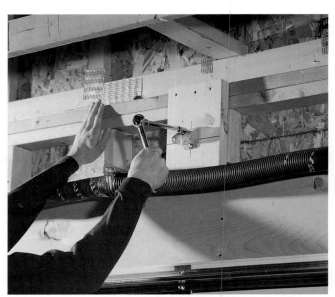

3 To locate the header bracket, first extend a vertical line from the center of the door onto the wall above. Raise the door and note the highest point the door reaches. Measure from the floor to this point. Add 2" to this distance and mark a horizontal line on the front wall where it intersects the centerline. If there is no structural support behind the cross point, fasten 2 × lumber across the framing. Then fasten the header bracket to the structural support with the included screws.

4 Support the opener on the floor with a board or box to prevent stress and twisting to the rail. Attach the rail pulley bracket to the header bracket above the door with the included clevis pin. Then place the opener on a stepladder so it is above the door tracks. Open the door and shim beneath the opener until the rail is 2" above the door.

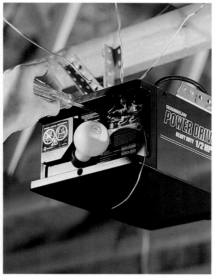

5 Hang opener from the ceiling joists with the included hanging brackets and screws. Angle at least one of the hanging brackets to increase stability of the unit while in operation. Attach the manual release cord and handle to the release arm of the trolley.

6 Strip ¼" of sheathing from the wall-console bell wire. Connect the wire to the screw terminals on the console, then attach it to the inside wall of the garage with included screws. Run the wires up the wall and connect them to the proper terminals on the opener. Secure the wire to the wall with insulated staples, being careful not to pierce the wire. Install the light bulbs and lenses.

7 Install the sensor-eye mounting brackets at each side of the garage door, parallel to each other, about 4" to 6" from the floor. The sensor brackets can be attached to the door track, the wall, or the floor, depending upon your garage layout. See the manufacturer's directions for the best configuration for your garage.

8 Attach the sensor eyes to the brackets with the included wing nuts, but do not tighten the nuts completely. Make sure the path of the eyes is unobstructed by the door tracks. Run wires from both sensors to the opener unit and connect the wires to the proper terminals. Plug the opener into a grounded receptacle and adjust the sensors until the indicator light shows correct eye alignment (inset), then tighten the wing nuts. Unplug the unit and attach the sensor wires to the walls with insulated staples.

9 Center the door bracket 2" to 4" below the top of the door. Drill holes and attach the bracket with the included carriage bolts. Connect the straight and curved arm sections with the included bolts. Attach the arm to the trolley and door bracket with the included latch pins. Plug the opener into a grounded receptacle and test the unit. See the manufacturer's directions for adjustment procedures.

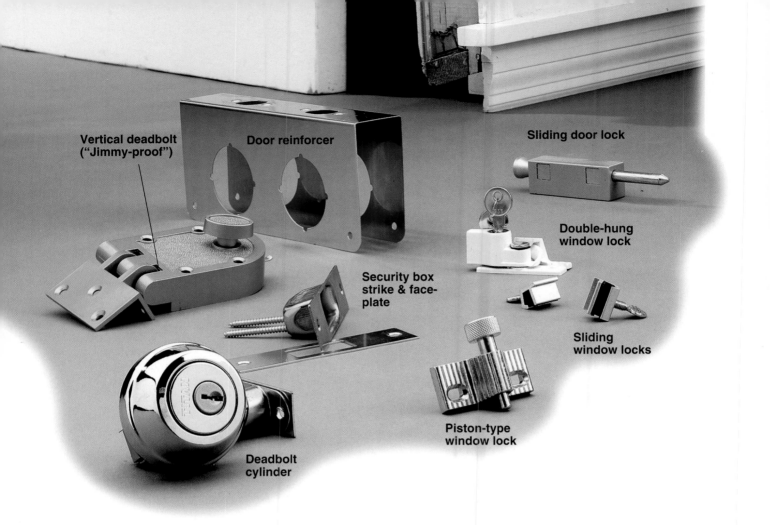

Vertical deadbolt ("Jimmy-proof")

Door reinforcer

Sliding door lock

Double-hung window lock

Security box strike & face-plate

Sliding window locks

Deadbolt cylinder

Piston-type window lock

Securing Windows & Doors

Securing windows and doors is often simply a matter of having the right hardware pieces. But skimping on strength or quality with any of them will undermine the security of the whole system.

Glass is both the strength and weakness of windows, in terms of security. An intruder can easily break the glass, but may not, since the noise it would make is likely to draw attention. Aside from installing metal bars, there's no way to secure the glass, so make sure your windows can't be opened from the outside.

Entry doors should be metal or solid wood—at least 1¾" thick—and each one in the home should have a deadbolt lock, as doorknob locks provide little security. Lock quality varies widely; just make sure to choose one that has a bolt (or bolt core) of hardened steel and a minimum 1" throw—the distance the bolt protrudes from the door when engaged.

Door hinges are easy to secure. Manufacturers

offer a variety of inexpensive devices that hold a door in place even when the hinge pins are removed.

Garage doors are structurally secure, but their locking devices can make them easy targets. When you're away from home, place a padlock in the roller track. If you have an automatic door opener, make sure the remote transmitter uses a rolling code system, which prevents thieves from copying your signal. An electronic keypad can make your garage door as secure and easy to use as your front door.

Everything You Need

Tools: hammer, drill, hole saw, spade bit, awl, screwdriver, chisel, utility knife.

Materials: plywood, casing nails, board, eye bolts, hinge, screws, dowel, security devices.

Tips for Securing Windows

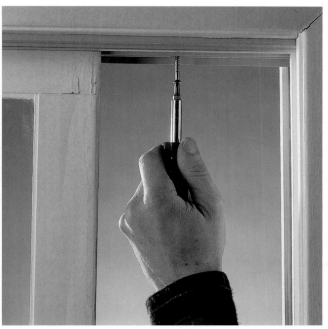

Pin together sashes of single- and double-hung windows with ¼ × 3" eye bolts. With the window closed, drill a ¼"-dia. hole, at a slight downward angle, through the top rail of the bottom sash and into the bottom rail of the top sash. Avoid hitting the glass, and stop the hole about ¾ of the way through the top sash. To lock the window in open positions, drill holes along the sash stiles (vertical pieces) instead.

Drive screws into the top channel of sliding windows to prevent intruders from lifting the window sash out of the lower channel. The screws should just clear the top of the window and not interfere with its operation. Use sturdy screws, and space them about 6" apart.

Block sash channels on sliding windows with a narrow board or a thick dowel.

Use auxiliary locks on sliding windows when a dowel or board won't work. Most types can be installed on the upper or lower window track.

Replace old sash locks on double-hung windows with keyed devices. Traditional sash locks can be highly vulnerable—especially on old windows. Be sure to store a key nearby, for emergency exits.

(continued next page)

Tips for Securing Windows (continued)

Removing the handles from casement and awning windows keeps intruders from cranking the window open after breaking the glass.

Security bars or gates can be installed in ground-floor windows to prevent intruders from gaining entry to your home.

Tips for Securing Sliding Glass Doors

Make a custom lock for your door track, using a thick board and a hinge. Cut the board to fit behind the closed door, then cut it again a few inches from one end. Install a hinge so you can flip up the end and keep the door secure while it's ajar. Attach knobs to facilitate use.

Drive screws into the upper track to keep the sliding panel from being pried up and out of the lower track. Use sturdy pan-head screws, spaced about every 8", and drive them so their heads just clear the top of the door. For metal door frames, use self-tapping screws and a low drill speed.

Attach a sliding-door lock to the frame of the sliding panel. Drill a hole for the deadbolt into the upper track. Then drill an additional hole a few inches away so you can lock the door in an open position.

Tips for Securing Doors

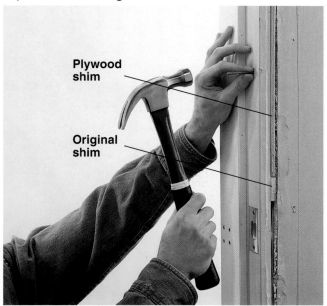

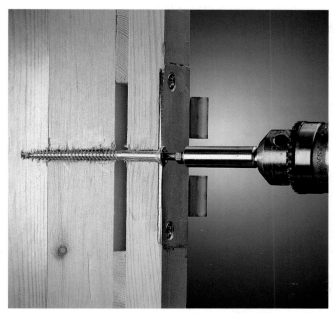

Install plywood shims in the gaps between the door frame and wall studs, to prevent pry-bar attacks. Remove the casing molding on the inside of the frame and inspect the gap; if it's wider than ¼", install new plywood shims in the spaces between the original shims. Be sure to shim directly above, below, and behind the strike plate. Drill pilot holes, and secure the shims with 10d casing nails.

Replace short hinge screws with longer screws (3" or 4") that extend through the door jamb and into the wall studs. This helps resist door kick-ins. Tighten the screws snug, but avoid overtightening them, which can pull the frame out of square.

Add metal door reinforcers to strengthen the areas around locks and prevent kick-ins. Remove the lockset (page 219) and slip the reinforcer over the door's edge. Be sure to get a reinforcer that is the correct thickness for your door.

Add a heavy-duty latch guard to reinforce the door jamb around the strike plate. For added protection, choose a guard with a flange that resists pry-bar attacks. Install the guard with long screws that reach the wall studs.

(continued next page)

Tips for Securing Doors (continued)

Have lock cylinders re-keyed to ensure that lost or stolen keys can't be used by unwanted visitors. Remove cylinder (see step 4, page 205), leaving bolt mechanism in door, and take it to a locksmith.

Putting a peephole into an exterior door is a quick and easy security measure. Simply drill a hole at the appropriate height, then screw the two halves of the peephole together.

How to Install a Security Box Strike

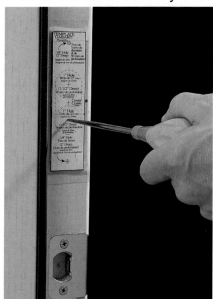

1 Mark the horizontal center of the deadbolt on the door jamb and tape the box strike template to the jamb, aligning the center marks. Use an awl to mark the drilling points, then use a utility knife to score a ⅛"-deep line around the outside of the template.

2 Drill pilot holes for the faceplate screws, and bore holes for the box mortise, using the recommended spade bit. To chisel the faceplate mortise, make parallel cuts ⅛" deep, holding the chisel at a 45° angle with the bevel side in. Flip the chisel over, and drive it downward to remove the material.

3 Insert the box strike into the mortise and install the screws inside the box. Angle the screws slightly toward the center of the wall stud, to increase their holding power. Position the faceplate and install the screws.

How to Install a Deadbolt Lock

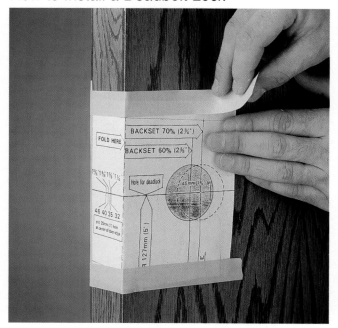

1 Measure up from the floor or existing lockset to locate the lock. Its center should be at least 3½" from the lockset center. Tape the template (supplied with lock) to the door. Use an awl to mark the centerpoints of the cylinder and deadbolt holes on the door. Close the door and use the template to mark the centerline for the deadbolt hole in the door jamb.

2 Bore the cylinder hole with a hole saw and drill. To avoid splintering the door, drill through one side until the hole saw pilot (mandrel) just comes out the other side. Remove the hole saw, then complete the hole from the opposite side of the door.

3 Use a spade bit to bore the deadbolt hole from the edge of the door into the cylinder hole. Be sure to keep the drill perpendicular to the door edge while drilling.

4 Insert the deadbolt into the edge hole. Fit the two halves of the lock into the door, aligning the cylinder tailpiece and connecting screw fittings with the proper holes in the deadbolt. Secure the two halves together with the connecting screws.

5 Use the centerline mark on the jamb to locate the hole for the deadbolt. Bore the hole, then chisel a mortise for the strike plate (see steps 1 and 2, page 202). Install the strike plate. Or, for greater security, install a security box strike (page 198), instead of the standard strike plate.

Repairing Windows & Doors

Window & Door Fix-ups

There probably isn't a home anywhere that doesn't have a sticking window or a door that won't close properly. Most windows suffer from a lack of lubrication; the same is true for locksets and other door hardware. The doors themselves, being typically made of wood, swell and warp with humidity, and their hinges loosen with everyday abuse and the force of gravity. Garage doors, although durable, usually suffer the most from neglect.

If a window is sticking or won't stay open, try one of the repairs in this section to improve its operation; the solution may be as simple as cleaning the tracks. Replacing glass and screen also are easy repairs that will improve your windows.

Door problems may require some investigation, but a quick inspection will tell you a lot. Check the gap between the door and the door frame: Is it wider on one side? Can you feel the door rub against the frame? Is the latchbolt missing the strike plate, or does it stick inside the door?

If your interior door rattles, it's probably not firmly seated against the stop molding. One fix is the same as for a severely warped door—adjust the stop molding. Or, add some weatherstripping, which works on rattling windows, too.

After new carpet is laid, you may find that your door drags. If the binding is minor, you may free it by simply planing the bottom of the door. If the binding is more serious, you may need to shorten the door.

As for garage doors, they thrive on a little routine maintenance. Tightening the bolts and lubricating the moving parts twice a year should prevent most problems. It's also important to check the springs and safety features of your garage door to prevent serious problems.

Cleaners and lubricants for windows and doors include, from left: spray lubricant with Teflon, penetrant/protectant spray, silicone spray, penetrating oil, and all-purpose household oil.

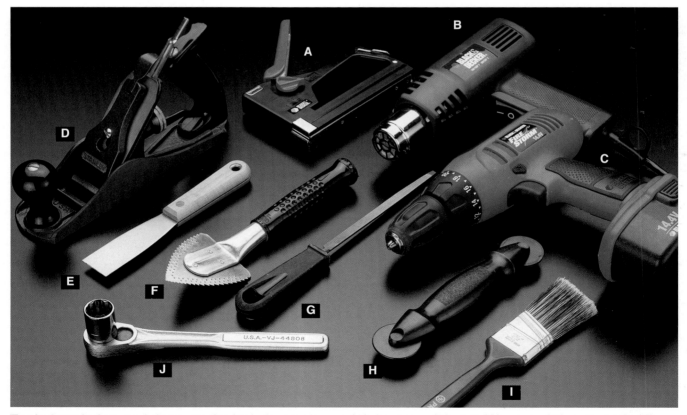

Tools for window and door repairs include: staple gun (A), heat gun (B), drill (C), plane (D), putty knife (E), window opener, sometimes called a "paint zipper" (F), metal file (G), spline roller (H), paintbrush (I), ratchet wrench (J).

Improving Window Operation

Problems with window operation—that is, opening and closing—are specific to the type of window you have. Windows stick if the wood is left unprotected and allowed to swell with moisture, or if someone has painted the window channels. Older windows that won't stay open probably have a broken sash cord or chain.

Newer double-hung windows with spring-loaded sash tracks need little maintenance. Clean the vinyl tracks to improve operation, and adjust the springs in (or behind) the tracks, following the manufacturer's directions.

Casement windows cause trouble when the crank mechanisms get dirty or rusty, or when the gears become stripped. If cleaning doesn't fix your casement window, replace the crank mechanism with new parts from the manufacturer or with a generic set you find at the hardware store.

For storm windows, especially the combination type, a little cleaning and lubrication goes a long way. Clean the accumulated dirt from the window track and apply a greaseless lubricant each time you switch the windows and screens.

Everything You Need

Tools: screwdrivers, paint zipper or utility knife, hammer, vacuum, small pry bar, scissors, stiff brush.

Materials: toothbrush, paint solvent, rags, sash cord, lubricant, wax candle, string, all-purpose grease.

How to Adjust Windows

Spring-loaded windows have an adjustment screw on the track insert. Adjust both sides until the window is balanced and opens and closes smoothly.

Spring-lift windows operate with the help of a spring-loaded lift rod inside a metal tube. Adjust them by unscrewing the top end of the tube from the jamb, then twisting the tube to change the spring tension: clockwise for more lifting power; counterclockwise for less. Maintain a tight grip on the tube at all times to keep it from unwinding.

Tips for Freeing Sticking Windows

Cut the paint film if the window is painted shut. Insert a paint zipper or utility knife between the window stop and the sash, and slide it down to break the seal.

Place a block of scrap wood against the window sash. Tap lightly with a hammer to free the window.

Clean the tracks on sliding windows and doors with a hand vacuum and a toothbrush. Dirt buildup is common on storm window tracks.

Clean weatherstrips by spraying with a cleaner and wiping away dirt. Use paint solvent to remove paint that may bind windows. Then apply a small amount of lubricant to prevent sticking.

Lubricate wood window channels by rubbing them with a white candle, then open and close the window a few times. Do not use liquid lubricants on wood windows.

How to Replace Broken Sash Cords

1 Cut any paint seal between the window frame and stops with a utility knife or paint zipper. Pry the stops away from the frame, or remove the molding screws.

2 Bend the stops out from the center to remove them from the frame. Remove any weatherstripping that's in the way.

3 Slide out the lower window sash. Pull knotted or nailed cords from holes in the sides of the sashes (see step 9).

4 Pry out or unscrew the weight pocket cover in the lower end of the window channel. Pull the weight from the pocket, and cut the old sash cord from the weight.

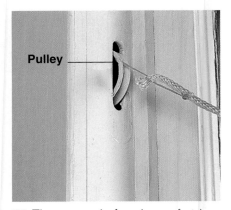

5 Tie one end of a piece of string to a nail and the other end to the new sash cord. Run the nail over the pulley and let it drop into the weight pocket. Retrieve the nail and string through the pocket.

6 Pull on the string to run the new sash cord over the pulley and through the weight pocket. Make sure the new cord runs smoothly over the pulley.

7 Attach the end of the sash cord to the weight, using a tight double knot. Set the weight in the pocket. Pull on the cord until the weight touches the pulley.

8 Rest the bottom sash on the sill. Hold the sash cord against the side of the sash, and cut enough cord to reach 3" past the hole in the side of the sash.

9 Knot the sash cord and wedge the knot into the hole in the sash. Replace the pocket cover. Slide the window and any weatherstripping into the frame, then attach the stops in the original positions.

210

How to Clean & Lubricate a Casement Window Crank

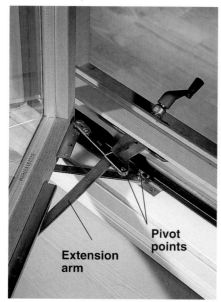

1 If a casement window is hard to crank, clean the accessible parts. Open the window until the roller at the end of the extension arm is aligned with the access slot in the window track.

2 Disengage the extension arm by pulling it down and out of the track. Clean the track with a stiff brush, and wipe the pivoting arms and hinges with a rag.

3 Lubricate the track and hinges with spray lubricant or household oil. Wipe off excess lubricant with a cloth, then reattach the extension arm. If that doesn't solve the problem, repair or replace the crank assembly (below).

How to Repair a Casement Window Crank Assembly

1 Disengage the extension arm from the window track (above), then remove the molding or cap concealing the crank mechanism. Unhinge any pivot arms connected to the window.

2 Remove the screws securing the crank assembly, then remove the assembly and clean it thoroughly. If the gears are badly worn, replace the assembly. Check a home center or call the manufacturer for new parts. Note which way the window opens—to the right or left—when ordering replacement parts.

3 Apply an all-purpose grease to the gears, and reinstall the assembly. Connect the pivot arms, and attach the extension arm to the window. Test the window operation before installing the cap and molding.

Replacing Window Glass & Screen

To replace broken glass in a single-pane window, break out the big pieces, wearing gloves and goggles, then wiggle the small pieces out of the glazing. Take the exact dimensions of the window frame opening to the hardware store. Purchase glass that is ⅛" less than the width and length of the opening, to allow for expansion.

Coat the window groove of wood frames with sealant to prevent rot and absorption of oils from the glazing compound. For an easier repair, use the type of glazing compound that comes in a tube.

Replace old screening with new fiberglass screen. It's cheap and easier to install than metal screening. Cut the screen larger than the frame so you'll have something to grip while stretching.

Everything You Need

Tools: heat gun, putty knife, caulk gun, sash brush, chisel or screwdriver, utility knife, stapler, hammer, spline roller.

Materials: gloves, goggles, sandpaper, wood sealer, glazing points and compound, glass, screen, vinyl spline.

How to Replace Window Glass

Putty

1 Remove the window sash, if possible. If not, you can repair it in place. With traditional glazing, soften the old putty with a heat gun, but be careful not to scorch the wood. Scrape away the soft putty with a putty knife. On newer windows, pry out the vinyl glazing strips. If you have metal windows, there should be "spring clip" molding that holds the glass in place; pry this out with a screwdriver.

2 Remove the broken glass and metal glazing points from the frame, then sand the L-shaped groove to clean away old paint and putty. Coat any bare wood with sealer and let it dry.

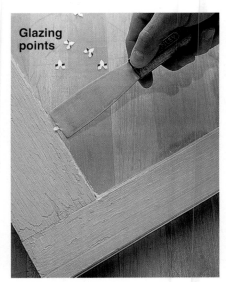

Glazing points

3 Apply a thin layer of glazing compound in the groove. Install the glass and press it lightly to embed it in the compound. Press in new glazing points every 10", using the tip of a putty knife.

4 Apply a bead of glazing compound around the edges of the glass. Smooth the glazing with a wet finger or cloth. When the glazing is dry, paint it to match the window frame. Overlap the paint onto the glass by ¹⁄₁₆" to create a good weather seal.

How to Replace a Screen in a Wood Frame

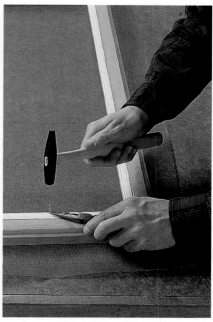

1 Pry up the screen molding with a small chisel or screwdriver. If the molding is sealed with paint, use a utility knife to cut the film. Cut the new screen 3" wider and longer than the frame.

2 Staple the screen along the top edge of the frame, then stretch it tight and staple it along the bottom edge. Stretch and staple the screen to the sides, one at a time.

3 Nail the screen molding back in place with wire brads or finish nails. Cut away excess screen, using a utility knife.

How to Replace a Screen in an Aluminum Frame

1 Pry the vinyl spline from the groove around the edge of the frame with a screwdriver. Retain the old spline if it is still flexible, or replace it with a new spline.

2 Stretch the new screen tight over the frame so that it overlaps the edges of the frame. Keeping the screen taut, use the convex side of a spline roller to press the screen into the retaining grooves.

3 Use the concave side of the spline roller to press the spline into the groove (it helps to have a partner for this). Cut away excess screen, using a utility knife.

Replacing a Storm Window

As old removable storm windows wear out, many homeowners elect to replace them with modern, combination storm windows. Designed to mount permanently in the existing opening, retrofit combination storm windows are very easy to install, and fairly inexpensive.

Most retrofit storm windows attach to the outside edges of the window stops on the sides and top of the window opening. Most windows do not have a bottom stop. Secure the bottom rail of the new window with caulk. Common window sizes are stocked at most building centers, but you may need to order custom-made windows. Have the exact measurements when you order the windows. You also will be asked to choose a finish color and a style. If you have operating double-hung windows, choose three-sash windows so you have the option of opening the top storm sash.

Retrofit storm windows attach to the window stops in the existing window opening. The easiest way to size them is to use the dimensions of old storm windows. Otherwise, measure narrowest point between side jambs to find the width, and measure the shortest point from the header to the sill (where it meets the front edges of the stops) to find the height.

Everything You Need

Tools: screwdriver, drill, tape measure.

Materials: replacement storm windows, caulk or panel adhesive, screws.

How to Install a New Combination Storm Window

1 Buy replacement storm windows to fit your window openings. Test-fit before installing them. To install, first apply a bead of exterior-grade panel adhesive or caulk to outside edges of the window stops at the top and sides.

2 Drill pilot holes for fasteners in mounting flanges, spaced 12" apart, making sure they will be centered over the stops. Press the new storm window into the opening, centered between the side stops, the bottom rail resting on the windowsill.

3 Drive fasteners (#4 × 1" sheet-metal screws work well), starting at the top. Make sure the window is squarely in the opening, then fill in fasteners on the side stops. Apply caulk along the bottom rail, leaving a ¼"-wide gap midway as a weep hole.

Weatherizing a Window

The secret to energy-tight windows is blocking air movement, creating a sealed-off dead air space between interior and exterior glass panes.

Modern double- and triple-paned windows often contain inert gases between panes to help create dead air spaces. You can create dead air spaces in older windows by using weatherstripping and a good storm window (or plastic window sheeting) to block air movement. Weatherstripping the inside gaps helps keep warm, moist air on the interior side of a window, minimizing condensation and frosting between the inner window and the storm window.

Everything You Need

Tools: tack hammer, aviator snips, putty knife, hair dryer, staple gun.

Materials: metal V-channel, compressible foam, tubular gasket, reinforced felt, brads, clear silicone caulk, siliconized acrylic caulk, peelable caulk, plastic sheeting (interior and exterior).

The primary heat loss areas in windows (shown highlighted) should be sealed with the appropriate weatherstripping material. This can increase the energy efficiency of a window by 100% or more.

Tips for Weatherizing a Window

Apply clear silicone caulk around the interior window casing. For added protection, lock the window in the closed position, and caulk the gaps around the interior edges of the sash with clear, peelable caulk (which can be removed easily).

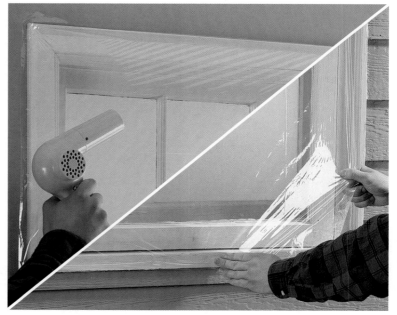

Add plastic sheeting or shrink-wrap product (left) on the interior to block drafts and keep moisture away from the window surfaces. Directions often include using a hair dryer to tighten the plastic and remove wrinkles, making it almost invisible. Install exterior plastic sheeting (right) on the outside of your window, following the manufacturer's directions.

(continued next page)

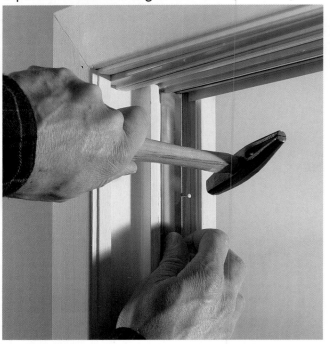

Sliding windows: Treat side-by-side sliding windows as if they were double-hung windows turned 90°. For greater durability, use metal tension strips rather than self-adhesive compressible foam in the sash track that fits against the edge of the sash when the window is closed.

Casement windows: Attach self-adhesive foam or rubber compression strips on the outside edges of the window stops.

Storm windows: Create a tight seal by attaching foam compression strips to the outside of storm window stops (left). After installing the storm window, fill any gaps between the exterior window trim and the storm window with caulk backer rope. Check the inside surface of the storm window during cold weather for condensation or frost buildup (page 25). If moisture is trapped between the storm window and the permanent window, drill one or two small holes through the bottom rail (right) to allow moist air to escape. Drill at a slight upward angle.

How to Weatherstrip a Window

1 Cut metal V-channel to fit in the channels for the sliding sash, extending at least 2" past the closed position for each sash (do not cover sash-closing mechanisms). Attach the V-channel by driving wire brads (usually provided by the manufacturer) with a tack hammer. Drive the fasteners flush with the surface so the sliding sash will not catch on them.

2 Flare out the open ends of the V-channels with a putty knife so the channel is slightly wider than the gap between the sash and the track it fits into. Avoid flaring out too much at one time—it is difficult to press V-channel back together without causing some buckling.

3 Wipe down the underside of the bottom window sash with a damp rag, and let it dry; then attach self-adhesive compressible foam or rubber to the underside of the sash. Use high-quality hollow neoprene strips, if available. This will create an airtight seal when the window is locked in position.

Bottom sash (raised)

Top sash (lowered)

4 Seal the gap between the top sash and the bottom sash on double-hung windows. Lift the bottom sash and lower the top sash to improve access, and tack metal V-channel to the bottom rail of the top sash using wire brads. TIP: The open end of the "V" should be pointed downward so moisture cannot collect in the channel. Flare out the V-channel with a putty knife to fit the gap between the sash.

Solving Common Door Problems

The most common door problems are caused by loose hinges. When hinges are loose, the door won't hang right, causing it to rub and stick, and throwing off the latch mechanism. The first thing to do is check the hinge screws. If the holes for the hinge screws are worn and won't hold the screws, try the repair on page 68.

If the hinges are tight but the door still rubs against the frame, sand or plane down the door's edge. If a door doesn't close easily, it may be warped—use a long straightedge to check for warpage. You may be able to straighten a slightly warped door, using weights, but severe warpage can't be corrected. Instead of buying a new door, remove the door stop and reinstall it following the curve of the door.

Door latch problems occur for a number of reasons: loose hinges, swollen wood, sticking latchbolts, and paint buildup. If you've addressed those issues and the door still won't stay shut, it's probably because the door frame is out of square. This happens as a house settles with age; you can make minor adjustments by filing the strike plate on the door frame. If there's some room between the frame and the door, you can align the latchbolt and strike plate by shimming the hinges. Or, drive a couple of extra-long screws to adjust the frame slightly (page 69).

Common closet doors, such as sliding and bi-fold types, usually need only some minor adjustments and lubrication to stay in working order.

Door locksets are very reliable, but they do need to be cleaned and lubricated occasionally. One simple way to keep an entry door lockset working smoothly is to spray a light lubricant into the keyhole, then run the key in and out a few times. Don't use graphite in locksets, as it can abrade some metals with repeated use.

Everything You Need:

Tools: Screwdrivers, nail set, hammer, drill, utility knife, metal file, straightedge, pry bar, plane, paintbrush.

Materials: Spray lubricant, wooden golf tees or dowels, wood glue, cardboard shims, 3" wood screws, finish nails, paint or stain, sandpaper, wood sealer.

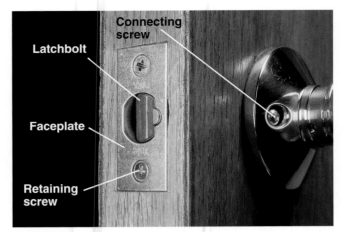

Latchbolts stick when they are dirty or in need of lubrication. Clean and lubricate locksets (page 67), and make sure the connecting screws aren't too tight—another cause of binding.

A misaligned latchbolt and strike plate will prevent the door from latching. Poor alignment may be caused by loose hinges, or the door frame may be out of square (page 69).

Sticking doors usually leave a mark where they rub against the door frame (page 71). **Warped doors** may resist closing and feel springy when you apply pressure. Check for warpage with a straightedge (page 70).

How to Disassemble & Lubricate a Lockset

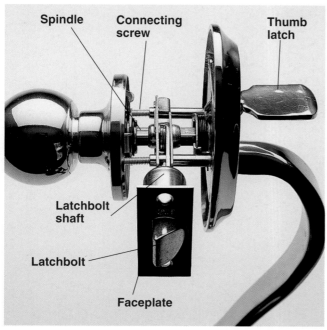

Modern locksets are sandwiched to the door with two connecting screws; remove these to disassemble the lockset. Spray the moving parts with lubricant, then reinstall the lockset. Tighten the connecting screws an equal amount, but don't overtighten them, which can cause binding.

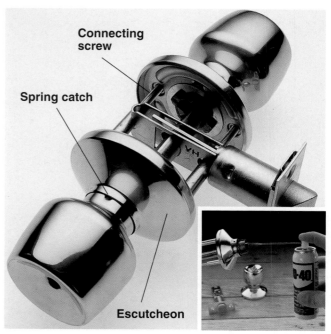

Some passage locksets have connecting screws hidden behind an escutcheon and often have handles held by a spring catch. To remove the handle, stick a pointed tool into the spring catch hole, then pop off the escutcheon with a screwdriver. Disassemble the lockset and lubricate the moving parts.

Mortise locksets, common in older homes, are held in place by screws in the faceplate. Remove the faceplate screws, then loosen the setscrew on one of the knobs. Remove the knob, then pull out the other knob and attached spindle, and pry the lockset from the door. Lay the lockset flat and remove the cover without disturbing the internal parts; if you do, just piece them back together. Replace any broken springs and lubricate all of the parts.

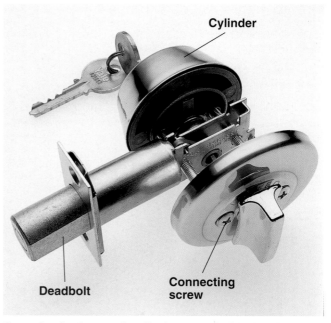

Security locks, or deadbolts, usually bind inside the keyed cylinder. Spray lubricant directly into the keyhole and around the deadbolt. Insert the key and turn it several times to spread the lubricant. If that doesn't work, take apart the lock by removing the connecting screws, then lubricate all of the parts.

How to Remove a Door

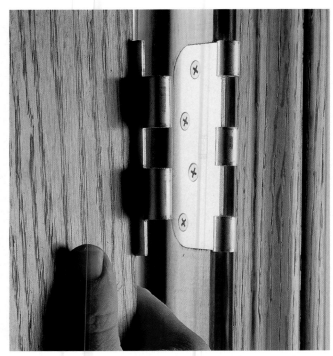

1 Drive the lower hinge pin out, using a screwdriver and hammer. Have a helper hold the door in place, then drive out the upper hinge pin. To help get the screwdriver tip under the pin head, use a nail set or small punch to tap the pin up from underneath.

2 Remove the door and set it aside. Clean and lubricate the hinge pins before reinstalling the door.

How to Tighten a Loose Hinge

1 Remove the door from the hinges. Tighten any loose screws. If the wood won't hold the screws tightly, remove the hinges.

2 Coat wooden golf tees or dowels with wood glue, and drive them into the worn screw holes. If necessary, drill out the holes to accept dowels. Let the glue dry, then cut off excess wood.

3 Drill pilot holes in the new wood, and reinstall the hinge.

Tips for Aligning a Latchbolt & Strike Plate

Check the door for a square fit. If the door is far out of square with the frame, remove it (page 220) and shim the top or bottom hinge (right). Or, drive long screws into one of the hinges (below).

Install a thin cardboard shim behind the bottom hinge to raise the position of the latchbolt. To lower the latchbolt, shim behind the top hinge.

Remove two hinge screws from the top or bottom hinge, and drive a 3" wood screw into each hole. The screws will reach the framing studs in the wall and pull the door jamb upward, changing the angle of the door. Add long screws to the top hinge to raise the latchbolt or to the bottom hinge to lower it.

Fix minor alignment problems by filing the strike plate until the latchbolt fits.

How to Straighten a Warped Door

1 Check the door for warpage, using a straight-edge. Or, close the door until it hits the stop and look for a gap (see below). The amount of gap between the door and the stop reveals the extent of warpage. The stop must be straight for this test, so check it with a straightedge.

2 If the warpage is slight, you can straighten the door using weights. Remove the door (page 220), and rest the ends of the door on sawhorses. Place heavy weights on the bowed center of the door, using cardboard to protect the finish. Leave the weights on the door for several days, and check it periodically with a straightedge.

How to Fix a Severely Warped Door

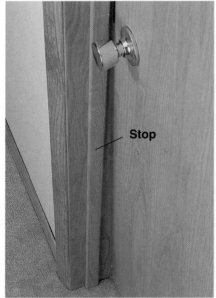

Stop

1 A severe warp cannot be corrected. Instead, you can adjust the door stop to follow the shape of the door. If you touch up the door jamb with paint or stain after you've finished, no one will notice the repair.

2 Remove the door stop, using a small pry bar. If it's painted, cut the paint film first with a utility knife to prevent chipping. Avoid splintering by removing nails from the stop by pulling them through the back side of the piece. Pull all nails from the door jamb.

3 Close the door and latch it. Starting at the top, refasten the stop, keeping the inside edge flush against the door. Drive finish nails through the old holes, or drill new pilot holes through the stop. Set the nails with a nail set after you've checked the door operation.

How to Free a Sticking Door

1 Tighten all of the hinge screws. If the door still sticks, use light pencil lines to mark the areas where the door rubs against the door jamb.

2 During dry weather, remove the door (page 220). If you have to remove a lot of material, you can save time by planing the door (step 3). Otherwise, sand the marked areas with medium-grit sandpaper. Make sure the door closes without sticking, then smooth the sanded areas with fine-grit sandpaper.

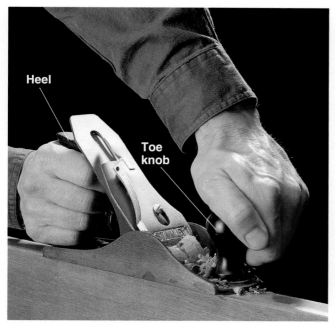

Heel

Toe knob

3 Secure the door on-edge. If the door has veneered surfaces, cut through the veneers with a utility knife to prevent splintering. Operate the plane so the wood grain runs "uphill" ahead of the plane. Grip the toe knob and handle firmly, and plane with long, smooth strokes. To prevent dipping, press down on the toe at the start of the stroke, and bear down on the heel at the end of the stroke. Check the door's fit, then sand the planed area smooth.

4 Apply clear sealer or paint to the sanded or planed area and any other exposed surfaces of the door. This will prevent moisture from entering the wood and is especially important for entry doors.

How to Maintain a Sliding Door

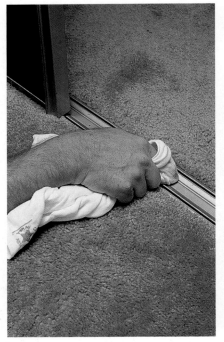  

1 Clean the tracks above and below the doors with a toothbrush and a damp cloth or a hand vacuum.

2 Spray a greaseless lubricant on all the rollers, but do not spray the tracks. Replace any bent or worn parts.

3 Check the gap along the bottom edge of the door to make sure it is even. To adjust the gap, rotate the mounting screw to raise or lower the door edge.

How to Maintain a Bifold Door

1 Open or remove the doors and wipe the tracks with a clean rag. Spray the tracks and rollers or pins with greaseless lubricant.

2 Check closed doors for alignment within the door frame. If the gap between the closed doors is uneven, adjust the top pivot blocks with screwdriver or wrench.

Adjustable pivot blocks are also found at the bottom of some door models. Adjust the pivot blocks until the gap between the door and the frame is even.

Weatherizing a Door

Door weatherstripping is prone to failure because it undergoes constant stress. Use metal weatherstripping that is tacked to the surfaces whenever you can—especially around door jambs. It is much more durable than self-adhesive products. If your job calls for flexible weatherstripping, use products made from neoprene rubber, not foam. Replace old door thresholds (see pages 230 to 233) or threshold inserts as soon as they begin to show wear.

Everything You Need

Tools: putty knife, tack hammer, screwdriver, backsaw, flat pry bar, chisel and mallet, tape measure, drill.

Materials: metal V-channel or tension strips, reinforced felt strips, door sweep, wood filler, nails or brads, caulk, threshold and insert.

The primary heat loss areas in doors (shown highlighted) are around jambs and at the threshold. Install weatherstripping on jambs, and update the threshold and threshold insert to reduce drafts.

Tips for Weatherizing a Door

Install a storm door to decrease drafts and energy loss through entry doors. Buy an insulated storm door with a continuous hinge and seamless exterior surface.

Adjust door frame to eliminate large gaps between door and jamb. Remove interior case molding and drive new shims between jamb and framing member on the hinge side, reducing size of door opening. Close door to test fit, and adjust as needed before reattaching case molding.

(continued next page)

Tips for Weatherizing a Door (continued)

Patio door: Use rubber compression strips to seal the channels in patio door jambs, where movable panels fit when closed. Also install a patio door insulator kit (plastic sheeting installed similarly to plastic sheeting for windows—page 215) on the interior side of the door.

Garage door: Attach a new rubber sweep to the bottom outside edge of the garage door if the old sweep has deteriorated. Also check the door jambs for drafts, and add weatherstripping, if needed.

Tips for Installing Fiberglass Insulation

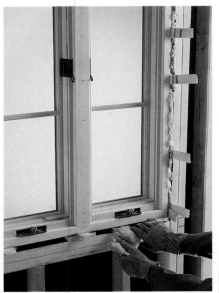

Never compress insulation to fit into a narrow space. Instead, use a sharp utility knife to trim it about ¼" wider and longer than the space. To trim the insulation, use a wall stud as a straightedge and cutting surface.

Insulate around pipes, wires, and electrical boxes by peeling the insulation in half and sliding the back half behind the obstruction. Then, lay the front half in front of the obstruction and trim it to fit snugly around the object.

Use scraps of insulation to fill gaps around window and door jambs. Fill the cavities loosely to avoid compressing the insulation. Fill narrow gaps with expanding spray-foam insulation, following manufacturer's instructions.

How to Weatherize an Exterior Door

1 Cut two pieces of metal tension strip or V-channel the full height of the door opening, and cut another to full width. Use wire brads to tack the strips to the door jambs and door header, on the interior side of the door stops. TIP: Attach metal weatherstripping from the top down to help prevent buckling. Flare out the tension strips with a putty knife to fill the gaps between the jambs and the door when the door is in the closed position (do not pry too far at a time).

2 Add reinforced felt strips to the edge of the door stop, on the exterior side. The felt edge should form a close seal with the door when closed. TIP: Drive fasteners only until they are flush with the surface of the reinforcing spine—overdriving will cause damage and buckling.

3 Attach a new door sweep to the bottom of the door, on the interior side (felt or bristle types are better choices if the floor is uneven). Before fastening it permanently, tack the sweep in place and test the door swing to make sure there is enough clearance.

Tip: Fix any cracks in wooden door panels with epoxy wood filler or caulk to block air leaks. If the door has a stain finish, use tinted wood putty, filling from the interior side. Sand and touch up with paint or stain.

Hollow-core doors have solid wood frames, with hollow center cores. If the entire frame member is cut away when shortening a door, it can be reinserted to close the hollow door cavity. Measure carefully when marking a door for cutting.

Shortening an Interior Door

Prehung interior doors are typically installed with a ⅜" to ¾" gap between the bottom of the door and the floor. This gap lets the door swing without binding on carpet or floor covering. If a thicker carpet or a larger threshold is installed, however, the door may need to be shortened.

If the door is solid wood, material can usually be removed by planing the edge, using a hand plane or power plane.

Shortening a hollow-core door requires a few more steps because the door consists of multiple pieces. Depending on the width of the cut, the pieces may need to be cut and then re-assembled.

Everything You Need

Tools: tape measure, hammer, screwdriver utility knife, sawhorses, circular saw, chisel, straightedge, clamps.

Materials: wood glue.

How to Cut Off a Hollow-core Interior Door

1 With the door in place, measure ⅜" up from the top of the floor covering and mark the door. Remove the door from the hinges by tapping out the hinge pins with a screwdriver and a hammer.

2 Mark the cutting line. Cut through the door veneer with a sharp utility knife to prevent it from chipping when the door is sawed.

3 Lay the door on sawhorses and clamp a straightedge to the door as a cutting guide. Saw off the bottom of the door. The hollow core of the door may be exposed.

4 To reinstall a cutoff frame piece in the bottom of the door, chisel the veneer from both sides of the removed portion.

5 Apply wood glue to the cutoff frame. Insert the frame piece into the opening of the door and clamp it. Wipe away any excess glue and let the door dry overnight.

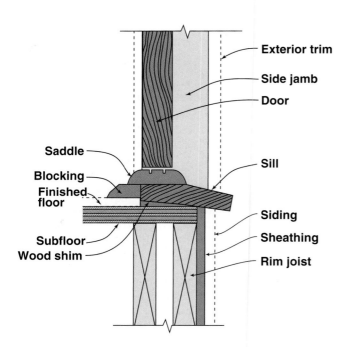

Exterior trim
Side jamb
Door
Saddle
Sill
Finished floor
Siding
Subfloor
Sheathing
Rim joist

Exterior trim
Side jamb
Door
Saddle
Sill
Blocking
Finished floor
Siding
Subfloor
Sheathing
Wood shim
Rim joist

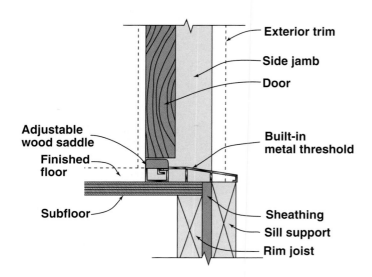

Exterior trim
Side jamb
Door
Adjustable wood saddle
Built-in metal threshold
Finished floor
Subfloor
Sheathing
Sill support
Rim joist

Replacing a Threshold

While construction varies from home to home, the part of a door that is generally referred to as the "threshold" is actually made up of two separate components: a *sill*, which serves as the bottom of the door frame and diverts water and dirt away from the home, and the threshold or *saddle*, which is attached to the sill and helps to seal the air space under a door. Due to constant traffic and exposure to the elements, sills and saddles may eventually require replacing.

Modern prehung doors often have a cast metal sill with an integrated saddle and are installed directly on top of the subfloor. Older homes often have thick wooden sills, and so are installed lower than metal sills, flush with the floor framing, with a separate saddle bridging the gap between the sill and the finished floor. Saddles are available in several styles and materials, such as wood, metal, and vinyl. Because the design of entry thresholds can vary, it is important to examine the construction of your door threshold to determine your needs. In this project, we replaced a deteriorating wooden sill and saddle with a new oak sill and a wooden weatherstripped saddle.

Besides replacing a deteriorating threshold, you might also choose to replace an existing threshold for increased accessibility. While standard thresholds are designed to keep mud and dirt out of a home, they deny access to people in wheelchairs and can cause people unsteady on their feet to trip. See page 233 for tips on making thresholds accessible.

Everything You Need

Tools: reciprocating saw, pry bar, hammer, drill with countersink bit, pencil.

Materials: 3" galvanized screws or 10d galvanized casing nails, 1½" galvanized screws or 8d galvanized nails, shims, putty, silicone caulk, sealer/protectant.

How to Replace an Exterior Door Threshold

1 Remove the old saddle. This may be as easy as unscrewing the saddle and prying it out. If necessary, cut the old saddle in two, using a reciprocating saw, then pry out the saddle. Be careful not to damage the flooring or door frame. Note which edge of the saddle is more steeply beveled; the new saddle should be installed the same way.

2 Examine the sill for damage or deterioration. If it needs replacing, use a reciprocating saw to cut the sill into three pieces, cutting as close to the jambs as possible. Pry out the center piece, then use a hammer and chisel to split out the pieces directly beneath the jambs. Remove any remaining nails from beneath the jambs, using a reciprocating saw with a metal cutting blade.

3 Measure and cut the new sill to size. If possible, use the salvaged end pieces from the old sill as a template to mark the notches on the new sill. Cut the notches using a jig saw.

4 Test-fit the new sill, tapping it into place beneath the jambs, using a hammer and wood block to protect the sill. Remove the sill and, if necessary, install long wood strips (or tapered shims) beneath the sill so it fits snugly beneath the jambs with a gentle slope away from the home.

(continued next page)

5 Apply a wood protectant/sealer to the sill and allow to dry. Apply several beads of caulk to the area beneath the sill. Tap the sill back in place. Drill countersunk pilot holes every 4" to 5" and fasten the sill with 10d galvanized casing nails or 3" screws.

6 Measure the distance between the jambs and cut the new saddle to length. Test-fit the saddle. Mark the ends and cut notches to fit around the door jamb stops, using a jig saw. Apply caulk to the bottom of the saddle and position it so it covers the gap between the sill and the finished floor. Fasten the saddle using 1½" galvanized screws.

Variation: If you are installing a metal saddle, instead of cutting notches in the saddle, use a hammer and chisel to notch the jamb stops to fit.

Tip: A threshold insert seals the gap between the door and the saddle. A door sweep attaches to the door bottom to help seal out drafts.

Variation: Making Thresholds Accessible

"No-threshold" entry door: Entry thresholds should be no higher than ¼" for square-edged sills and ½" high for beveled sills.

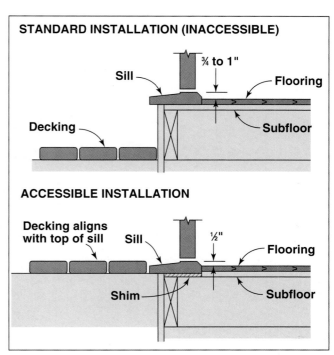

Accessible thresholds: There are many ways to modify standard thresholds for accessibility. Often, the first step is to raise the exterior surface or decking to the same level as the threshold.

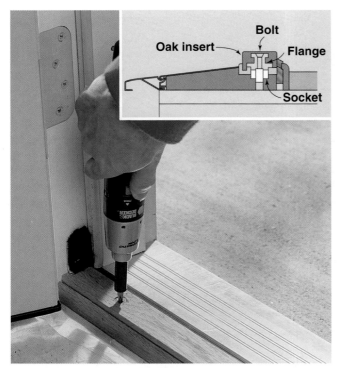

Adjustable sills: Many prehung doors have an aluminum sill with an adjustable wood saddle. Some versions can be made accessible without additional modification by lowering the saddle as far as possible. Other types can be adapted by recessing the sill into the subfloor.

Mini-ramps: The slide channels on most sliding glass doors present a major obstacle for wheelchair users. The height difference can be as much as 2" from the bottom to the top of the track. Commercially available mini-ramps can make standard sliding glass door thresholds accessible.

233

Maintaining Storm Windows & Doors

Build a storage rack for removable screens and storm windows. Simply attach a pair of 2 × 4s to the rafters of your garage or the ceiling joists in your basement. Attach window-hanger hardware to the top rails of the screen and storm windows, if they do not already have them. Space the hangers uniformly. Then, attach screw eyes to the 2 × 4s in matching rows to fit the window hangers.

Removable storm windows and doors are excellent insulators and removable screens provide full ventilation.

Simple wood-sash construction and a lack of moving parts make removable storms and screens easy to repair and maintain. Replacing screening or glass, tightening loose joints, and applying fresh paint are the primary maintenance jobs.

Combination storms and screens offer convenience, and can be repaired easily if you have a little know-how and the right replacement parts.

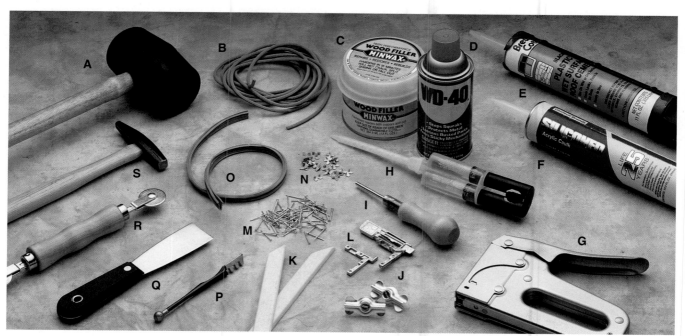

Tools and materials for repairing and maintaining storm windows and doors include: rubber mallet (A), spline cord for metal sash (B), epoxy wood filler (C), penetrating lubricant (D), roof cement (E), siliconized acrylic caulk (F), staple gun (G), epoxy glue (H), brad pusher (I), turnbuttons (J), retaining strips for wood sash (K), metal sash replacement hardware (L), wire brads (M), glazier's points (N), rubber window gasket for metal sash (O), glass cutter (P), putty knife (Q), spline roller (R), tack hammer (S).

Tips for Maintaining Storm Windows & Doors

Replace turnbuttons and window clips that do not hold storm windows tightly in place. Fill old screw holes with wood putty or toothpicks and glue before driving screws.

Lubricate sliding assemblies on metal-framed combination storm windows or doors once a year, using penetrating lubricant.

Replace deteriorated glazing around glass panes in wood-framed windows. Sound glazing makes windows more energy-efficient and more attractive.

Tighten storm door latches by redriving loose screws in strikeplate. If latch does not catch on strikeplate, loosen the screws on the strikeplate, insert thin wood shims between the plate and the jamb, and retighten the screws.

Add a wind chain if your storm door does not have one. Wind chains prevent doors from blowing open too far, causing damage to the door hinges or closer. Set the chain so the door will not open more than 90°.

Adjust door closer so it has right amount of tension to close the door securely, without slamming. Most closers have tension-adjustment screws at end of cylinder farthest from hinge side of the door.

Repairing Wood Storm Windows & Screens

Because they are installed, removed, transported, and stored so frequently, removable wood storm windows need repair and maintenance regularly. Broken glass, loose joints or hangers, dry or missing glazing, and failed paint are the primary problems. Fortunately, fixing wood storm windows and screens is simple, and maintaining them well has a high payback in the appearance and efficiency of your home.

Everything You Need

Tools: utility knife, clamps, mallet, scissors, drill, putty knife, staple gun, tack hammer.

Materials: epoxy glue, screening, caulk, glazier's points, glazing compound, replacement glass, dowels, wire brads.

Clean out recesses for glass and screening by carefully removing old glass, glazing compound, and glazier's points (or screening and retaining strips). Scrape residue from the recess with an old chisel, then paint with a coat of primer or sealer before installing new glass or screen.

How to Repair Loose Joints in a Wood Sash Frame

1 Remove the glass or screening, then carefully separate the loose joint, using a flat pry bar if necessary. Scrape the mating surfaces clean. Inject epoxy glue into the joint (plain wood glue should not be used for exterior work). Press the mating surfaces back together and clamp with bar clamps, making sure the frame is square.

2 After the glue is dry, reinforce the repair by drilling two ³⁄₁₆"-dia. holes through the joint. Cut two ³⁄₁₆"-dia. dowels about 1" longer than the thickness of the frame, and round over one end of each dowel with sandpaper. Coat dowels with epoxy glue, and drive them through holes. After glue dries, trim ends of dowels with a hacksaw, then sand until they are flush with sash. Touch up with paint.

How to Replace Glass in a Wood Storm Window

1 Clean and prepare the glass recess (page 236). From outside shoulders of the glass recess, measure the full width and height of the opening, subtract ⅛" from each dimension, and have new glass cut to fit. Apply a thin bead of caulk in the recess to create a bed for the new pane of glass.

2 Press the new glass pane into the fresh caulk. Use a putty knife or screwdriver blade to push glazier's points into the frame every 8" to 10" to hold the glass in place.

3 Roll glazing compound into ⅜"-dia. "snakes" and press the snakes into the joint between the glass and the frame. Smooth the compound with a putty knife held at a 45° angle to create a flat surface. Strip off the excess. Let the compound dry for several days before painting.

How to Replace Screening in a Wood Frame

1 Completely clean and prepare the recess. Cut a new piece of screening at least 3" longer in height and in width than the opening. TIP: Use fiberglass screening for residential windows—it is easy to work with, and will not rust or corrode.

2 Tack the top edge of the screening into the recess with a staple gun. Stretch the screen tightly toward the bottom. Tack the bottom into the recess. Tack one side in place. Then stretch the screening tightly across the frame, and tack the other side.

3 Attach retaining strips over the edges of the screening. Do not use old nail holes; drill ½₂"-dia. pilot holes in the retaining strips, then drive 1" wire brads. Trim off the excess screening with a sharp utility knife.

Repairing Metal Storm Windows & Doors

Compared to removable wood storm windows and screens, repairing combination storm windows is a little more complex. But there are several repairs you can make without too much difficulty, as long as you find the right parts. Take the old corner keys, gaskets, or other original parts to a hardware store that repairs storm windows so the clerk can help you find the correct replacement parts. If you cannot find the right parts, have a new sash built.

Everything You Need

Tools: tape measure, screwdriver, scissors, drill, utility knife, spline roller, nail set, hammer.

Materials: spline cord, screening, glass, rubber gasket, replacement hardware.

Remove metal storm window sash by pressing in the release hardware in the lower rail (like the slide tabs above), then lifting the sash out. Sash hangers on the corners of the top rail should be aligned with the notches in the side channels before removal.

How to Replace Screening in a Metal Storm Window

1 Pry the vinyl spline from the groove around the edge of the frame with a screwdriver. Retain the old spline if it is still flexible, or replace it with a new spline.

2 Stretch the new screen tightly over the frame so that it overlaps the edges of the frame. Keeping the screen taut, use the convex side of a spline roller to press the screen into the retaining grooves.

3 Use the concave side of the spline roller to press the spline into the groove (it helps to have a partner for this). Cut away excess screen, using a utility knife.

How to Replace Glass in a Metal Storm Window

1 Remove the sash frame from the window, then completely remove the broken glass from the sash. Remove the rubber gasket that framed the old glass pane and remove any glass remnants. Find the dimensions for the replacement glass by measuring between the inside edges of the frame opening, then adding twice the thickness of the rubber gasket to each measurement.

2 Set the frame on a flat surface, and disconnect the top rail. Remove the retaining screws in the sides of the frame stiles where they join the top rail. After unscrewing the retaining screws, pull the top rail loose, pulling gently in a downward motion to avoid damaging the L-shaped corner keys that join the rail and the stiles. For glass replacement, you need only disconnect the top rail.

3 Fit the rubber gasket (buy a replacement if the original is in poor condition) around one edge of the replacement glass pane. At the corners, cut the spine of the gasket partway so it will bend around the corner. Continue fitting the gasket around the pane, cutting at the corners, until all four edges are covered. Trim off any excess gasket material.

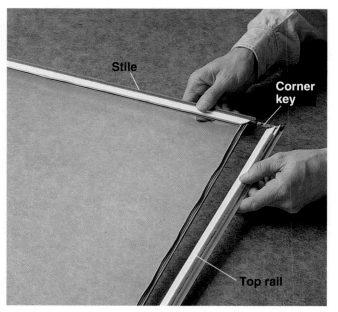

4 Slide the glass pane into the channels in the stiles and bottom rail of the sash frame. Insert corner keys into top rail, then slip the other ends of the keys into the frame stiles. Press down on the top rail until mitered corners are flush with stiles. Drive retaining screws back through the stiles and into the top rail to join frame together. Reinsert frame into the window.

How to Disassemble & Repair a Metal Sash Frame

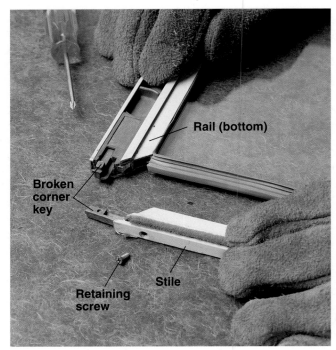

Rail (bottom)

Broken corner key

Retaining screw

Stile

Crimp

Broken corner key

Shown cut away for clarity

1 Metal window sashes are held together at the corner joints by L-shaped pieces of hardware that fit into grooves in the sash frame pieces. To disassemble a broken joint, start by disconnecting the stile and rail at the broken joint—there is usually a retaining screw driven through the stile that must be removed.

2 Corner keys are secured in the rail slots with crimps that are punched into the metal over the key. To remove keys, drill through the metal in the crimped area, using a drill bit the same diameter as the crimp. Carefully knock the broken key pieces from the frame slots with a screwdriver and hammer.

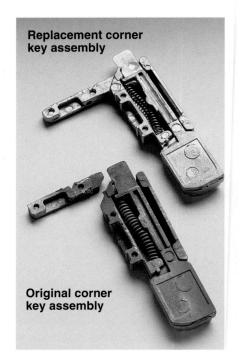

Replacement corner key assembly

Original corner key assembly

3 Locate matching replacement parts for the broken corner key, which is usually an assembly of two or three pieces. There are dozens of different types, so it is important that you save the old parts for reference.

4 Insert the replacement corner key assembly into the slot in the rail. Use a nail set as a punch, and rap it into the metal over the corner key, creating a new crimp to hold the key in place.

5 Insert the glass and gasket into the frame slots (page 239), then reassemble the frame and drive in retainer screws (for screen windows, replace the screening).

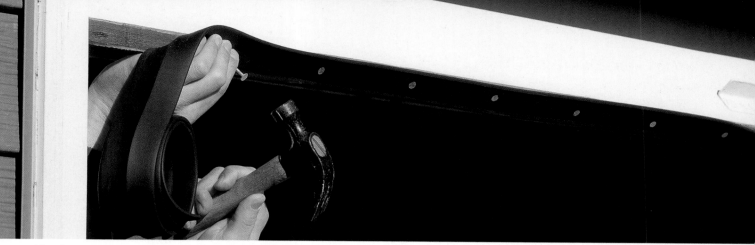

Replace worn or damaged weatherstripping along the bottom of your garage door. Weatherstripping stops drafts and water, and it protects the door from moisture damage and rot. Nail new stripping in place with galvanized roofing nails. Keep the door panels well sealed with paint or wood sealer to prevent moisture penetration.

Repairing a Garage Door

Most garage door problems are due to moisture, dirt, and neglect. Common symptoms include rusted or rotted panels, loose hinges, squeaky or stuck rollers, and a door that binds or seems heavier than usual. Except for work on the lift springs, you can easily make any garage door repair yourself.

Start your routine maintenance by cleaning and lubricating the moving parts and tightening all of the hardware. If the door binds or doesn't open smoothly, check the rollers and the track adjustment. Also check the lift springs—a well balanced door should stay open about three feet above the ground. Above or below that position, it should open or close by itself. If your door fails this test, call a professional to have the lift springs adjusted or replaced.

Most replacement parts for garage doors, such as rollers, hinges, locks, cables, and hardware, are inexpensive and commonly available at home centers. If you have an automatic garage door opener, always disengage the lifting mechanism by pulling the emergency release cord before making any repairs on the door.

Everything You Need

Tools: hammer, ratchet wrench, rubber mallet, level, pliers.

Materials: weatherstripping, galvanized roofing nails, spray lubricant or oil, replacement hardware.

Tips for Repairing Garage Doors

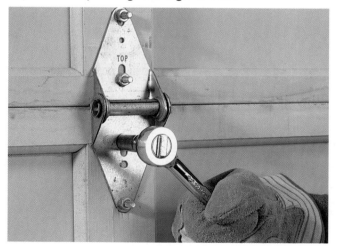

Tighten all hinge screws or bolts, using a ratchet wrench. Replace any missing or broken hardware and loose or bent hinges.

Adjust the lock so the lock bar meets the lock hole in the door track. Loosen the mounting screws or bolts on the lock to adjust the position of the bar. Center-mounted locks with long lock bars have guides near the door edges. Move the lock bar guides to align the bars with the track holes.

How to Lubricate a Garage Door

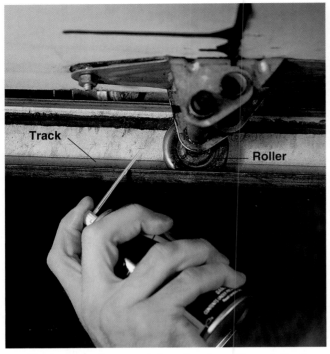

1 Clean the rollers and door tracks with a cloth, then spray them with a greaseless lubricant or apply a small amount of oil. Don't use grease, which attracts dirt. Lubricate door locks, cable pulleys, and hinges.

2 Clean and lubricate the chain and track of chain-driven automatic door openers. Check the manufacturer's instructions for additional maintenance directions.

How to Adjust a Garage Door Track

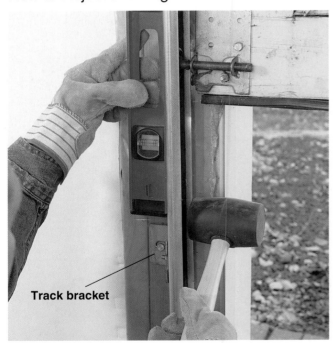

If the door binds in the tracks, loosen the screws securing the lower track brackets to the door framing. Tap the bottom of the track with a rubber mallet to adjust it. Use a level to make sure the track is plumb, then retighten the screws. Adjust both tracks.

If the door rubs against the stop molding, or if there is a large gap, loosen the bolts securing the tracks to the lower track brackets. Adjust the tracks so there's a slight gap between the door and the stop, then retighten the bolts.

How to Replace Garage Door Rollers

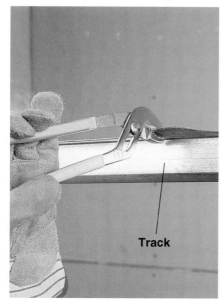

1 Locate the access area on the horizontal portion of each track. Have a helper lift the door until the damaged roller is aligned with the access area. If you can't find an access area, use pliers to bend out a few inches of the top side of the track.

2 Loosen the screws or bolts of the roller hinge, using a ratchet wrench. Tilt the hinge so you can pull the roller out of the track. Replace the hinge if it is bent.

3 Insert the stem of the new roller into the barrel of the hinge, then work the roller into the track. Tighten the hinge mounting screws or bolts.

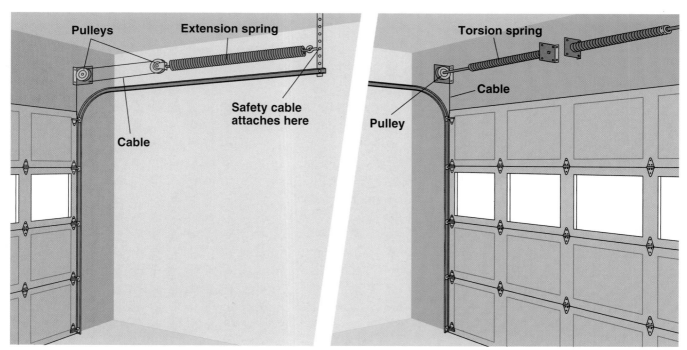

Garage door lifting mechanisms use powerful steel springs and pulleys and cables to help carry the door's weight. Roll-up doors use one of two spring types. Extension springs (left) run parallel to the tracks. The springs are fully "loaded," or under tension, when the door is closed and should be "relaxed" when the door is open. With the door open, check the springs, cables, and pulleys routinely for wear, and call a professional to fix potential problems or to balance the door. Extension springs should have a safety cable that runs through the center of the spring and attaches to the track supports. If you don't have these, get some installed: they prevent the spring from lashing out in the event of a break. Torsion springs (right) mount to the wall framing above the door. These are constantly under tremendous tension and should be handled only by a professional.

Decorative Window Treatments

Decorating with Style

When most people think about window treatments, they think of variations of conventional curtains and drapes. These elements are surely an integral part of a room's theme or mood. Windows that are beautifully dressed enrich the style of a room. These kinds of window treatment can filter sunlight during the day and close out the nighttime darkness. They can allow fresh air to circulate into the room or provide weather and noise insulation. They can frame a magnificent view or obscure a poor view and offer privacy. They also can emphasize architectural details or add visual width and height to a window. Depending on the color and style, the room's ambience can seem more casual or more formal.

Within this section is information on the types of hardware these treatments may employ, such as rods, finials, and tiebacks. Projects include installing a mounting board as an alternative to drapery rods, and creating a cornice as an additional finishing top treatment.

Within a home, you will often find a combination of conventional and alternative kinds of window treatment. Some may use no fabric components at all. The projects included here are simple to follow and include lots of photos and step-by-step instructions.

For an open and casual feel, you might build shelves above the windows, or suspend hanging plant shelves in front of the window. For a bit more privacy, you may install antique stained-glass panels or etch the window glass. Some interior windows are enhanced with decorative shutters. And for protection against the elements, many homeowners install exterior storm shutters.

Whether you are starting with bare windows or adding to existing treatments, you can select a window treatment that reflects your personal taste. Careful matching of window style and treatment style is sure to make your project a success.

Straw hats, adorned with flowers and ribbons, are hung from a peg rail to create a seasonal window valance.

Sports pennants create a fitting treatment for a young sports fan. The pennants are secured to the wood pole with double-stick tape.

Seining net and creels balance each other in a rustic display for the enthusiastic angler.

Decorative sheets with printed borders create curtains with a tailored look. For best results, purchase good-quality sheets with a high thread count. The border may be used as a tieback and as an accent at the top. A separate piece of fabric is stitched on the wrong side of the sheet for the rod pocket.

For kitchen windows, towels can become creative window treatments, giving a casual, carefree look. They are available in coordinating patterns, some with contrasting borders to make curtains with the look of banding. Linen or linen-blend towels work well for small rod-pocket curtain panels and valances.

Selecting Window Treatment Hardware

If you choose a conventional curtain or drapery window treatment, it may be stationary or traversing, and the hardware you select can be decorative as well as functional.

For ornate treatments, traditional wood or metal poles with detailed finials are available, as well as decorative tieback holders. And sleek, contemporary hardware is available for a more understated look. Some hardware styles, such as curtain rods, sash rods, and tension rods, are

designed to be covered completely by the fabric. Poles for rod-pocket window treatments can also be made from PVC plastic pipe available at hardware stores.

Select and install the hardware you want before measuring for a window treatment. The cut length of fabric panels for curtains, draperies, and valances depends on the style and placement of the hardware.

Decorative Hardware

Metal rods and wood poles (A) in various finishes and diameters are used with rings for hand-drawn traversing or stationary treatments when part or all of the rod or pole is always exposed. Without rings, rods and poles are suitable for several styles. Stylish finials accompany metal rods; wood poles may have finials or elbows. Unfinished wood poles can be painted, stained, or covered with fabric to fit your decor.

Decorative traverse rods (B) have a built-in mechanism of carriers and cording for opening and closing the treatment. Most often used for pleated draperies, the rods can have plain carriers or ring carriers. Tab carriers are also available, for hanging traversing tab curtains.

Utility Hardware

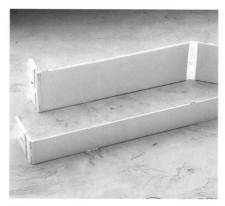

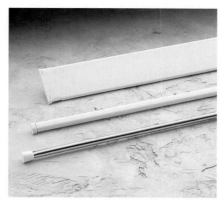

Narrow curtain rods are used for rod-pocket window treatments. They are available in various projections in single- and double-rod styles.

Wide curtain rods are available in several widths. They add depth and interest to rod-pocket window treatments. Corner connectors make these rods suitable for bay and corner windows, also.

Tension rods, used inside window frames for rod-pocket curtains and valances, are held in place by the pressure of a spring inside the rod. Because mounting brackets are not used, the woodwork is not damaged by screws.

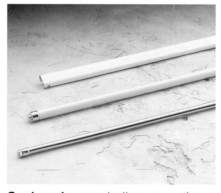

Sash rods use shallow mounting brackets so the window treatment hangs close to the glass. Available flat or round, they are commonly used for stretched door curtains.

Conventional traverse rods, designed for pleated draperies, are available in white, ivory, and wood tones. Drapery hooks are inserted so the pleats conceal the rod when the treatment is closed. Valances or cornices are used over the top of the draperies to completely conceal the rod. Flexible traverse rods are used for pleated draperies on bow windows.

Hardware Accessories

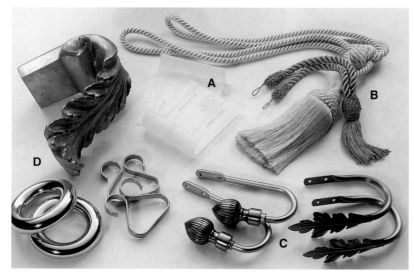

Concealed tieback holders (A) fit behind the last fold of pleated or rod-pocket draperies to prevent the tieback from crushing the draperies. The projection is adjustable.

Cord-and-tassel tiebacks (B) are used with concealed or decorative holders to hold draperies in place.

Holdbacks (C), as the name implies, are decorative accessories that hold back a stationary curtain or drapery without the use of tiebacks.

Swag holders (D) support the draped fabric in swag window treatments. Some styles are meant to be concealed, while others are quite obviously decorative.

Installing Hardware

Window treatment hardware is packaged complete with mounting brackets, nails or screws, and installation instructions.

If nails are supplied with the hardware you purchased, use them only for lightweight treatments installed directly on the window frame. Otherwise, substitute screws or molly bolts that fit through the holes in the brackets.

Use screws alone if installing through wallboard or plaster directly into wall studs. When brackets are positioned between wall studs, support the screws for lightweight treatments with plastic anchors in the correct size for the mounting screw. If the brackets must support a heavy window treatment, use plastic toggle anchors or molly bolts.

To prevent drapery rods from bowing, support them with center brackets. The brackets are usually positioned at intervals of 45" or less, across the width of the rod. Whenever possible, screw the brackets into wall studs.

Everything You Need

Tools: tape measure, hammer, screwdriver, drill with bits.

Materials: window treatment hardware.

How to Install Hardware Using Plastic Anchors

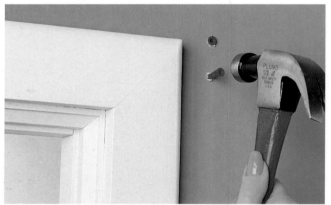

1 Mark screw locations on wall. Drill holes for plastic anchors, using a drill bit slightly smaller than the diameter of plastic anchor. Tap anchors into drilled holes, using a hammer.

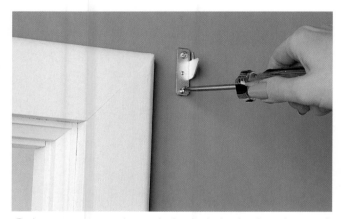

2 Insert a screw through the hole in the bracket and into the installed plastic anchor. Tighten the screw securely; anchor expands in wallboard, preventing it from pulling out of wall.

How to Install Hardware Using Plastic Toggle Anchors

1 Mark screw locations on wall. Drill holes for plastic toggle anchors, using a drill bit slightly smaller than the diameter of toggle anchor shank.

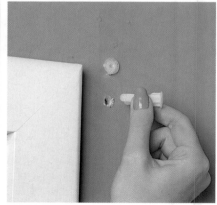

2 Squeeze wings of the toggle anchor flat, and push it into the hole. Tap in with hammer until it is flush with wall.

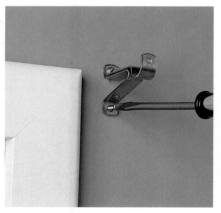

3 Insert a screw through the hole in bracket and into the installed anchor. Tighten the screw. Wings spread out and flatten against the back side of wallboard.

How to Install Hardware Using Molly Bolts

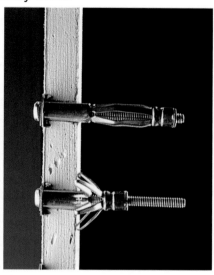

1 Mark screw locations on wall. Drill holes for molly bolts, using drill bit slightly smaller than the diameter of the molly bolt.

2 Tap molly bolt into drilled hole, using hammer; tighten screw. Molly bolt expands and flattens against back side of wallboard.

3 Remove screw from molly bolt; insert the screw through hole in bracket and into installed molly bolt. Screw the bracket securely in place.

Photo courtesy of Kolbe & Kolbe Millwork Company, Inc.

Colorful, print fabric makes this cozy nook a fun place for reading or relaxing. A decorative curtain rod has been casually draped with a large piece of coordinating fabric for a whimsical valance. The tiebacks can be loosened to cover the window and gain privacy.

Light, flowing fabric is softly draped and held in place with curtain tiebacks. The casements are lightly framed while the uniquely shaped fixed window above has no window treatment. This style lends a formal look to the room.

Making a Mounting Board

Many window treatments are mounted on boards rather than on drapery hardware. The mounting board is usually covered with fabric to match the window treatment, or with drapery lining, and the window treatment is then stapled to the board. The mounting board can be installed as an inside mount by securing it inside the window frame. Or, the board may be installed as an outside mount, securing it directly to the window frame or to the wall above and outside the window frame.

For an inside-mounted window treatment, the depth of the window frame must be at least 1½" to accommodate a 1 × 2 mounting board. Cut the mounting board ½" shorter than the inside measurement across the window frame, to

ensure that the board will fit inside the frame when it is covered with fabric.

For outside-mounted treatments, use a 1 × 4 board. Cut the mounting board at least 2" wider than the ouside measurement across the window frame. Install the board using angle irons that measure more than one-half the projection of the board.

Everything You Need

Tools: level, stapler, screwdriver, drill with bits.

Materials: fabric, board, angle irons, screws.

How to Cover the Mounting Board with Fabric

1 Center board on wrong side of fabric. Staple one long edge of fabric to board, placing staples about 8" apart. Do not staple within 6" of ends. Wrap fabric around board. Fold under ⅜" on long edge. Staple to board, placing staples about 6" apart.

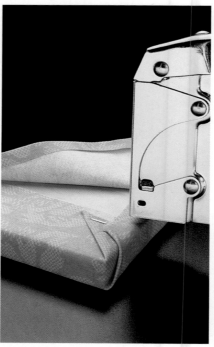

2 Fold and tuck fabric at corners on side of the board with the unfolded fabric edge. Finger-press. Staple in place near raw edge.

3 Fold and tuck fabric at corners on side of the board with folded fabric edge. Finger-press. Fold under excess fabric at ends. Staple near fold.

How to Install an Inside-mounted Board

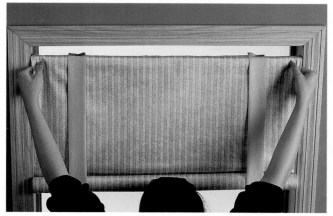

1 Hold board in place against upper window frame, with wide side of board up. Align front edge to frame.

2 Predrill screw holes through the board and up into window frame, using ⅛" drill bit. Drill holes within 1" of each end of board and in center for wide treatments. Secure board, using 8 × 1½" roundhead screws.

How to Install an Outside-mounted Board

1 Mark and predrill screw holes for angle irons on bottom of board, positioning angle irons within 1" of each end of board and at intervals of 45" or less.

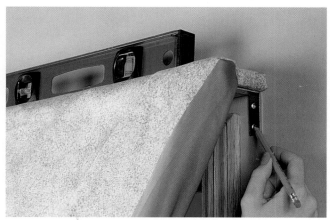

2 Hold board at desired placement, making sure it is level. Mark screw holes on wall or window frame. Remove angle irons from board.

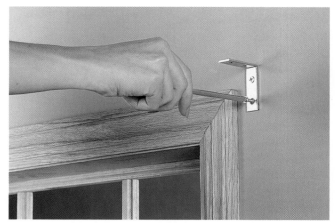

3 Secure angle irons to the wall, using 1½" flat-head screws. If angle irons are not positioned at wall studs, use molly bolts or toggle anchors instead of flat-head screws.

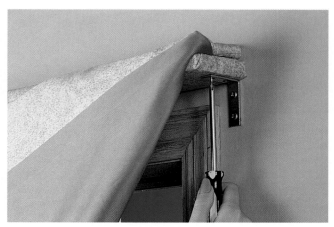

4 Reposition window treatment on angle irons, aligning screw holes. Fasten screws.

Creating a Cornice

A cornice is a wooden frame used as a top treatment. It can be used alone, or to frame and finish another window treatment, hiding the hardware.

This cornice is trimmed with decorative moldings, available in a variety of designs and sizes. Crown molding or chair rail frames the upper edge, and outside corner molding finishes the lower edge.

To avoid piecing the fabric, choose a design that also can be turned sideways and used lengthwise.

Take the measurements for the cornice after any drapery hardware is in place. The cornice should clear any undertreatment rod by at least 3", and it should extend at least 2" beyond the end brackets of the rod on each side.

The cornice should completely cover any drapery headings and hardware. Also, the height of the cornice should be in proportion to the total length of the window or window treatment, but to keep the window treatment from appearing top-heavy or overpowering, smaller cornices are sometimes desired. Smaller cornices also look sleek, making them especially suitable for contemporary rooms.

Everything You Need

Tools: miter box and backsaw or miter saw, hammer, heavy-duty stapler and staples, nail set.

Materials: ½" plywood, outside corner molding, crown molding or chair rail, finish nails, angle irons, flat-head wood screws, wood glue, paint or stain and matching putty, decorator fabric, lining, batting, spray adhesive, fabric glue.

How to Create a Cornice

1 Glue and nail each side piece to the top piece, aligning the upper edges. Repeat for front piece, aligning it to the top and side pieces.

2 Place corner molding on lower edge of cornice. Mark a line on the cornice front and sides at the edge of the molding. Repeat for crown molding or chair rail at the upper edge of the cornice.

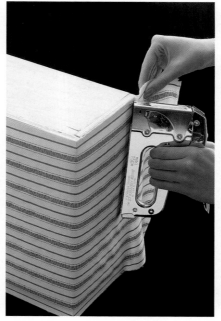

3 Cut a strip of decorator fabric as wide as the height of the cornice, and as long as the distance around outside of cornice plus 8". If necessary, fabric may be pieced and seamed together, pressing seams open. Cut batting to fit between molding lines by the distance around cornice. Affix batting to the cornice using spray adhesive.

4 Position fabric, right side up, centered on cornice front. Secure with staples at the center front, close to the upper and lower edges. Pull fabric taut to one end of cornice. Secure with staples near the end. Repeat for opposite side.

5 Wrap fabric around the side piece to inside of cornice, trimming corner at upper edge. Glue in place. Repeat for opposite side. Allow the glue to dry, then remove staples.

(continued next page)

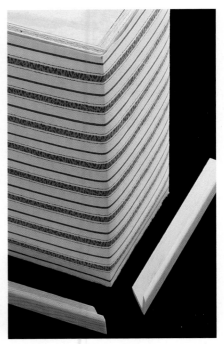

6 Glue raw edge of fabric to cornice along lower edge. Allow glue to dry. Smooth fabric taut to upper edge, and glue in place.

7 Cut a piece of lining to inside height of cornice plus ½". Secure lining to inside of cornice, using spray adhesive, aligning one long raw edge at the top. Clip lining at corners, then glue to lower edges of boards. Cut a piece of lining to fit cornice top. Affix, using spray adhesive.

8 Miter corner molding for sides of cornice at front corners. Leave excess length on the molding strips. Miter one corner on molding for the front of the cornice, leaving excess length.

9 Position mitered front and side molding strips at one corner. Mark the finished length of the side piece for a straight-cut end.

10 Place side molding at opposite end. Using a straightedge, mark outside edge of front molding where miters will meet. Mark angle of cut. Cut miter.

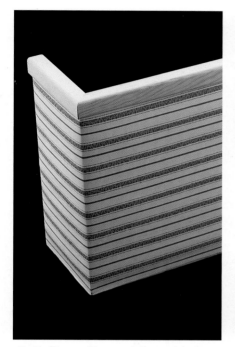

11 Reposition moldings. Mark and straight-cut second side piece to fit.

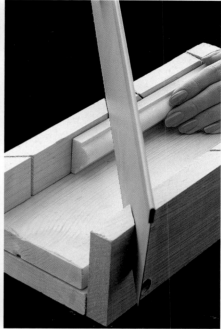

12 Cut crown molding or chair rail to fit around upper edge of cornice, following same sequence used for corner molding. To miter crown molding, place upper edge of molding tight against bottom of miter box. Cornice side should be tight against back of miter box (left). To miter chair rail, place its flat side against back of miter box (right).

13 Paint or stain molding as desired. Secure molding to cornice, using finish nails, pre-drilling nail holes with 1/16" drill bit. Use glue to secure mitered ends of moldings.

14 Secure upper edges of crown molding, if used, with one nail at each corner. Countersink nails, using a nail set. Fill holes with putty to match stain, or touch up with paint.

15 Install cornice as for out-side-mounted board on page 253. Whenever possible, screw angle irons into wall studs instead of using molly bolts.

Shelf Variations

Add larger supports at the shelf ends to accommodate a dowel for hanging dried flowers and herbs. A coordinating "backsplash" provides a way to attach the shelf to the wall. Attach hooks to the underside of the shelf to hang other collectibles or keepsakes.

Building a Window Shelf

Shelves may be hung above windows as novelty top treatments to showcase plants and collections. They can be used alone or in combination with other window treatments, such as curtains. In that case, mount the shelf with brackets hidden under the valance.

Although the end pieces in this project act as supports for the shelf, also secure the shelf to a horizontal support piece. Then, attach the whole unit to the wall with wood screws. If heavy items are to be displayed, drill more pilot holes for the wood screws to be closer together for added strength.

Whatever the size of the items to be displayed, you can adjust the depth of the shelf unit to accommodate them.

Everything You Need

Tools: hammer, drill and bits, circular saw, jig saw, router, sander, nail set.

Materials: 1 × 8 and 1 × 2 lumber, 2" wood screws, 6d casing nails, paint or stain.

How to Build a Window Shelf

1 Cut the 1 × 8 shelf board and the 1 × 2 horizontal support piece the same length as the total width of the window unit, including the outer casing. Attach the shelf to the support at a 90° angle, using 2" wood screws spaced every 6" to 10".

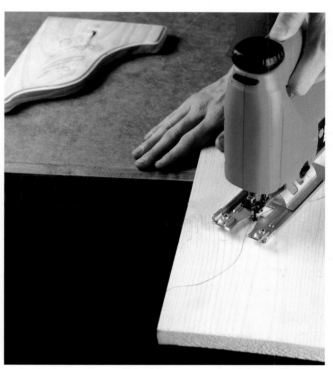

2 Cut out the two end pieces from 1 × 8 lumber. If the design has only straight lines, use a circular saw. If it includes curves, use a jig saw.

3 Add a design to the end supports, using a router. Sand smooth the faces and edges that will be exposed. Attach end supports to shelf unit using wood glue and 6d casing nails. Use a nail set to recess the nail heads. Finish the unit by staining or painting.

4 Drill pilot holes in the support piece every 6" to 10", avoiding screws attaching the shelf to the horizontal support. Attach shelf unit to wall just above window casing, using 2" wood screws driven through pilot holes. Plug and finish screw holes, if desired.

Making Hanging Plant Shelves

Plants have a delightful way of adding charm and hospitality to a room, no matter what the decorating scheme may be.

The shelves in this project are made from 1 × 6 stock lumber, cut to a length equal to the outside measurement of the window frame. They are braced with two 7" lengths of parting stop at each end, and suspended with rope from a wooden pole. When the pole is mounted at the top of a wide window, an additional brace and rope can be added to the center, along with a center support bracket for the pole.

The length of each rope equals twice the distance from the top of the pole to the bottom of the lowest shelf, plus 6" for the upper knot, plus 6" for each knot under a shelf, plus an extra 6" to 10".

If desired, holes can be cut into the shelf to hold pots that have slanted sides and collars, such as standard clay pots.

Vary the number and placement of shelves to alter the style. A double or triple hanging shelf, covering the entire window or just the lower half, acts as a curtain when filled with plants. Located near the top of the window, a single hanging shelf with several hanging or climbing plants becomes a valance.

Everything You Need

Tools: screwdriver, jig saw, ³⁄₃₂" combination drill and countersink bits, drill, ⁵⁄₁₆" twist bit, level.

Materials: 1 × 6 boards, parting stops, sandpaper, 1³⁄₈" dia. wood pole, 6 × 1" wallboard screws, finials, pole brackets, ³⁄₁₆" nylon or polyester rope, sponge applicator, paint or stain, clear acrylic finish.

How to Make Hanging Plant Shelves

1 Mark placement of holes for the rope on the wide side of the braces, ½" from each end. Drill holes using 5/16" drill bit. Sand all wood surfaces, using 180-grit or 220-grit sandpaper. Round the corners of the shelves and braces slightly. NOTE: If the shelves are more than 36" wide, cut and drill holes in a third brace for the center of each shelf.

2 Mark lines on underside of shelf 2" from each end. On wide side of braces, mark placement for screws, 1½" from ends. Place braces, wide side up, on shelf, with outer edges along lines, and ends extending equally beyond each side of the shelf. Position a third brace, if needed, at center of board. Repeat for braces on any additional shelves.

3 Adjust 3/32" combination drill and countersink bit so wallboard screw head will be recessed below surface of wood. Drill screw holes, holding the brace firmly in place as positioned in step 2. Drill through brace and into underside of shelf, up to point on drill bit indicated by white line. Insert 6 × 1" wallboard screw. Repeat for remaining braces.

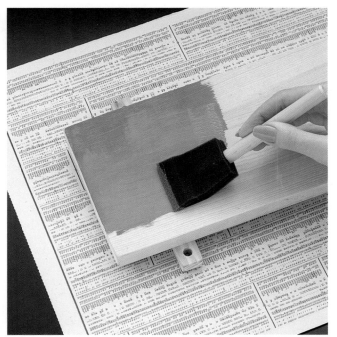

4 Stain the shelves to coordinate with the color of the window casing, or paint them to complement the decor of the room. In either case, apply clear acrylic finish to avoid damage from any inadvertent water spills. Colored rope cord is available, also.

(continued next page)

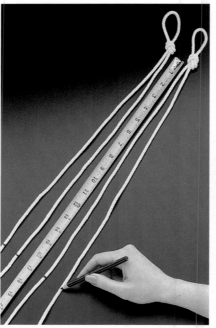

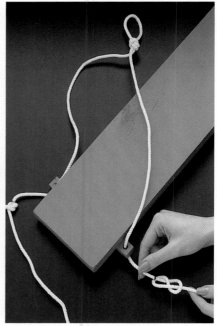

5 Fold the ropes in half. Tie each together in an overhand knot near the folded end, leaving a 2½" loop. Tie all knots in the same direction so they look the same.

6 Measure from the overhand knots to the desired location for the first set of shelf support knots, allowing 1¼" for the thickness of the shelf and braces. Mark the ropes with a pencil.

7 Thread the rope down through the holes in the braces of the shelf until the pencil marks are below the braces. As shown, tie a figure-eight knot at each location, just under the pencil mark.

8 Mount brackets for the wood pole, either on the window frame or just outside the frame. Use molly bolts or toggle anchors if not installing the brackets into window frame or wall studs. If a center support bracket is needed, mount it with one side of another bracket pair at the center.

9 Slide the pole through loops in the rope, and attach finials to the ends. Mount the pole on the brackets. Check to see that the shelves are level and resting on knots. Adjust the knots if necessary. Trim excess rope under the knots for the bottom shelf.

Variation with Inserted Pots

Holes cut into the hanging plant shelf hold potted plants of various colors, sizes, and shapes. This style works especially well to help stabilize small-bottomed clay pots.

1 Mark placement for the ropes and drill holes as on page 261, step 1. Measure the circumference of the flowerpot just under the collar. Divide this measurement by 6.28 to determine the radius. Draw a circle with this radius on paper, using a compass. Cut out the circle and slide it up from the bottom of the pot to the collar. Adjust the hole size if necessary.

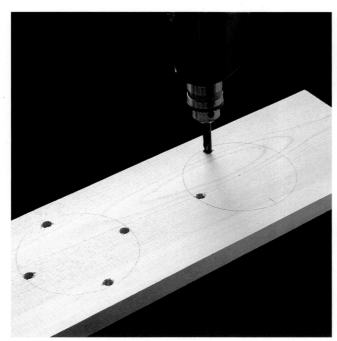

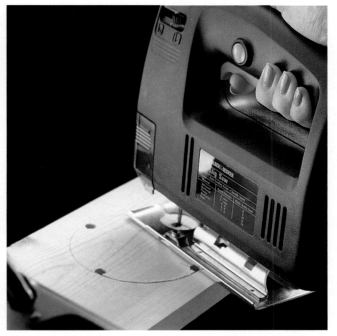

2 Determine the number of pot holes you wish, and the spacing between them. The outer edge of the first and last holes should be at least 3½" from the end of the shelf; minimum spacing between holes is 2". Mark circles for the holes on the top of the shelf. Drill some evenly spaced holes at the inner edge of each circle, using a large drill bit. We drilled four.

3 Use a jig saw to cut out the openings, cutting from one drilled hole to the next. Complete the plant shelf as on pages 261 and 262, steps 2 to 9.

Etching Glass

Create a charming, custom embellishment for a window or door by etching the glass. A subtle design can draw attention to a beautiful view or enhance a special molding. Etching may be the only treatment that is used on some windows or door glass. Depending on the design used for the etching, the effect can be classic or contemporary.

The etching cream, available from craft stores, is applied over a stencil to create the etched glass. You may make your own custom stencil or you may use precut etching stencils, also available from craft stores. If precut stencils are used, apply the stencil and etch the glass according to manufacturer's instructions. The amount of time the etching cream remains on the glass varies with the type of stencil.

For best results, use a simple design with small areas for etching; large, solid areas of glass may look blotchy. To become familiar with the technique, practice on a scrap of glass before etching the window.

Etching may be done on either the inside or outside of the window. Because it is easier to work on glass placed on a work table, remove the glass or the window, if possible.

Before you apply the stencil, clean and dry the window thoroughly, using a lint-free cloth. Also plan how you will rinse the project, so areas of woodwork or wall do not come in contact with the rinse water.

Everything You Need

Tools: mat knife, soft-bristle brush.

Materials: precut stencils or self-adhesive vinyl (such as Contact), etching cream, smudgeproof carbon paper or graphite paper, masking tape, drop cloth, lint-free cloths, rubber gloves.

How to Make & Apply a Custom Stencil

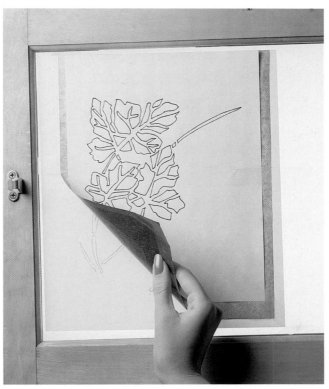

1 Cut self-adhesive vinyl 2" larger than design. Remove the paper backing, and affix vinyl to window, pressing out any air bubbles. If more than one width of vinyl is needed, overlap edges ½".

2 Position the design on the window, with carbon or graphite paper under it. Tape the design securely in place. Trace the design onto the vinyl.

3 Cut around design areas to be etched, using a mat knife, applying just enough pressure to cut through vinyl. At corners, do not cut past intersecting lines.

4 Remove the vinyl in the design areas to be etched, using the tip of the knife blade to loosen the edge of the vinyl.

5 Press firmly on all cut edges of the remaining vinyl, using a lint-free cloth.

How to Etch Window Glass

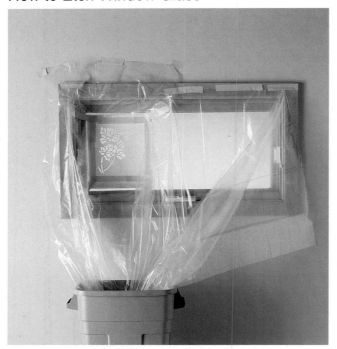

1 Use masking tape and plastic drop cloth to cover woodwork, walls, or any areas of the glass not protected by the stencil. Place the ends of the plastic in a nearby container to catch the rinse water.

2 Apply a thick layer of etching cream over entire design area, wearing rubber gloves and using soft-bristle brush. Allow etching cream to remain on design 6 to 10 minutes—or follow manufacturer's instructions. While cream is reacting, gently move cream with brush to make sure there are no air bubbles or uncovered areas.

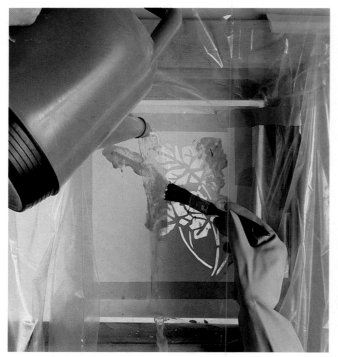

3 Rinse design thoroughly to remove all etching cream, working from top to bottom. Use brush to aid in removal of cream, being careful not to tear stencil. Do not allow rinse water to come in contact with woodwork or walls.

4 Pat area dry, using a lint-free cloth. Carefully remove stencil.

Etching Variations

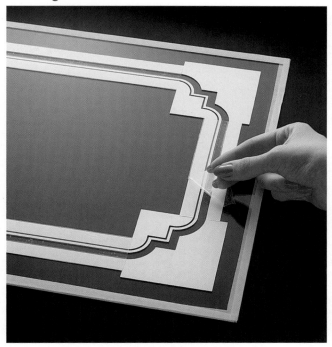

Precut adhesive etching stencil. Separate the stencil from the backing sheet and position it with the adhesive side touching the glass. Remove the top sheet, checking to see that the stencil is completely adhered. Follow steps 4 and 5 on page 265.

Precut rub-off etching stencil. Secure the stencil temporarily with masking tape. Rub entire stencil firmly but gently, using a wooden stick, to transfer stencil to glass. Remove the top sheet carefully, checking to see that the stencil is completely adhered.

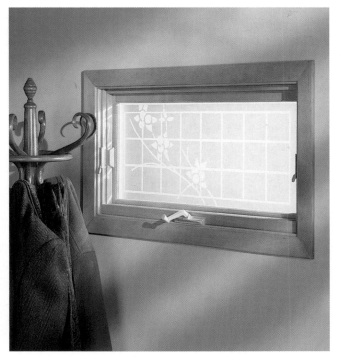

An etched border design decorates this window without obstructing the view. The homeowner has chosen to use no other window treatment, letting in the maximum amount of natural light.

An etched grid design, interrupted with floral motifs, gives this awning window a frosted effect. The result is that a good amount of diffused daylight enters the room, while preserving privacy.

Framing an Antique Stained-glass Window

Beautiful antique stained-glass windows are readily found in flea markets and antique stores. Prized because of their delicate craftsmanship and the ever-changing play of light through the glass, a unique stained-glass piece makes a striking addition to a room. Unfortunately, though, most antique leaded stained glass tends to be drafty and not energy-efficient, making it impractical to install in place of standard window glass.

However, you can still enjoy the beauty of your stained-glass treasures by re-framing the piece and mounting it to the interior sash of a standard window. This simple, yet attractive, frame is built from 2 × lumber and decorative molding and doesn't require any specialized woodworking tools.

Fixed transom windows, door sidelights, or picture windows often make attractive showcases for stained glass. Because of the delicacy of most stained glass, don't install this project on a working, openable window.

If you plan to stain your frame, be sure to use a finish-grade wood in 2 × dimensions. If you are painting the frame to match the existing trim, standard 2 × lumber is sufficient. If you are concerned about the strength of your stained glass, or notice any bowing when the piece is held up-right, cut a piece of clear Plexiglas® to match the size of the stained glass and install it behind the glass piece in the frame.

Because of its fragile nature, removing paint or other grime from old stained glass should always be done with a very gentle touch. Acetone or alcohol-based paint removers are safe to use on most unpainted stained-glass pieces. Always test cleaning solutions in an inconspicuous area of the glass. Avoid acidic, abrasive, or corrosive cleaners (including ammonia), as they can react with putty or the metallic cames. Antique painted glass should always be taken to a professional restorer for cleaning.

Everything You Need

Tools: putty knife, screwdriver or small pry bar, razor blade, tape measure, circular saw, straightedge cutting guide, pipe clamps, drill and bits, paintbrush, miter saw, hammer.

Materials: antique stained-glass window, mineral spirits, 0000 steel wool, glass cleaner, 2 × lumber, quarter-round trim molding, wood glue, 3½" screws, 4d finish nails, paint, 2" finish screws, decorative washers, standard washers.

How to Frame an Antique Stained-glass Window

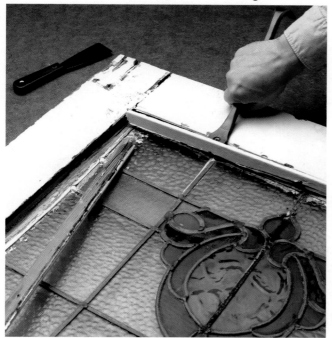

1 If the stained glass is framed, score the paint around the edges of the molding, using a putty knife or utility knife. Carefully pry the molding from the frame, using a screwdriver or small pry bar. Loosen any caulk or paint with the knife and pull out any nails. Gently lift the stained glass from the frame.

2 Remove old paint from the glass by applying mineral spirits with a clean rag, then scraping away the paint with a putty knife. Dirty lead cames can be cleaned by rubbing with 0000 steel wool, but take care not to scratch the glass. Clean the glass of any residual dirt and debris using an ammonia-free glass cleaner.

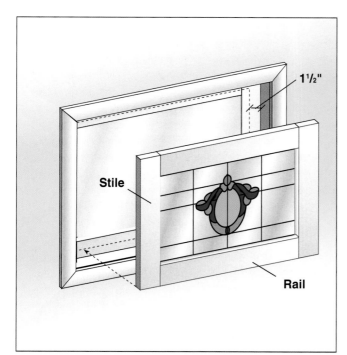

3 Determine the width of the rails and stiles for the new frame by subtracting the dimensions of the stained-glass piece from the dimensions of the existing window and dividing each result by two. Subtract an additional 1½" from each dimension for a gap around the frame to allow for airflow.

4 Cut the 2 × frame pieces to length. The rail length should be equal to the width of the stained-glass piece. The length of the stiles equals the height of the stained glass plus the width of the top and bottom rails. Once the boards are cut to length, rip each rail and stile to its determined width.

(continued next page)

5 Apply wood glue to the ends of the rails and assemble the frame. Clamp the joints with pipe clamps, then double-check the dimensions of the opening and adjust if necessary. Secure the joints by driving 3½" screws at an angle at the joints.

6 When the glue has dried, paint or stain the frame to match the trim around your window. Also paint or stain the molding pieces before you cut and install them.

7 Cut two pieces of decorative molding for the sides of the inside frame to length, making 45° miter cuts at the ends. Install the side molding pieces to the inside of the frame by drilling pilot holes and attaching it with 4d finish nails. Make sure the molding edge is flush with the front of the frame.

8 Measure between the side pieces and cut top and bottom molding pieces to length, making 45° miter cuts at the ends. Test-fit the molding into the frame, and make new cuts if necessary. There should be no discernable gap in the corner joints. When the molding fits well, drill pilot holes and attach it to the frame using 4d finish nails.

9 Turn the frame over. Carefully lay the glass piece in the frame so that it rests on the front molding. Cut and install the rear molding around the frame. Using extreme caution so as not to damage the glass, drill pilot holes and attach the rear molding with 4d finish nails.

10 Center the newly framed stained glass within the existing window frame. Drill pilot holes and attach the stained glass, using 2" finish screws and decorative washers. Use two to three standard washers as spacers between the new frame and the existing window sash to promote airflow and prevent condensation (inset).

Variation: Add decorative hooks to the top of the stained-glass frame and to the top of the window frame, predrilling the holes. Hang the panel from chains secured to the hooks. Use chains and hooks that are strong enough to support the weight of the panel.

©Smith-Baer Photography

Installing Interior Shutters

Wooden shutters have long been a popular window treatment, adding charm to any window setting. Accordion-fold shutters may be used on almost any window. They offer privacy and open neatly to expose the full width of the window. Shutters with louvers offer greater light control than many other window treatments.

If the exact size of ready-made shutters isn't available, select a pair that is slightly larger than your measurements. Half-shutters on a double-hung window usually reach (but do not extend past) the top of the lower sash.

You can trim the shutters to the correct height with a miter saw, radial arm saw, or table saw. If you're removing ¾" or less, take it all off the bottom of the shutters. If you need to remove more, take half off the top and half off the bottom.

Make sure the window frame is square before installing the shutters. Tape two shutters together and stand them in the window opening with the left-hand shutter touching the left jamb. Be sure the bottoms of the shutters are flat on the window stool. If there's no gap between the jamb and the shutter, that side is square. Tape the other two shutters together and check the right side the same way.

If there is a gap, the window is out of square and you must taper the shutters to accommodate the variance before installing them.

Everything You Need

Tools: miter saw, radial arm saw, or table saw; jointer, belt sander, or hand plane; screwdriver; paintbrush; tape measure; pencil compass.

Materials: shutters, tape, ⅛"-wide shims, 120-grit sandpaper, 2½" non-mortising hinges, screws, paint or varnish, latch.

How to Install Interior Shutters

1 Adjust a pencil compass to the widest part of the gap. Hold the pivot point against the jamb and slide the compass down from top to bottom, marking a corresponding line. Use a jointer, belt sander, or hand plane to trim the shutter to the pencil line. Repeat for other side, and test-fit both sides in the window.

2 Stand all four shutters in position, adding ⅛"-thick shims beneath them and along both sides. Check for uniform spaces. If necessary, trim the shutters to fit. Remove from window and lightly sand each shutter with 120-grit sandpaper. Paint, stain, or varnish, using a narrow brush to reach between the louvers.

3 Join each pair of shutters with two 2½" non-mortising hinges, so that they fold outward and swing away from sash. Attach two hinges to each shutter edge that abuts side jamb. If middle gap is not uniform when shutters are closed, shim behind the jamb hinge to adjust it. Attach a small latch to hold the shutters closed.

Nonfunctional shutters serve as decorative side panels. They are simply mounted on the wall. They can be painted or "pickled" with a colored stain (as shown here). Instead of matching the window frame, the shutters may be finished to match one of the fabrics in the room.

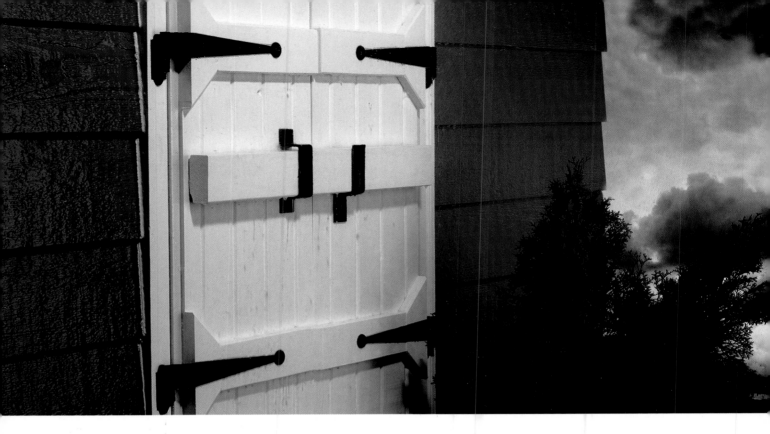

Building Custom Exterior Storm Shutters

These customized shutters are designed to protect your windows from the high winds and flying debris of severe storms. Working exterior shutters are a permanent alternative to the frenzied rush of installing plywood over your windows in the hours before an approaching storm, only to have to remove it again once the danger has passed. For those of you far from the threat of coastal storms, working shutters provide a quick and easy way to protect the windows on summer cabins or cottages while you are away.

These easy-to-construct shutters are built from exterior-grade tongue-and-groove boards. Their simple, rustic design is offset with stylish beveled cleat-and-fan battens. A customized decorative trim, visible when open, can turn these utilitarian shutters into a fashionable complement to your home's exterior.

Everything You Need

Tools: tape measure, pipe clamps, straight-edge, circular saw, router with chamfer bit, paintbrush, drill.

Materials: 1 × 8 tongue-and-groove lumber, 1 x 4 dimensional lumber, wood glue, 1¼" and 3" galvanized deck screws, paint, shutter hardware.

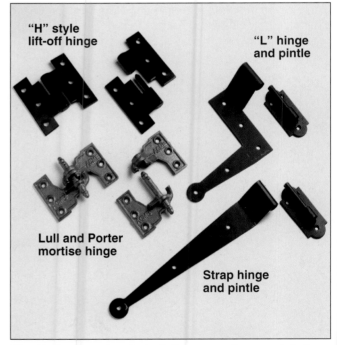

"H" style lift-off hinge

"L" hinge and pintle

Lull and Porter mortise hinge

Strap hinge and pintle

Tip: Before you begin building your shutters, it is important to locate the proper hinges. Shutter hardware may not be readily available in all regions of the country and may have to be ordered from shutter manufacturers. Shutter hinges are available in a wide range of styles, and installation will vary depending upon the hinge and your window design. Always consult with the manufacturer to determine the hardware that will work best for your needs.

How to Build Custom Exterior Storm Shutters

1 To determine dimensions for your shutters, first measure the height of the window opening. Because windows may not be square, it's best to take both a right- and left-side measurement. Subtract ½" from the actual height to allow for clearance. To find the width of each shutter, measure the width between the inside edges of the window jamb, divide by two, and subtract ⅜" to allow for hinge clearance.

2 Assemble two to four tongue-and-groove 1 × 8s so that each shutter is slightly larger than its determined width. Hold the 1 × 8s together with pipe clamps, then use a straightedge to mark the dimensions on the face of each shutter. Cut the shutters to length, using a circular saw.

3 Remove the clamps. Use a circular saw to rip the shutters to width, removing the grooved edge from one side of each shutter and the tongue edge from the other. Reattach the clamps.

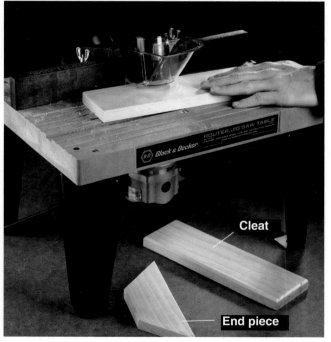

Cleat

End piece

4 Cut four cleats 3" shorter than the shutter width from 1 × 4 exterior-grade lumber. Also cut four end pieces, mitering the ends at 45°. Bevel all edges that will not butt another piece, using a router and chamfer bit.

(continued next page)

5 Attach the cleats and end pieces using waterproof wood glue and countersunk 1¼" galvanized screws. Allow glue to fully dry before installing the shutters.

Variation: To spruce up the simple design and construction of these shutters, consider a customized decorative trim design for the side that is visible when open. Ideas for trim include a sawtooth design or a traditional barn door Z- or X-style. Each design can be cut from 1 × 4 material and attached with wood glue and screws.

6 Paint or stain the shutters as desired and allow to dry. Drill pilot holes and attach the shutter hinges to the cleats with included fasteners or 1¼" galvanized screws.

7 Measure from the top of the shutter to the lower edge of the upper hinge and add ¼". Measure down this distance from the edge of the top jamb and make a mark. Align the bottom of the pintle's pin with the mark. Attach the pintle to the window molding, using 3" galvanized screws.

Add ¼"

Measure this distance

© Karen Melvin

8 Set the top hinge on the pintle. Support the shutter until both hinges are attached. Align the lower pintle with the lower hinge, and attach it with 3" galvanized screws. Repeat steps 7 and 8 for the other shutter. NOTE: Hinge installation may vary due to hinge style and window design. Always follow manufacturer's directions.

9 Install decorative holdbacks (also called shutter dogs) to hold the shutters in the open position. A slide latch can be installed inside or outside the shutters. An inexpensive alternative to latches is to install a pair of bar holders on the outside of the shutters and secure them with a 2 × 4 during the storm (inset).

Variation: Manufactured Storm Shutters

Photo courtesy of AGI Group

Photo courtesy of Wheatbelt, Inc.

Photo courtesy of AGI Group

Manufactured storm shutters are available in many traditional styles, including louvered, raised panel, and board-and-batten.

Rolling shutters adjust to any position to provide storm protection or light control. They can be controlled manually or automatically.

Bahama-style shutters function as sun awnings when open and provide wind and impact protection when closed.

Glossary

Apron — Flat trim piece placed just below a windowsill or stool.

Backband — Trim surrounding window or door casing, usually for the purpose of increasing depth.

Balloon framing — A type of framing construction in which each exterior wall stud runs from the sill plate on the foundation to the roof framing in one continuous piece. Used most commonly in house construction before 1930.

Bevel cut — An angled cut through the width or thickness of a board or other piece of stock.

Brick molding — A thick, exterior wood casing traditionally used with brick, which covers the frame and the exterior finish.

Buck — Lumber pieces used to serve as a window frame for fastening a window to concrete or concrete block.

Building code — A set of building regulations and ordinances governing the way a house may be built or modified. Most building codes are controlled by the local municipality.

Casing — The interior and exterior trim surrounding the frame of a window or door.

Cladding — A skin or sheathing, typically vinyl or metal, covering the exterior portions of a door or window unit.

Clerestory — A window near the top of a wall. Typically several are arranged in a series to provide indirect lighting.

Cornice — A wooden frame used as a window top treatment.

Cripple stud — The short wall studs that fall over window and door headers and beneath windowsills.

Dormer — A building element that projects from a sloping roof and contains a vertical window.

Drip edge — Preformed weather flashing installed above door or window trim.

Egress window — A window meeting specific requirements for use as an emergency exit.

Elevation drawing — An architectural drawing showing the side view of a room or exterior, usually with one wall per drawing.

Endnailing — Joining two boards by driving nails through the face of one board and into the end of another.

Facenailing — Joining two boards by driving nails through the faces of both boards.

Flashing — A thin sheet, usually metal or plastic, designed to divert water from a joint or building surface.

Floor plan — An architectural drawing showing a room as seen from above.

Furring strip — Wood strips used to level or add thickness to a surface.

Gable wall — The triangular exterior end wall underneath a two-sided pitched roof.

Grille — Ornamental or simulated window muntins that don't actually divide the glass.

Head — The area at the top of a window or door.

Header — A horizontal framing member over a window or door opening that supports the structural load above.

Jack stud — A wall-framing member used to support a header in a doorway or window opening.

Jambs — The pieces that make up a window or door frame.

Joist — The horizontal framing member of a floor or ceiling.

King stud — The first stud on either side of a framed opening to span from the sole plate to the top plate.

Level — Perfectly horizontal.

Light (or lite) — Glazing (glass) framed by muntins and/or sashes in a window or door.

Low-E glass — Glass that has low emissivity due to a film or metallic coating restricting the passage of radiant heat.

Miter cut — A 45° angled cut in the end of a piece of molding or a framing member.

Mullion (or mullion post) — A vertical member that divides multiple windows within a single unit.

Muntin — A smaller, secondary member that divides the glass or openings in a sash or door.

Nail set — A pointed metal rod used in finish carpentry for driving finish nails or casing nails below the wood surface.

Platform framing — A type of framing construction in which the studs only span a single story, and each floor acts as a platform to build and support the next level. Used in most homes built after 1930.

Plumb — Standing perfectly vertical. A plumb line is exactly perpendicular to a level surface.

Prehung door — A door already mounted with hinges in a frame.

R-value — The measure of resistance of a material to the passage of heat.

Rail — The horizontal member of a window sash or door panel frame.

Rough opening — An opening in framing made to fit a manufactured unit such as a window or door.

Saddle — The shaped strip or board that lays over the doorsill and seals the gap beneath the door.

Sash — The outermost frame that holds glass in a window unit.

Sash cord — A rope connecting the window sash to a weight inside the window frame. The cord travels on a pulley that rotates as the window is opened or closed.

Sheathing — A layer of plywood or other sheet good covering the wall or roof framing of a house.

Shim — Wood wedge used to align a window or door unit in its rough opening.

Sidelight — A tall, narrow window beside a door.

Sill — The framing member at the bottom of a window or door, or the sloped exterior base of a window or door unit.

Sole plate — A 2 × 4 or 2 × 6 board nailed flat on the floor to support the bottom ends of wall studs.

Stile — The vertical side member of a window sash or door panel frame.

Stool — A horizontal shelf-like trim piece at the interior base of a window.

Stop — Small molding strips attached to window or door jambs to guide moving sashes and stop swinging doors.

Stud — The vertical member of a wall.

Threshold — The base of any exterior door frame, made up of the sill and saddle. Also, the saddle itself.

Toenailing — Joining two boards at a right angle by driving nails at an angle through one board and into the other.

Wallboard (or drywall) — Paper-covered gypsum panels used for most interior wall and ceiling surfaces.

Weatherstripping — Strips of metal, plastic, felt, or other material, used to seal windows and doors to prevent air leakage and water intrusion.

Whaler — A temporary support beam used in the modification of balloon framing.

Additional Resources

American Institute of Architects
800-242-3837
www.aia.org

American Society of Interior Designers
202-546-3480
www.asid.org

Construction Materials Recycling Association
630-548-4510
www.cdrecycling.org

Energy & Environmental Building Association
952-881-1098
www.eeba.org

International Residential Code (book) published by **International Conference of Building Officials**
800-284-4406
www.icbo.com

National Association of the Remodeling Industry (NARI)
847-298-9200
www.nari.org

U.S. Environmental Protection Agency—Indoor Air Quality
www.epa.gov/iedweb00/pubs/insidest.html

Universal Design Resources

ABLEDATA
800-227-0216 (phone)
301-608-8958 (fax)
www.abledata.com

Access One, Inc.
800-561-2223
www.beyondbarriers.com

Adaptive Environments Center, Inc.
617-695-1225 (phone)
617-482-8099 (fax)
www.adaptenv.org

American Association of Retired Persons (AARP)
800-424-3410
www.aarp.org

Center for Inclusive Design & Environmental Access School of Architecture and Planning—University of Buffalo
716-829-3485 ext. 329 (phone)
716-829-3861 (fax)
www.ap.buffalo.edu/~idea

Center for Universal Design NC State University
919-515-3082 (phone)
919-515-3023 (fax)
www.design.ncsu.edu/cud

National Association of Home Builders (NAHB) Research Center
800-638-8556 (phone)
301-430-6180 (fax)
www.nahbrc.org

Contributors

Access One, Inc.
800-561-2223
www.beyondbarriers.com

AGI Group, Inc.
800-823-6677
www.agigroup.com

Andersen Windows, Inc.
800-426-4261
www.andersenwindows.com

Architectural Stairs, Inc.
787-274-0922
www.architecturalstairs.com

The Bilco Company
203-934-6363
www.bilco.com

Craftmaster Manufacturing, Inc.
800-405-2233
www.craftmasterdoorsdesign.com

Designer Doors
715-426-1100
www.designerdoors.com

JELD-WEN, Inc.
800-877-9482
www.jeld-wen.com

Kolbe & Kolbe Millwork Co., Inc.
800-955-8177
www.kolbe-kolbe.com

Kwikset Corporation
714-535-8111
www.kwikset.com

Larson Manufacturing
800-411-larson
www.larsondoors.com

Madawaska Doors, Inc.
800-263-2358
www.madawaska-doors.com

Marvin Windows and Doors
888-537-8268
www.marvin.com

Milgard Windows
800-MILGARD
www.milgard.com

Peachtree Doors and Windows
800-732-2499
www.peach99.com

Pittsburgh Corning Corporation
800-624-2120
www.pittsburghcorning.com

Roto Frank of America
800-787-7709
800-243-0893

Simpson Door Company
800-952-4057
www.simpsondoor.com

SuntunnelSkylights
800-369-7465
www.suntunnel.com

VELUX America, Inc.
800-888-3589
www.velux-america.com

Wheatbelt, Inc.
800-264-5171
www.rollupshutter.com

Woodport Interior Doors Heritage Veneered Products
715-526-2146
www.woodport.com

Photographers

Brad Daniels Photography
St. Paul, MN
©Brad Daniels p. 43, and for the following builders/designers: Ostrom Construction: pp.12, 40 (top right); Enerjac Construction: p.18; Paramount Homes: p. 39; Barrington Homes: p. 40 (top center); Hoffman Homes: p. 40 (bottom center); Bright Keys: p.164

Smith-Baer Photography
Port Chester, NY
©Smith-Baer: p. 272

Karen Melvin
Architectural Stock Images, Inc.
©Karen Melvin: p. 276

Andrea Rugg Photography
Minneapolis, MN
©Andrea Rugg: pp.13,14,15,17,40

Bill Tijerina Photography
Columbus, Ohio
© Bill Tijerina: pp. 4-5

Conversion Charts

Converting Measurements

To Convert:	To:	Multiply by:
Inches	Millimeters	25.4
Inches	Centimeters	2.54
Feet	Meters	0.305
Yards	Meters	0.914
Square inches	Square centimeters	6.45
Square feet	Square meters	0.093
Square yards	Square meters	0.836
Cubic inches	Cubic centimeters	16.4
Cubic feet	Cubic meters	0.0283
Cubic yards	Cubic meters	0.765
Ounces	Milliliters	30.0
Pints (U.S.)	Liters	0.473 (Imp. 0.568)
Quarts (U.S.)	Liters	0.946 (Imp. 1.136)
Gallons (U.S.)	Liters	3.785 (Imp. 4.546)
Ounces	Grams	28.4
Pounds	Kilograms	0.454

To Convert:	To:	Multiply by:
Millimeters	Inches	0.039
Centimeters	Inches	0.394
Meters	Feet	3.28
Meters	Yards	1.09
Square centimeters	Square inches	0.155
Square meters	Square feet	10.8
Square meters	Square yards	1.2
Cubic centimeters	Cubic inches	0.061
Cubic meters	Cubic feet	35.3
Cubic meters	Cubic yards	1.31
Milliliters	Ounces	.033
Liters	Pints (U.S.)	2.114 (Imp. 1.76)
Liters	Quarts (U.S.)	1.057 (Imp. 0.88)
Liters	Gallons (U.S.)	0.264 (Imp. 0.22)
Grams	Ounces	0.035
Kilograms	Pounds	2.2

Lumber Dimensions

Nominal - U.S.	Actual - U.S.	METRIC
1 × 2	¾ × 1½"	19 × 38 mm
1 × 3	¾ × 2½"	19 × 64 mm
1 × 4	¾ × 3½"	19 × 89 mm
1 × 5	¾ × 4½"	19 × 114 mm
1 × 6	¾ × 5½"	19 × 140 mm
1 × 7	¾ × 6¼"	19 × 159 mm
1 × 8	¾ × 7¼"	19 × 184 mm
1 × 10	¾ × 9¼"	19 × 235 mm
1 × 12	¾ × 11¼"	19 × 286 mm
1¼ × 4	1 × 3½"	25 × 89 mm
1¼ × 6	1 × 5½"	25 × 140 mm
1¼ × 8	1 × 7¼"	25 × 184 mm
1¼ × 10	1 × 9¼"	25 × 235 mm
1¼ × 12	1 × 11¼"	25 × 286 mm
1½ × 4	1¼ × 3½"	32 × 89 mm
1½ × 6	1¼ × 5½"	32 × 140 mm
1½ × 8	1¼ × 7¼"	32 × 184 mm
1½ × 10	1¼ × 9¼"	32 × 235 mm
1½ × 12	1¼ × 11¼"	32 × 286 mm
2 × 4	1½ × 3½"	38 × 89 mm
2 × 6	1½ × 5½"	38 × 140 mm
2 × 8	1½ × 7¼"	38 × 184 mm
2 × 10	1½ × 9¼"	38 × 235 mm
2 × 12	1½ × 11¼"	38 × 286 mm
3 × 6	2½ × 5½"	64 × 140 mm
4 × 4	3½ × 3½"	89 × 89 mm
4 × 6	3½ × 5½"	89 × 140 mm

Liquid Measurement Equivalents

1 Pint	= 16 Fluid Ounces	= 2 Cups
1 Quart	= 32 Fluid Ounces	= 2 Pints
1 Gallon	= 128 Fluid Ounces	= 4 Quarts

Converting Temperatures

Convert degrees Fahrenheit (F) to degrees Celsius (C) by following this simple formula: Subtract 32 from the Fahrenheit temperature reading. Then, multiply that number by 5/9. For example, 77°F - 32 = 45. 45 × 5/9 = 25°C.

To convert degrees Celsius to degrees Fahrenheit, multiply the Celsius temperature reading by 9/5. Then, add 32. For example, 25°C × 9/5 = 45. 45 + 32 = 77°F.

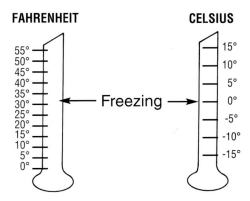

Drill Bit Guide

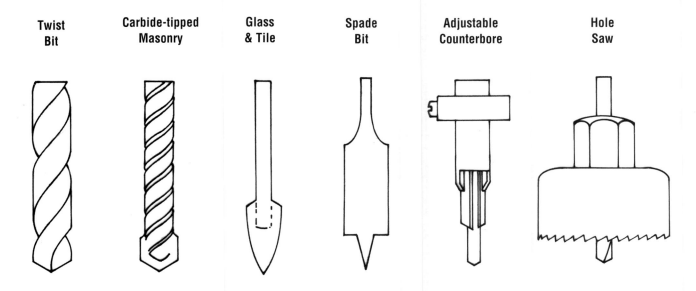

| Twist Bit | Carbide-tipped Masonry | Glass & Tile | Spade Bit | Adjustable Counterbore | Hole Saw |

Counterbore, Shank & Pilot Hole Diameters

Screw Size	Counterbore Diameter for Screw Head	Clearance Hole for Screw Shank	Pilot Hole Diameter	
			Hard Wood	Soft Wood
#1	.146 (9/64)	5/64	3/64	1/32
#2	1/4	3/32	3/64	1/32
#3	1/4	7/64	1/16	3/64
#4	1/4	1/8	1/16	3/64
#5	1/4	1/8	5/64	1/16
#6	5/16	9/64	3/32	5/64
#7	5/16	5/32	3/32	5/64
#8	3/8	11/64	1/8	3/32
#9	3/8	11/64	1/8	3/32
#10	3/8	3/16	1/8	7/64
#11	1/2	3/16	5/32	9/64
#12	1/2	7/32	9/64	1/8

Nails

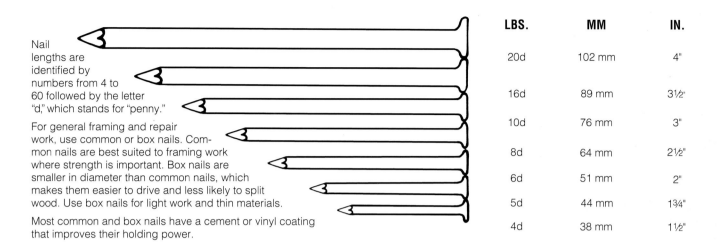

Nail lengths are identified by numbers from 4 to 60 followed by the letter "d," which stands for "penny."

For general framing and repair work, use common or box nails. Common nails are best suited to framing work where strength is important. Box nails are smaller in diameter than common nails, which makes them easier to drive and less likely to split wood. Use box nails for light work and thin materials.

Most common and box nails have a cement or vinyl coating that improves their holding power.

LBS.	MM	IN.
20d	102 mm	4"
16d	89 mm	3½"
10d	76 mm	3"
8d	64 mm	2½"
6d	51 mm	2"
5d	44 mm	1¾"
4d	38 mm	1½"

Metric Plywood Panels

Metric plywood panels are commonly available in two sizes: 1,200 mm × 2,400 mm and 1,220 mm × 2,400 mm, which is roughly equivalent to a 4 × 8-ft. sheet. Standard and Select sheathing panels come in standard thicknesses, while Sanded grade panels are available in special thicknesses.

STANDARD SHEATHING GRADE		SANDED GRADE	
7.5 mm	(5/16 in.)	6 mm	(4/17 in.)
9.5 mm	(3/8 in.)	8 mm	(5/16 in.)
12.5 mm	(½ in.)	11 mm	(7/16 in.)
15.5 mm	(5/8 in.)	14 mm	(9/16 in.)
18.5 mm	(¾ in.)	17 mm	(2/3 in.)
20.5 mm	(13/16 in.)	19 mm	(¾ in.)
22.5 mm	(7/8 in.)	21 mm	(13/16 in.)
25.5 mm	(1 in.)	24 mm	(15/16 in.)

Lumber Dimensions

NOMINAL - U.S.	ACTUAL - U.S.	METRIC
1 × 2	¾" × 1½"	19 × 38 mm
1 × 3	¾" × 2½"	19 × 64 mm
1 × 4	¾" × 3½"	19 × 89 mm
1 × 5	¾" × 4½"	19 × 114 mm
1 × 6	¾" × 5½"	19 × 140 mm
1 × 7	¾" × 6¼"	19 × 159 mm
1 × 8	¾" × 7¼"	19 × 184 mm
1 × 10	¾" × 9¼"	19 × 235 mm
1 × 12	¾" × 11¼"	19 × 286 mm
1¼ × 4	1" × 3½"	25 × 89 mm
1¼ × 6	1" × 5½"	25 × 140 mm
1¼ × 8	1" × 7¼"	25 × 184 mm
1¼ × 10	1" × 9¼"	25 × 235 mm
1¼ × 12	1" × 11¼"	25 × 286 mm
1½ × 4	1¼" × 3½"	32 × 89 mm
1½ × 6	1¼" × 5½"	32 × 140 mm
1½ × 8	1¼" × 7¼"	32 × 184 mm
1½ × 10	1¼" × 9¼"	32 × 235 mm
1½ × 12	1¼" × 11¼"	32 × 286 mm
2 × 4	1½" × 3½"	38 × 89 mm
2 × 6	1½" × 5½"	38 × 140 mm
2 × 8	1½" × 7¼"	38 × 184 mm
2 × 10	1½" × 9¼"	38 × 235 mm
2 × 12	1½" × 11¼"	38 × 286 mm
3 × 6	2½" × 5½"	64 × 140 mm
4 × 4	3½" × 3½"	89 × 89 mm
4 × 6	3½" × 5½"	89 × 140 mm

Index